STUDIES IN RELIGION

Also by Glyn Richards

A SOURCEBOOK OF MODERN HINDUISM

BEYOND TRAGEDY (*editor*)

THE PHILOSOPHY OF GANDHI

THEMES IN COMPARATIVE RELIGION (*editor*)

TOWARDS A THEOLOGY OF RELIGIONS

Studies in Religion

A Comparative Approach to Theological and Philosophical Themes

Glyn Richards
formerly Head of Department of Religious Studies
University of Stirling

St. Martin's Press

First published in Great Britain 1995 by
MACMILLAN PRESS LTD
Houndmills, Basingstoke, Hampshire RG21 6XS
and London
Companies and representatives
throughout the world

A catalogue record for this book is available from the British Library.

ISBN 0–333–64492–1

10	9	8	7	6	5	4	3	2	1
04	03	02	01	00	99	98	97	96	95

Printed and bound in Great Britain by
Ipswich Book Co Ltd, Ipswich, Suffolk

_____

First published in the United States of America 1995 by
Scholarly and Reference Division,
ST. MARTIN'S PRESS, INC.,
175 Fifth Avenue,
New York, N.Y. 10010

ISBN 0–312–12676–X

Library of Congress Cataloging-in-Publication Data
Richards, Glyn.
Studies in religion / Glyn Richards.
p.   cm.
Includes bibliographical references and index.
ISBN 0–312–12676–X (cloth)
1. Religion—Philosophy.   2. Hinduism—Philosophy.
3. Christianity—Philosophy.   Buddhism—Philosophy.
5. Religions.
BL51.R435   1995
200—dc20   95–5584
                                                   CIP

Er Cof am Fy Mhriod Annwyl

In Memory of Helga

In freta dum fluvii current, dum montibus umbrae
Lustrabunt convexa, polus dum sidera pascet
Semper honos nomenque tuum laudesque manebunt

(Virgil, *Aeneid*, i, 607)

Contents

Acknowledgements

Many of the essays contained in this work originally appeared in journals and books over the past years and are included in this collection with modifications and additions. The author gratefully acknowledges the permission given by the editors and publishers listed below to include them in this collection:

'Symbols and Religious Language', *Humanities: Christianity and Culture*, 18, May 1984, International Christian University Publication, IV-B; *Symbols in Art and Religion*, edited by Karel Werner, Curzon Press & Riverdale Press, 1990.

'Paul Tillich and the Historical Jesus', *Religious Sciences/Sciences Religieuses*, 4:2, 1974/5. By permission of the Canadian Corporation for Studies in Religion.

'Gandhi's Concept of Truth and the *Advaita* Tradition', *Religious Studies*, Vol. 22, No. 1 March, 1986, Cambridge University Press.

'*Śūnyatā*: Objective Referent or *Via Negativa?*', *Religious Studies*, Vol. 14, No. 2, June, 1978, Cambridge University Press.

'Liberation Theology: Bonhoeffer and Gandhi', *Modern Theology*, Vol. 3, No. 4, July, 1987, Blackwell Publishers.

'The One and the Many: Radhakrishnan's Concept of Religion', *The Scottish Journal of Religious Studies*, Vol. X, No. 2, Autumn, 1989; 'Radhakrishnan's Essentialist View of the Nature of Religion', *Radhakrishnan: Centenary Volume*, edited G. Parthasarathi and D.P. Chattopadhyaya, Oxford University Press, 1989.

'Towards a Theology of Religions', *The Journal of Theological Studies*, Vol. XXXI, Part I, April, 1980. By permission of Oxford University Press.

'Conceptions of the Self in Wittgenstein, Hume, and Buddhism', *The Monist*, Vol. 61, No. 1, January, 1978. Copyright © 1978, *The Monist*, La Salle, Illinois 61301. Reprinted by permission.

'Gandhi and Education', *The Scottish Journal of Religious Studies*, Vol. XIV, No. 1, Spring, 1993.

'Modern Hinduism', *The World's Religions*, edited by Stewart Sutherland, Leslie Houlden, Peter Clarke, Friedhelm Hardy. Routledge, 1988.

'Vivekānanda and Essentialism', *The Scottish Journal of Religious Studies*, Vol. XV, No. 2, Autumn, 1994.

'A Wittgensteinian Approach to the Philosophy of Religion', *The Journal of Religion*, Volume 58, Number 3, July, 1978. Copyright © by The University of Chicago. All rights reserved.

Every effort has been made to contact all the copyright-holders, but if any have been inadvertently overlooked the publishers will be pleased to make the necessary arrangement at the earliest opportunity.

Introduction

A collection of studies in religion which includes observations on what is sometimes called comparative religion, might give rise to misgivings in the minds of some readers because of deep-rooted misconceptions concerning the nature of comparative religion. It is often maintained, for example, that comparisons are odious; that religious comparisons are more odious than most; and that those who are concerned with comparative religion are only comparatively religious. The aim of this collection, however, is not to present a comparatively religious outlook, nor to engage in odious comparisons which could result in one religious tradition being elevated to a position of superiority over others. Its aim rather is to look at the spiritual insights and the theological and philosophical reflections to be found in the writings of prominent thinkers from different religious traditions, and where appropriate to examine the resemblances and differences that exist between them.

The essays in this collection embrace Hindu, Buddhist, and Christian themes and where comparisons are drawn every effort is made to maintain an empathetic approach. That is, themes are examined, where appropriate, from within the religious traditions concerned and in a way that would meet with the approval of adherents of those religions.

It is my hope that this open-ended, comparative approach to theology and religion, which has dominated my thinking for a quarter of a century, will prove helpful to the enquiring mind. In the pluralistic religious situation of today, with its infinite variety of religious experiences, we ought to be able to escape from the small island of our own cultural tradition, and from the ghetto mentality that would confine us to the insights of a single religious tradition. It would be a tragedy if such a mentality were to isolate us from the richness and diversity of other cultures and from the deep, spiritual insights of different religious traditions.

GLYN RICHARDS

1 Towards a Theology of Religions

I INTRODUCTION

Religious pluralism has become a stock phrase and there have been a variety of approaches to what has been called the pluralistic situation of today. It is not at all clear in what way the religious pluralistic situation of today differs from the religious pluralistic situation of yesterday. The variety of religious experiences pertaining today shows no substantial increase on that of yesterday, but what has occurred during the last hundred years is a growth in awareness of religious pluralism. Reference is made, for example, to a 'planetary culture', by which in all probability is meant that the world has grown smaller as a result of improved communications, and that it is no longer possible for man to confine himself to the small island of his own culture and tradition and not recognise the significance of other cultures. Reference is also made to the ghetto mentality of those who attempt to work within the confines of their own religious traditions in isolation from the spiritual insights of other religious traditions. It might be argued that we can only work effectively within our own culture and that to talk of a 'planetary culture' really makes no sense. Similarly it can be argued that since commitment is involved in the case of religions we can only come to a full understanding of our own religious tradition and that to talk about a theology of religions is nonsense. Is not the concept of a theology of religions as much an abstraction as the concept of a 'planetary culture', and does it not make more sense to talk about theologies of religions rather than a theology of religions? It may make sense, for example, to speak of a Christian theology of religions, or a Hindu theology of religions, or a Buddhist theology of religions, but does it really make sense to talk about such an abstraction as a theology of religions as if such a theology could be constructed in isolation from particular religious traditions?

II　APPROACHES TO RELIGIOUS PLURALISM

What I propose to do in this essay is to examine some of the problems involved in seeking to construct a Christian theology of religions. It is evident that there has been a growing concern with the plurality of religions in the world. First, it is implicit if not explicit in the declaration of the Second Vatican Council of the Roman Catholic Church of 1963–65, which states that 'Those who through no fault of theirs are still ignorant of the Gospel of Christ and of his Church yet sincerely seek God and, with the help of divine grace, strive to do his will as known to them through the voice of their conscience, those men can attain to eternal salvation'.[1] This is a change, albeit a tentative one, from the apparently clear pronouncement of Pius in 1854, which takes this form: 'It is to be held by faith that outside the apostolic Roman Church no one can be saved; it is the only ark of salvation and anyone who does not enter it will perish in the flood. But it is also to be considered certain that those who labour under invincible ignorance of the true religion are not guilty in this matter in the eyes of the Lord'.[2] The Second Vatican declaration may be regarded as a confirmation of the anti-Jansenist pronouncement of the Church which could be expressed positively as *extra ecclesiam conceditur gratia*. But if there is divine grace *extra ecclesiam* and yet no salvation *extra ecclesiam*, how are these two pronouncements to be reconciled? If the declaration of the Second Vatican Council is to make sense and if the pronouncement of Pius IX is not going to stand out like a sore thumb in this new theological context, then some kind of non-exclusive interpretation of *extra ecclesiam salus non est* would seem to be called for. One attempt at such an interpretation is the suggestion that *extra ecclesiam salus non est* refers to a 'principle defining a category' and not 'a principle concerning persons' and that if people are saved by divine grace, they are saved because of the representative capacity of the Church, that is to say, the Church represents God's grace.[3] I must admit that the logic of this interpretation escapes me, but even if we were to grant its validity, questions concerning the Church's teaching concerning the necessity of the sacraments of baptism and the eucharist for salvation, and whether the saving grace of the Church works retrospectively, would still need to be answered. If the sacraments are essential for salvation in what sense are they essential in view of the possibility of eternal salvation through grace for those non-Christians who, according to the declaration of Vatican II, strive to do God's will as revealed to them through their conscience, that is, those who live in accordance with high ethical principles and whose morality is referred to as taking the place of baptism.[4] But consideration of these questions takes us beyond the limited scope of this essay. They arise as a consequence of our concern for a theological study of non-Christian religions. Yet it has to be said that they are not unrelated to the formulation of a Christian theology of religions.

Secondly, various theologians have shown concern for a Christian theology of religions as a result of increasing acquaintance with the major religions of the world. This is true, for example, of Paul Tillich. Eliade refers to his *re-awakened* interest in the history of religions as a result of his visit to Japan in 1960 and his encounter with living representatives of Buddhism and the Shinto religion.[5] The use of the term *re-awakened* is apposite because his initial attraction to the subject of the history of religions was during his student days when his teacher Martin Kähler showed him the dangers of doctrinal narrowness and exclusivism with the loss of openness and spiritual freedom that entailed. His acquaintance with the works of Jacob Boehme and Ernst Troeltsch revealed the mystical and social aspects of religion, and it was the latter who first indicated to him the value of religious cross-fertilisation which, together with Rudolf Otto's analysis of the concept of the holy, helped him to formulate his dynamic–typological approach to the study of religions. This approach analyzed the interrelation of what he considered to be the three main elements of religion, namely, the sacramental, mystical and prophetic, and I shall examine this in greater detail in the next section.[6]

The Catholic theologian Karl Rahner has described today's pluralistic religious situation as qualitatively new and an insurmountable fact, while John Hick somewhat picturesquely describes it as representing a change from a Ptolemaic religion-centred situation to a Copernican God-centred situation.[7]

Thirdly, the phenomenological approach to the study of religion may also be taken as indicative of an interest in religious diversity. This is comparatively recent and has been called a child of the Enlightenment. It seeks to apply scientific methods to the study of religious traditions and strives to be neutral, objective and disinterested in its approach. To what extent it succeeds is a moot point and a recurring theme in methodological discussions. Clearly an empirical approach to the study of religion has its limitations. It cannot, for example, raise questions about the truth or validity of religious claims nor make judgments as to their value or merit. When it does so it ceases to be a scientific and neutral approach. The tendency to move from the phenomenological study of religion to the philosophy of religion is a natural one, although there are those who maintain that the distinction can be maintained and that the methodology of the science of religion is quite autonomous. They maintain that an objective, neutral, unbiased, phenomenological approach to religious beliefs can be justified. Doubts arise, however, when we ask whether it is possible to be totally neutral and unbiased, or to bring a totally disinterested mind to bear on the investigation of religious beliefs. We may ask whether there can be an open-ended, objective approach to the study of religion. Are there not, in actual fact, degrees of bias, and would it not be advantageous for us to acknowledge them? Phenomenologists might be persuaded to admit that a open-ended, unbiased approach to the study of religion is an impossibility, but they might still want to draw a distinction between a phenomenological approach and certain philosophical and theological approaches with their preconceptions and *a priori* notions. But the distinction is one of degree and not of kind. Should the phenomenologist wish to proceed with his open-ended approach on the assumption that all religions contain relative not absolute truth, then his assumption is as much an *a priori* notion as, for example, a Christian theological claim would be that only Christianity is true and all other religions false.

It may be that the kind of interest exemplified by a phenomenological approach to religious pluralism is incompatible with the search for a theology of religions which is an explicitly theological undertaking. We might ask if faith can be studied scientifically. Is there not an uniqueness in the experience of faith which makes a scientific, empirical investigation of it impossible? Is Cantwell Smith's observations relevant here, namely, that a man cannot be 'an observer *vis-à-vis* the history of the diverse religions of distinct or even close communities but rather a participant in the multiform religious history of the only community there is, humanity'?[8] And does not Smith echo Otto who insists that while a phenomenological approach examines the external expressions of religious experience from without, a true understanding of religion is achieved only from within and consequently demands a theological approach?[9]

To put the question in another way: can one draw a distinction between religious traditions and the faith which finds expression in those traditions? Is it possible to confine the study of religion to a scientific examination of the truth *about* religion as distinct from theological concern with the truth *of* a religion? Does intellectual openness, which is sometimes regarded as synonymous with a phenomenological approach to the study of religion, necessarily involve ignoring the implications of a theological concern with the truth of religion?[10] Phenomenology may be a necessary condition, but is it a sufficient condition for the understanding of religious beliefs? What can be said, of course, in this context is that it is indicative of the current concern with religious pluralism.

Fourthly, concern for some kind of assessment of the plurality of religions takes the form of an attempt to seek the essence of religion. It was Hegel who was one of the first to state that religion is an entity preceding historical manifestations, a prototype as it were of all particular instances. Schleiermacher also conceived of religion as pre-existing particular historical manifestations which are grounded in the fundamental unity of religion, an *a priori* condition.[11] The transcendental unity of religion is necessary for the existence of positive historical religions which are the concrete expressions of the primordial form described by Schleiermacher as 'the sense and taste of the infinite'. No finite, positive form of religion can encapsulate the universality of religion so the idea that a finite form of religion can be regarded as universally valid is inappropriate.[12] But it does not follow that finite forms are superfluous and that all we need is a kind of natural religion. Religion has to find expression in historical forms and the plurality of particular religions is necessary for the complete manifestation of religion. Antipathy to religious pluralism should be avoided. According to Schleiermacher, each positive religion contains something of the true nature of religion, and the essence, the primordial form, or the transcendental unity of religion, is comprehended not by deducing it from the common elements of particular religions as a kind of abstraction, but in and through the language and traditions of particular religions. Historical religions are true in so far as they succeed in expressing the primordial form of religion which in turn is apprehended only in the depths of particular religions.[13]

But is it possible to maintain the existence of a primordial element which is the essence of all particular religious traditions? And how do we isolate such an element or determine the truth of historical religions by means of it? How do we distinguish between degrees or grades of numinosity for example? Is it possible that the quest for the essence of religion may simply lead us further away from a true understanding of religious traditions. Cantwell Smith seems to think that such is the case. Our inability to define the term 'religion' adequately, he maintains, indicates that we should dispense with it since it does not correspond to an entity which can be determined.[14] He describes it further as 'confusing, unnecessary, and distorting [and not something] that can be formulated and externalised into an observable pattern theoretically abstractible from the persons who live it.'[15] Whether the failure to define religion adequately is a sufficient reason for dropping the term altogether is highly debatable. It is only when religion is used as referring to an essence that it becomes difficult to define. When it is used to refer to particular religious traditions the same difficulty does not apply. Smith cites Karl Barth as one of the foremost antagonists of the concept of religion and regards it as surprising that we should want to view religion as the Aristotelian essence of all particulars as if all particular instances must of necessity have a common element.[16] This is not to deny that there may be much in common between religions or that there are family resemblances, but that is a far cry from claiming that there is a primordial element common to all particular religions which can be called religion. Smith clearly points out that there are problems in seeking to postulate 'a transcendental ideal of which the historical actualities are a succession of mundane and therefore imperfect, compromised manifestations.'[17] In place of religion Smith substitutes the twin concepts of faith and cumulative tradition, that is, the religious experience of people on the one hand, and the historical data of the religious life of the people on the other. The latter is a human construct; it is the expression of faith and can take many forms. The former is the impinge-ment of the transcendent on the lives of people. What we call religion in Smith's view is not an essence or a primordial ele-ment but the dialectic that takes place between faith and tra-dition.[18] Critics of Smith would say that if he has difficulty with the notion of an essence or primordial element would he not have equal difficulty in giving an account of 'the impingement of the transcendent' on people's lives, for is not this simply a different version of the attempt to find an 'essence' of reli-gion? Smith might reply that the faith of a Muslim or Buddhist or Christian has to be measured in terms of their participation in a way of life rather than in terms of its approximation to an essentialist ideal, but such a reply does not remove the prob-lem posed by 'the impingement of the transcendent'.

Here then are four indications of the growing concern with religious diversity and religious pluralism in theological cir-cles: the statement of the Second Vatican Council; increased theological interest in world religions; concern with the phe-nomenology of religion; and the quest for the essence of re-ligion underlying religious diversity. The question that arises is what will count as an adequate Christian theological response to religious pluralism?

III THEOLOGICAL RESPONSES TO RELIGIOUS PLURALISM

A number of theological responses to religious pluralism can be referred to. First there is the response that depends on a sharp distinction being drawn between religion and faith. The favourable attitude to the history and plurality of religions suffered a reverse in the early decades of the twentieth cen-tury as a result of the theological climate prevalent at the time. Tillich refers to the sense of theological isolation experienced by his friends Otto and Heiler and of the attacks levelled against his own views during a seminar on Schleiermacher at Marburg.[19] The neo-orthodox attitude which predominated then defined faith as revelation and religion as arrogant and futile human attempt to reach God. It was the modern version of the older orthodox attitude that distinguished between *vera religio* and *religiones falsâe*. The issue is that of distinguishing between revelation and religion, or between revealed theology and natural theology. The point is made that the revelation of God in Christ is not just an extension of natural religion but a consequence of the gracious activity of God. The emphasis is on discontinuity rather than continuity and on radical displacement of other religions by the Christian faith. This attitude is best represented in the writings of Karl Barth who defines religion as unbelief. At worst it is a manifestation of man's revolt against God, and at best it is man's perverted response to God's initiative. The Church, in Barth's view, is the locus of true religion, but not because it is the result of a process of differentiation conducted on the basis of an analysis of the concept of religion, rather as a result of the grace of God's self-revelation. Revelation is God's self-manifestation and religion is simply man's attempt to come to know God by means of his own efforts and is the antithesis of revelation. Religion cannot be interpreted as man's attempt to cooperate with God or as man's appropriation of God's grace; it is man's substitute for revelation and cannot provide knowledge of God. For Barth there can be no continuity between religion and revelation; the one radically displaces the other.

Can we infer from this that Barth considers Christianity to be the true faith or the true religion and that other non-Christian religions are false? On the face of it that does seem to be the case, but in fact he insists that the Christian religion is true only in so far as it listens to divine revelation and recognises religion in the generally accepted sense of the term as unbelief. A distinction has to be drawn, in his view, between religion and faith. If Christian believers were to assume that the definition of religion as unbelief applied only to non-Christian religions and not to Christianity itself as a religion then it fails to understand the discontinuity that exists between religion and revelation. The Christian religion, as well as non-Christian religions, stands under the judgement of unbelief pronounced on all manifestations of religion. The Church must never forsake its belief in the sufficiency of God's grace, nor must it seek to resist other religions by appeals to religious experience or religious self-consciousness. Its truth does not rest in its inherent holiness, or in its religious self-consciousness, or in religious experience (an implicit criticism of Schleiermacher), but in the knowledge of God's grace and revelation through faith.[20]

Barth may be providing the Church with a salutary reminder of its status, but the question arises: what is one to make of the claim of other religious traditions, or the faiths of other men, that God reveals himself to them in an act of grace? We are very much aware of philosophical positivism but can it be said that what we have here is an example of theological positivism? Must it be assumed that a different God is involved in the revelatory experience of other religions? Is it the case that true revelation applies only to the Christian tradition? If so then the question that has to be asked is by what independent criterion do we determine that revelation is true in one instance and not in another? Or can it be that there is no independent criterion and that revelation itself enables us to determine what is true and what is false? If that is the case what are we to make of the anti-Jansenist pronouncement of the Church *extra ecclesiam conceditur gratia?* If divine grace is believed to operate *extra ecclesia* then it operates in spheres other than the Christian tradition unless the claim is made that it operates only through the Church in its representative capacity. We shall have the opportunity of returning to this claim later.

Secondly, a different theological reaction to religious pluralism is that which regards Christianity as the fulfilment of the religious development of mankind, the culmination of a progressive evolutionary development from a lower to a higher form of religious experience. This assessment can take different forms. There is the form that arranges religions in an ascending scale of importance linked to the evolutionary development of man's religious consciousness from primitive forms of nature and idol worship, polytheism, through henotheism to monotheism, of which Islam, Judaism and Christianity are the primary representatives. An expression of this assessment is to be found in the writings of Schleiermacher for whom Christianity is the most perfect and highly developed form of religion. As we have seen he pointed to the need for a multiplicity of positive, historical religions in order that the essence of religion might be manifested. These positive religions are for him a manifestation of the progressive work of the spirit, and while they contain much that is corrupt and degenerate yet they possess, to a greater or lesser degree, something of the true nature of religion. Of all the positive religions the intuition of Christianity is for him the most penetrating, yet the possibility of even more impressive and glorious forms of religion cannot be ruled out.[21]

The third theological reaction that can be noted points to an assessment of religions in terms of fulfilment and is related to the concept of salvation history. It is claimed that all non-Christian religions have a place in God's plan of salvation. They manifest God's grace but their role is preparatory: the plenitude of grace and the fullness of salvation is to be found only within the Christian tradition. This view presupposes that salvation means the same thing in different religious traditions though why this assumption should be made is not clear. It also presupposes that the concept of God as the Lord of history, which has a particular meaning within the Christian tradition, must have a similar meaning and be applied in the same way in other religious traditions. Hans Küng expresses this view very well and it is sometimes referred to as representing a liberal Catholic attitude towards non-Christian religions. It is the view that favours dialogue rather than radical displacement. Küng claims that it rests on a wider vision of God than that which would confine God to a single religion. Denzinger's *Enchiridion* raises difficult questions for those liberal Catholics familiar with the testimony of Hindus and Buddhists, according to Küng, for it makes it almost impossible for them to continue to maintain the doctrine *extra ecclesiam nulla salus est*, as normally interpreted, or to engage in missionary activity in the usual way. It is not possible for them either to interpret non-Christian religions as indications of human autonomy in the quest for God after the fashion of dialectic theology, for 2000 years of Christian mission and testimony has not brought about any significant change in the pluralistic religious situation.[22] Küng's view is that the theological solution to the problem lies in assessing the significance of non-Christian religions in God's plan of salvation and the place of the Church in that plan. It involves a move from an ecclesiocentric to a theocentric view (what Hick calls a Copernican revolution) and setting aside the misleading axiom *extra ecclesiam nulla salus est*. Knowledge of God in non-Christian religious traditions must not be

assumed to be 'natural' religion rather a human response to
the revelation of divine grace. That is, God revealed himself to
man prior to the Christian revelation. As the Declaration on
the Relation of the Church to Non-Christian Religions of the
Second Vatican council affirms:

> His manifestation of goodness, his saving design, extend to
> all men until that time when the elect will be united in the
> Holy City ... where all the nations will walk in his light.[23]

Küng is at pains to point out that this does not automatically
lead to the affirmation of a relativism of religious forms expressing an absolute religious or mystical experience common
to all religious traditions. An affirmation of that sort is as much
an affirmation of faith as the affirmation that God has revealed himself fully and completely in Christ. The impersonal
approach is no less dogmatic than the personal approach. But
given the dogmatic presuppositions of the Christian tradition,
how are other non-Christian religions to be regarded? From
the dogmatic standpoint, says Küng, it can be claimed that
they are (a) in error; (b) though in error proclaim the truth
of God when they acknowledge man's need of salvation, recognise God's grace, and listen to the voice of the prophets; (c)
ordinary ways of salvation as distinct from the extraordinary
way of salvation of the church. That is, they exemplify universal salvation history as distinct from special salvation history,
since man is intended to find salvation within his own historical milieu and his own religious tradition. Real salvation and
true communion, however, is revealed only through the gospel
of Christ. Religions are structures which contain both the light
of revelation and the darkness of human error and failure.
They are pre-Christian rather than non-Christian and stand in
need of the gospel. On the basis of this analysis Küng claims
that he is not proposing the domination of one religion or a
syncretism of religions, yet he regards the church as a sign of
fulfilment, as the work of God, and as a challenge to the adherents of non-Christian or pre-Christian religions to unite
with it in witnessing to Christ. In fact the church by its very
existence extends an invitation to Christians *de jure* to become
Christians *de facto*.[24]

Schlette expresses a similar viewpoint when he refers to
salvation history as the basis for a theological interpretation of

religions. A general salvation history can be discerned in the non-Christian religious traditions, but special salvation history is occasioned by the revelation of God in Christ which points to an extraordinary way of salvation as distinct from ordinary ways of salvation. For Schlette Christ is the eschatological event indicative of special sacred history. The extraordinary way of salvation provided by the revelation of God in Christ is definitive and perfect and those who walk in this way are chosen. What occurred prior to this revelation was preparatory; it was not insignificant or unimportant but it was less than perfect, hence the need for a transition from religion to faith.[25] This is Schlette's way of justifying conversion from non-Christian religions to Christianity without given the impression of being too exclusive. He actually disapproves of conversion apologetics while at the same time acknowledging the need for a move from religion to faith in order to achieve fulfilment. Or, to put the matter more positively, it is his way of preserving the uniqueness of Christianity. He recognises in fact that his theological interpretation of non-Christian religions does not detract in any way from the uniqueness of Christianity or from its claim to possess absolute truth.

Whether it faces the problem of the truth claims of non-Christian religions is another matter. The same point could be made of Küng's views. The move towards a more open or radical approach to non-Christian religions is barely perceptible in either case. It could be regarded as a step forward in some ways from the neo-orthodox view that classifies all religions as unbelief, but does it differ substantially from that view in respect of the claim to the absoluteness and finality of the Christian faith? Schlette it has to be said characterises dialectic theology as too simplistic and extreme. It is far too frivolous, in his view, to classify the positive elements of non-Christian religions as isolated, illusory or subjective, since they bear witness to genuine religious sensitivity and experience. Yet he is ready to acknowledge the positive contribution of dialectic theology in stressing the uniqueness of God's revelation in Christ. The Christian faith for him, as for the neo-orthodox, is not an extension of natural theology but something attainable only through God's grace, and his insistence on the need of a transition from religion to faith means that he is not far removed from the neo-orthodox position.[26]

A fourth theological response to religious diversity is to be found in the theology of Paul Tillich who reminds us of the basic requirements of a Christian theologian engaged in the task of constructing a theology of religions. In the first instance he would have to reject the distinction often drawn between *vera religio* and *religiones falsae* or the notion that we have revelation on the one hand and religion on the other. In other words he would have to reject the exclusivist approach to religions and accept the view that revelatory experiences are universal and received by man within those specific human situations which tend to distort revelation.[27] Tillich, however, qualifies this position by making the claim, which was more tentative in his later writings, that there is a central event in religious history which makes possible a particular theology of universal significance. He refers to this central event as the *kairos* of the appearance of Jesus as the Christ. There are other *kairoi* in the history of religions, but the relation of the *kairos* to the *kairoi* is 'the relation of the criterion to that which stands under the criterion and the relation of the source of power to that which is nourished by the source of power'.[28] The *kairos* is unique and *kairoi* are rare symbolic moments, or momentous events of great religious significance, but together they determine the dynamics of religious history. If we ask Tillich on what grounds he is able to justify the claim that the appearance of Jesus as the Christ is unique, 'a moment in history for which everything before and after is both preparation and a reception', his reply is that it an expression of the daring courage of the Christian faith which without the risk of error would not be faith.[29] Yet even the possibility of error seems to be removed when he confidently asserts that despite empirical investigations there is no other event in history for which this claim could be made, and that the appearance of Jesus as the Christ 'is not only the centre of the history of the manifestation of the Kingdom of God [but] also the only event in which the historical dimension is fully and universally affirmed'.[30] The implication of this statement is that history can only be fully understood from that point where history reveals its meaning, namely, the appearance of Jesus as the Christ as the centre of history. This is Tillich's Christological interpretation of history which was given an enthusiastic welcome by D.M. Baillie, who compared it to the time scheme worked out by Barth.[31]

Tillich is guilty here of the same kind of misuse of religious language as when he seeks to give a fiducial guarantee for the historicity of Jesus as the Christ. On the question of the historical Jesus he distinguishes between the element of probability in our knowledge of the historical Jesus and the certainty we have concerning the facticity or factualness of the Christ event, or the personal life lying behind the biblical picture of Jesus as the Christ. It is difficult to understand why the personal life behind the biblical picture should not be subjected to the same kind of historical investigation as the historical Jesus, but Tillich insists on applying one criterion of historical truth to the historical Jesus and another to the factual element of the Christ event. He accepts the necessity for radical historical investigation of the historical Jesus, yet guarantees on the grounds of faith the historical life behind the biblical picture of Jesus as the Christ. Such a fiducial guarantee seeks to shelter the Christian faith from the harsh winds of historical investigation and is a misuse of religious language. To say that the experience of the reality of the New Being guarantees the factual element of the biblical picture of Jesus as the Christ as distinct from the historical Jesus, is to make a religious experience the criterion for establishing an historical truth. The question why Tillich should want to make the historical basis of the Christian faith immune from the normal investigatory processes of historical research is answered by the explanation that his interpretation of the meaning of history rests, as we have seen, on a Christological foundation, so he cannot afford to allow the historical basis of Christianity to be dependent on the uncertainties of historical research. The Christ event is the *kairos*, the momentous event, which affirms the historical dimension and reveals its meaning.[32]

What is not clear is how Tillich can deny to other religious traditions a similar interpretation of history based on what they conceive to be *kairos* of revelation, and which for them is an expression of the daring courage of their faith. The appearance of Jesus as the Christ may be decisive for Christians, and the Christ event may be their criterion of truth, but what is to prevent similar claims being made for other *kairoi* by other religious traditions? How do we distinguish between *kairoi*, and on what grounds do we determine which is the correct criterion?

Tillich's response to religious diversity results in what he calls a dynamic–typological approach in which he distinguishes three main elements in man's religious experience of the holy, namely, the sacramental, the mystical and the prophetic. These elements, when harmoniously united, produce what he calls the religion of the concrete spirit, which occurs in fragmentary form only in the depth of particular, historical religions. He refuses to conceive of an universally valid religion of the spirit existing in the abstract as it were, unrelated to, and divorced from, particular religions. He insists rather that the religion of the concrete spirit, as the phrase implies, exists concretely in the depth of particular, historical religions. So the future of theology lies in an interpenetration of theological and religious studies and not in the promotion of a ghetto mentality that would confine theological investigation to a single religious tradition.[33]

Tillich was not entirely happy with his dynamic–typological approach to the history of religions.[34] He recognises that to talk of types is to talk of abstractions,[35] which is why he rejects the notion of an ideal religion of the spirit unrelated to particular religious traditions where the sacramental, mystical and prophetic elements of man's experience of the holy are harmonised.[36] Yet this does not prevent him from hypostatising an ideal form of religious experience of which particular religious experiences are partial and fragmentary manifestations. In this respect he is akin to Schleiermacher for whom the essence of religion is comprehended in the language and traditions of particular religions.

IV THE SEARCH FOR INDEPENDENT CRITERIA

Four theological responses to religious pluralism have been noted: the distinction between religion and faith; Christianity as the fulfilment of the religious development of mankind; Christianity as part of God's plan of salvation; and the dynamic–typological approach together with the *kairos–kairoi* distinction. This brings us back to the question posed earlier: what are we make of the problem of competing truth claims? Is it not the case that a valid awareness of the divine occurs in all religions, and that the love of God in Christ is not incompatible with the love of God in other forms, at other times, and in other places? What then determines whether a religious claim is true or false? Is there an independent criterion of truth that can be appealed to? Christians claim that Jesus is the only-begotten Son of God while Hindus look upon Krishna as an *avatar* of Vishnu. Is there an independent criterion of truth, external to and independent of the religions in question, which can be invoked to settle the matter? The following suggestions might be made:

First, we might claim that the truth of a religion can be established eschatologically. But if it is the case that what determines the truth of the Christian claim is its eschatological verification in the lives of believing Christians, does it not follow that the truth of the Hindu claim that Krishna is an *avatar* of Vishnu is its eschatological verification in the lives of Vaishnavite believers? If the principle of eschatological verification is regarded as an universally acceptable criterion of truth, it is difficult to see what sense we can make of the claim of believers that all religious truths embodied in their respective religions are self-evident.

Secondly, it might be claimed that morality can be made an independent criterion of truth. If immoral action belies my confession of faith then it could be argued that my religious beliefs have been proved to be false by an appeal to the independent criterion of moral acceptability. This suggestion presupposes that we know what is moral or immoral apart from and independent of participation in a way of life. But is that the case? Do we not learn to identify what is right and wrong within a form of life rather than as neutral observers? Some of the early practices of the Hebrews, however, might be considered to be barbaric and some of the comparatively recent practices of the Hindus to be distinctly immoral, but could it not be argued that they simply reflect the nature of their beliefs and the kind of activities they have tended to regard as acceptable at certain stages in the development of their religious tradition? Prophets and reformers within the religions concerned have, after all, drawn attention to the barbaric and immoral nature of these religious and social practices. Can it be that there are different moral attitudes related to different beliefs which are grounded in different forms of life at different times, and that this means there is no justification for regarding morality as an independent criterion?

There are those, however, who are reluctant to let go completely the criterion of moral acceptability. For example, when Kierkegaard says that ethically speaking what Abraham planned for Isaac was murder, one is inclined to agree and to ask whether anything makes murder palatable. If Kierkegaard is correct in his account of Abraham then he has given us one very good reason for rejecting the claim that religious beliefs and practices should not be subject to moral evaluation. But does this mean that morality is an independent criterion of the truth of a religion? Is it not something that is inextricably bound up with religious beliefs as the actions of prophets and reformers have shown? Can it really be regarded as the means of distinguishing between the truth claims of competing religions?[37]

Thirdly, we might be tempted to regard religious experience as a criterion of truth against which religious beliefs and traditions can be checked and assessed. It is precisely this tendency to regard religious experience as having a life of its own, independent of particular historical expression of religious belief and apart from the context of religious language and tradition, that may have been one of the reasons for the revolt against natural theology in the first place. For if we regard religious experience as an independent criterion of truth then it might make sense to seek to construct a theology of religious experience. But is it possible to speak of religious experience in the abstract in this way? Does not reference to religious experience have meaning only when it is used in the context of religious traditions? If we maintain that religions are true when they clarify and illuminate religious experience are we not assuming that religious experience has a reality of its own independent of religious traditions?[38]

The problem of establishing an external independent criterion of truth is illustrated by accounts that are sometimes given of primitive cultures. Peter Winch, for example, poses the question: what criteria do we have for saying something is true or false, and does or does not make sense? He cites the Zande practice of consulting oracles as an example. It might appear to us to be unintelligible, but not to the Zande even when contradictions are pointed out to him. The question is: are we right and the Zande wrong? It could be argued that the Zande wallows in a sea of mystical notions while we are immersed in a sea of scientific notions. Is it possible to maintain, as Evans-Pritchard does, that we are confronted here with two fundamentally different languages and two concepts of reality and that our concept of reality is true and the Zande concept false? Winch points out that it is difficult to see what true and false can mean in this context. What we are confronted with here are different forms of understanding and different standards of intelligibility. In order to understand another person's way of life we should extend our way of life into the orbit of the other way of life rather than seeking to see everything in terms of our own distinctions between scientific and non-scientific. What appears to us to be irrational and unintelligible might be both rational and intelligible to the Zande. But does it follow that we are right and the Zande wrong? Winch's point is that when a society has a language and a tradition it also has a concept of rationality and intelligibility.[39] The parallels that can be drawn between accounts of primitive cultures and accounts of religious beliefs are evident. It could be said that judgments concerning the truth or falsity of religious beliefs sometimes ignore the role they play in the different forms of life involved.

Are we to conclude from what has been said that there is no independent criterion of truth? Barth's view is that the criterion of truth of the Christian faith is not religious experience, or its inherent holiness, but the self-revelation of God. It is a revealed criterion and not something that man discovers for himself. So it is not a criterion external to, or independent of, a particular form of religious belief, a criterion that can be applied as a measuring line to all other religious traditions. Schlette also refers to the absolute nature of the Christian experience as does Küng. For both of them, as for Barth, the criterion of truth is the revelation of God in Christ. Our basic problems it would seem remain.

V   WITTGENSTEINIAN PERSPECTIVES ON RELIGION

Recent Wittgensteinian approaches in the philosophy of religion may help us to see why the search for independent criteria of truth is itself confused. This approach refers to the absolute nature of God and religious beliefs. In the same way as we do not look outside mathematics to determine whether what is done in mathematics is correct or not, so we do not look outside religious beliefs in order to determine whether or not they are true. The criteria for the meaningfulness of religious belief lie within religion itself. We do not verify the truth of religious discourse by reference to an external criterion of truth. What kind of knowledge of God could we possibly have which was not in itself religious? To give a non-religious account of the reality of God is like giving a non-musical account of the reality of music or a non-scientific account of the reality of science. When we affirm the existence of God are we not making a confession of faith rather than a factual statement which is open to verification or falsification? Someone might want to deny the existence of God but in Wittgenstein's view that denial does not contradict the believer's affirmation that God exists. Contradiction is not involved because the believer and the non-believer do not share the same mode of discourse. A denial of the existence of God is not a denial of a particular fact but an indication of one of a variety of different ways a man may stand in relation to the affirmation of belief in God's existence.[40] This is what is meant by saying that religious belief is absolute. From the Wittgensteinian perspective belief in God is not an hypothesis which can be revised or discarded in the light of further evidence. We understand the meaning of the term through stories, pictures and catechisms and as Wittgenstein points out 'the whole *weight* may be in the picture'.[41]

From this viewpoint attempts to prove the existence of God by reference to an external criterion of truth are mistaken. When a believer says he believes in God he is not making the same kind of statement as someone who say that he believes there is a chair in the next room. The second proposition can be verified, but the same kind of verification cannot be applied to the first statement because it does not belong to the same class of propositions. The reality of God is not to be construed as if it is akin to the reality of an object. God's reality gets its unshakeable character 'from all the activities that hold it fast. Above all, those activities involving the language of praise and worship'.[42] If the concept of God's identity is to have any meaning it has to be found in the context of religious traditions since it is a confession of faith and not a factual statement. The problem, however, is that even after we

have established that there is no single paradigm of rationality
to which all modes of discourse must conform, and delineated
the religious mode of discourse in question, that is not the
same as establishing the truth of God's reality.

The similarity between the Wittgensteinian approach and
the theological approach of Barth is evident. Emphasis on the
absolute reality of God and religious beliefs is similar in both
cases. To an extent the same applies to their respective attitudes to natural theology. Barth draws a clear line of demarcation between natural and revealed theology. Similarly the
Wittgensteinian approach to religion would reject, for example, cosmological arguments for the existence of God on the
grounds that they presuppose the God whose existence is
proved by the use of reason, that is, the God of natural theology, is the same God who graciously reveals himself and who
is apprehended through faith. For both Barth and Wittgenstein
the believer has no need to reason from the world to God
since his attitude to the world is religious from the beginning.[43] Where Wittgenstein differs from Barth is in relation to
what is sometimes called the positivism of revelation. The
Wittgensteinian reply to any form of religious exclusivism is
that there can be no philosophical justification for speaking as
if there is only one true religion. There are different religions
and different moralities grounded in different forms of life.
What can be concluded, therefore, from the Wittgensteinian
perspective is that there are no independent criteria of truth
to enable us to adjudicate between different religious traditions.

VI POSSIBILITIES OF JUDGEMENTS

If the search for independent criteria of truth is mistaken or
confused it follows that there can be no grounds for seeking
to adjudicate between religions. Yet this does not preclude the
possibility of judgements being made about all forms of life
from within particular religious traditions.

There is, in the first place, the question of consistency. Given
the Christian concept of love, for example, it might be argued
that certain attitudes ought to be regarded as unacceptable.
There could be no justification for the use of force, for instance, in order to convert men to the Christian way of life for

that would indicate a greater love of dogma than of man, as Simone Weil correctly maintains. If the end justifies the means is not the Christian concept of love distorted? Certain inquisitorial and missionary methods might be considered unacceptable in this respect. Not that the right of anyone to engage in missionary activity is questioned. A Christian may, even when he understands the Zande practice of consulting oracles, still want to change them or put a stop to them. This is a matter of religious judgement. But the way in which he puts a stop to them and the attitude he adopts towards them could well be unacceptable if inconsistent with the Christian concept of love.

Again it may be considered inconsistent with the Christian belief that man is created in the image of God to treat certain racial groups as inferior. Christian propounders of the doctrine of apartheid might argue that far from being treated as inferior, certain racial groups are being encouraged to develop their own culture and traditions and establish their own homelands. But whatever the long-term objectives of the policy of racial segregation is it not the case that in the short term it has to be regarded as inconsistent with Christian belief about the nature and destiny of man?

The Hindu practice of infanticide and suttee, the self-immolation of widows on the funeral pyres of their husbands, may be considered by some Hindus to be consistent with their beliefs about *dharma* or duty. Yet other Hindus, especially reformers, might regard it as belonging to a degenerate form of Hinduism and inconsistent with the teaching of classical and reformed Hinduism. It would certainly be regarded as inconsistent with Christian beliefs about the nature and destiny of man. So from within the tradition concerned, and certainly from without, these practice would be regarded as inconsistent and unacceptable.

Secondly, there is the question of factual correctness. It may be factually incorrect for one group of believers to claim that their religion alone has certain features. They would have to acknowledged this when confronted with similar features in other religions which they claim to be unique to their own religion. The distinction drawn between religion and revelation is a case in point. It is a fact that in the judgement of Hindus revelation occurs in their tradition, and they draw a distinction between *śruti* (that which is revealed), and *śmriti* (tradition). As the *Bhagavadgītā* relates, Krishna, by an act of grace, reveals himself to Arjuna in a theophany that leaves Arjuna in do doubt a to the status of Krishna as an *avatar* of Vishnu. Again in the Māhāyana Buddhist tradition the *Bodhisattva*, or Enlightened Being, is presented as having all the characteristics of a saviour. In view of the similarities of these revelatory features in different religious traditions it might be considered arbitrary to classify religion as unbelief or as man's futile attempt to reach God, and revelation as specifically Christian. Similarly it might be regarded as factually incorrect to say that there is but one saviour for all men.

Yet while there may be grounds for judgments to be made when discussing questions of consistency and factual correctness, the fact remains that so far as competing truth claims are concerned there appears to be no independent criterion of truth to enable us to adjudicate between them. This is clearly something that the Christian theologian has to bear in mind as he seeks to formulate a theology of religions.

VII   CONCLUSION

This analysis of the different responses to religious pluralism has clarified some of the problems involved in seeking to construct a theology of religions. What has emerged is that it is no longer possible for any theologian to ignore the existence of different religious traditions, nor is it possible to disregard the occurrence of features in other religions similar to those hitherto considered unique to our own tradition. Tillich's rejection of the *vera religio religiones falsâe* distinction shows an awareness of this. Yet in his endeavour to preserve the universality of revelatory experiences and the uniqueness of the revelation in Jesus as the Christ, he resorts to distinguishing between preparatory and final revelation. The fact that he uses the term final in a normative sense does not really make any difference and the problem he has to face is that what is considered normative in one religious tradition need not necessarily be accepted as normative in another tradition.

Küng and Schlette show an awareness similar to Tillich when they suggest the rejection of the misleading axiom *extra ecclesiam nulla salus est* and the recognition of the significance of all religions in God's plan of salvation. Yet in their endeavour to ensure a place for non-Christian religions and to preserve the uniqueness of the Christian revelation, they resort to distinguishing between ordinary and extraordinary ways of salvation and between general and special sacred history. The problem is that what is regarded as extraordinary and special in one tradition need not be accepted as such in another tradition. Indeed they might make contrary claims based on their own religious judgments and, as we have tried to show, there is no independent criterion of truth whereby we might distinguish between them. It is with these problems in mind that the Christian theologian has to move towards a theology of religions.

2 A Wittgensteinian Approach to the Philosophy of Religion

The Wittgensteinian approach to the philosophy of religion owes much to the influence of Rush Rhees but is best exemplified in the work of D.Z. Phillips, whose writings have given a new direction to the philosophical discussion of religious issues. His work has prompted much opposition and critical comment which in the main has been of two kinds. On the one hand he has been attacked for seeking to provide religion with a haven from the harsh winds of philosophical analysis, which has prompted some to refer to him as the protagonist of what Nielsen calls Wittgensteinian fideism.[1] On the other hand he has been referred to by some religious believers as a reductionist who seeks to attenuate the faith of the fathers. I hope to examine both of these criticisms in the course of elucidating Phillips's position in this essay.

It may be appropriate to begin by asking what it is that Phillips finds inadequate in the traditional approach to the philosophy of religion. This is not simply a negative exercise because his reasons for rejecting the traditional approach sheds light on his own views as to what the philosophical discussion of religious issues ought to be. In the first place he has difficulty in understanding what is meant by the philosophical quest for a justification of religious experience. He is puzzled by the search for rational grounds for religious belief so characteristic of philosophical traditionalists and he expresses his misgivings thus: 'The requests for a "foundation" for religion as such are but another example of seeking justifications beyond the stage where it makes sense to do so.'[2] While it might seem eminently right and proper at first sight to establish the existence of God before embarking in the study of the philosophy of religion, the basic presupposition of such an approach, from the Wittgensteinian standpoint, is that we already know what is meant by the reality of God whose existence we seek to verify. Yet what kind of knowledge of God can we possibly have that is not basically religious? When philosophers insists that they able to give a non-religious account of the reality of God whose existence they seek to verify, it is similar, according to Phillips, to seeking to give a non-musical account of the reality of music or a nonscientific account of the reality of science.[3] The point he is making is that the reality of God cannot be considered in a non-religious context and that traditional philosophers of religion fail to distinguish between philosophical doubt and practical doubt. The latter can be settled in the case of the existence of material objects, a tree, for example, by proceeding to where a tree is located and verifying its existence. Philosophical doubt as to what it means to say that a tree exists cannot be resolved by standing in front of a tree. That is, philosophical doubt is not an extension of practical doubt; it is not resolved by an appeal to empirical facts. While the distinction may not be as clear in the case of moral values yet a philosophical analysis of what it might mean to hold certain moral values can be distinguished from the practical activity involved in making moral judgements.[4]

The reality of what is being investigated in the case of material objects and moral values is not questioned; but when it comes to the reality of God doubt is expressed as to whether there is such a reality, and the philosopher sees his primary task as determining whether or not God exists. That is, his philosophical doubt is an extension of his practical doubt. He no longer seeks to know what it might mean to say that one believes in God but tries to resolve the practical question whether there is a God. Phillips's argument is that God cannot be conceived as one reality among other realities, or as a being among other beings; God's existence cannot be proved as one proves the existence of things or the truth of matters of fact. His reality is absolute and requires no external justification; it is its own measuring line and determines what is comprehensible and incomprehensible within a particular form of life.

'The point is not that for believers *as a matter of fact* God will always exist, but that it *makes no sense* to say that God might not exist. The idea of God is such that the possibility of the non-existence of God is logically precluded.'[5]

We may ask what can possibly be meant by saying that the reality of God is absolute, or that the idea of God is such that the possibility of his non-existence is logically precluded? Is it not the case that God's existence is questioned, doubted and often rejected? How can rejection of the existence of God be reconciled with the claim that his non-existence is logically precluded? Does not the non-believer, or the believer who has lost his faith, deny the existence of God when he says 'There is no God'? Does not such a denial refute the claim that the reality of God is absolute? The answer would appear to be yes, but Phillips's response is to maintain with Wittgenstein that the non-believer who says 'there is no God' is not contradicting the believer who says that there is a God because they do not share the same mode of discourse. The denial of God's existence is a rejection of a whole mode of discourse rather than a contradictory statement within the same mode of discourse. The example given is that if you say to someone that handling a ball in a game amounts to a foul you both have to be playing the same game. The believer and the non-believer do not contradict one another because they do not share a common understanding.[6]

We may argue that talk of religious and non-religious modes of discourse and sharing a common understanding simply obscures the real issue. Does not the religious mode of discourse presuppose the reality of God, and is it not the existence of God which is under discussion? The assumption of such an argument, according to Phillips, is that the reality of God is akin to the reality of physical objects, a substantive, whereas the affirmation 'God exists' is really a confession of faith rather than a statement in the indicative mood. Similarly, the statement 'God does not exist' indicates one of many possible negative relationships in which a man may stand with regard to the affirmation of faith rather than a statement in the indicative mood. It is on these grounds that the claim is made for the absolute reality of God and his necessary existence.[7]

But does seeking to determine the existence of God necessarily rest on the assumption that the reality of God is akin to the reality of physical objects? Hick maintains that to ask whether God exists is clearly not to ask whether there is a particular physical object out there, so that the enquirer cannot be accused of assuming that the reality of God is akin to the reality of physical objects. It is no solution of the problem, according to Hick, to assert the necessary existence of God or his absolute reality because 'we do not learn what it is to exist by being told that some things exist necessarily and others contingently'. His solution of the problem of God's existence involves the notion of 'making a difference'. That is, the meaning of the affirmation 'God exists' must be sought in the difference such an affirmation makes within human experience. What Hick means by this is that although the term 'God' has an objective referent he does not wish to specify the nature of this referent other than to say that it is not a physical object, and that in fact God is known in his effects rather than in his essence.[8]

Phillips's argument is that to regard religious language as referential, whether the referent is specified or not, is fundamentally mistaken. When we do so we are guilty of grammatical confusion and of mistaking one kind of language for another. But has not the orthodox Christian tradition steadfastly upheld the referential character of religious language and consequently is not the accusation of reductionism often levelled against the Wittgensteinian position justified? From the orthodox point of view the answer is clearly yes, but for Phillips the real reductionists are those who insist on the referential nature of religious language and who by so doing distort the nature of religious belief.[9]

In pursuit of further clarification of this position we may ask whether religious discourse as a whole is non-referential. For example, is talk of Jesus non-referential? Surely the historicity of Jesus, or Muhammad, or other religious leaders, is not in dispute if their lives can be verified by the same process of historical investigation and principles of verification that are applied to other historical facts? On the other hand, the historicity of Jesus would justifiably be in dispute if it were claimed, as Tillich does, that the factual element of Jesus as the Christ is guaranteed by the faith of the believer. That would be a fiducial guarantee of the historicity of Jesus and an example of the misuse of religious language and of mistaking one kind of language for another that Phillips objects to.[10] A similar type of grammatical confusion applies when the last judgement is referred to as a future event that must necessarily take place. Not that belief in the last judgement is mistaken; it is simply that the account given of it as a future event is grammatically confused. A possible reinterpretation might be to regard this belief as a form of language which makes it possible for a man to have certain thoughts about a completed life.[11] But when this kind of reinterpretation is suggested it is made clear that it is a religious and not a philosophical judgement.

A second reason Phillips gives for rejecting the traditional approach to the philosophy of religion is the attempt it makes to posit general criteria of meaning for all significant utterances and every situation. Some philosophers insist on fitting religious beliefs into what they consider to be intelligible categories, which Wittgenstein refers to as empirical propositions and human attitudes. So, from the traditional standpoint, if religious beliefs are not classifiable as empirical statements then it is assumed that they must be human attitudes. But the problem with this approach is that questions that might reasonably be asked concerning religious beliefs are ignored. Phillips's argument is that positivism and empiricism – what he calls Hume's legacy – have had a profound effect on the way certain philosophers of religion think. Some of them find the criteria of meaningfulness in the ordinary use of language, and it follows that in religious discourse ordinary language is either stretched to breaking point (Hepburn), or eroded by a thousand qualifications on the part of the believer (Flew). The basic presupposition is that the ordinary use of language is the paradigm for its use in other contexts. But what does the ordinary use of language mean? Winch claims that 'When philosophers say "this is the meaning a word *must have*" without specifying any context, they are guilty of arbitrary linguistic legislation. The "must" is not a logical "must" but simply the "must" of their own preferences, or the "must" of one context which they have elevated, consciously or unconsciously, to be a standard for all others.'[12]

The fundamental mistake is to assume that there is a single paradigm of rationality to which all modes of discourse must conform. It amounts to a failure to distinguish between what Wittgenstein calls the surface grammar and the depth grammar of religious discourse. The point is that there are different contexts for the use of language and each language game has its own rules and criteria of meaningfulness including religion, and the 'criteria for the meaningfulness of religious concepts are to be found within religion itself.'[13]

What needs be to asked here is whether the notion of language-games simply obscures the whole issue. Is religious language cut off from ordinary language as Hick maintains, and social life divided into separate compartments as Nielsen would argue, by all this talk of language-games? Such criticisms are understandable and Phillips expresses misgivings himself about the use of the phrase 'language-games'. However, he does not want his misgivings to be construed as an admission that he considers religious discourse to be self-sufficient and isolated, or an esoteric language enjoyed by initiates but having no significance outside the believers circle. Nor does he want to suggest that religious beliefs are immune from criticism on the grounds that the criteria of the meaningfulness of religious beliefs lie within religion itself. On the other hand, he does not want his misgivings to be interpreted as justifying attempts to seek rational grounds for religious belief: 'Misgivings about treating religious beliefs as language-games can lead to an attempt to show why religious beliefs are important which distorts the nature of the values involved in such beliefs.'[14]

In the light of these qualifications we may ask what kind of misgivings are really being expressed here about the use of the phrase 'language-games'? Phillips admits that if the analogy between language and games is overdrawn religious discourse would become self-contained with an equivocal terminology.[15] In this respect he accepts the point Nielsen makes yet without accepting his accusation of Wittgensteinian fideism. If religion were to be considered apart from other modes of life and isolated from the joys and sorrows of normal existence, then it could not possibly have the significance and importance it has in the lives of people. Following Rush Rhees's argument in his paper on 'Wittgenstein's Builders', he points out that every language is a family of language-games and that the unity a language has is the unity of a family of language-games. What this means is that no language-game is autonomous in the sense that it is cut off completely from all other language-games and that what is said in one context by means of a particular statement must be related to the use of that statement in other contexts. That is, language-games are played by men who live lives with a variety of interests which influence one another. The significance of what a man does depends on whether he sees a unity in his many interests, activities, and relationships. Some language-games would not make sense unless there were other language-games independent of them. For example, how could the statement of Jesus, 'Not as the world gives give I unto you' have any force if religion were conceived of as an esoteric language-game? The significane of the statement depends on understanding the contrast referred to. What is being claimed here is that terms used in religious discourse have a connection with what lies outside religious discourse, and that the significance of their use in religious discourse is decided by the way they are used in other contexts.[16] The question is whether the concept of a family of language-games really constitutes an adequate explanation of the interrelation of religious discourse with other modes of discourse. Does it completely resolve the misgivings previously expressed concerning the use of the phrase? If the criteria for the meaningfulness of religious concepts are to be found within religion itself, what further significance can they acquire from being related to other modes of discourse? Does it mean that there are criteria of meaningfulness apart from those to be found within religion? If, as Rush Rhees maintains, it is the way in which we have come to know words in other connections that determines whether it makes sense to put them together in religious discourse for example, then the meaning they have within religious discourse is not confined to their use in that language-game.

We have seen that Phillips does not want to suggest that religious beliefs are immune from criticism because the criteria of the meaningfulness of those beliefs lie within religion. He maintains, for example, that if religious beliefs 'violate facts' or 'distort our apprehension of situations' then the fact that it is religious discourse is not sufficient to justify it. But does not this imply an external criterion whereby the adequacy or intelligibility of religious discourse is being judged? In one sense it has to be admitted that this is so. We can determine whether religious beliefs are confused or mistaken by checking those beliefs with what we know to be true in other circumstances. Phillips's argument, however, is that to say religious discourse should not violate or distort facts and situations is one thing, and to claim that religious beliefs are justified by those facts is another. The latter claim is based on the assumption '*that the relation between beliefs and non-religious facts is that between what is justified and its justification or that between a conclusion and its ground*'.[17] He rejects that assumption on the grounds that to insist what is considered intelligible in one context must be intelligible in the same way in all contexts is an example of philosophical prejudice and falsifies the absolute nature of religious beliefs.[18]

In view of what has been said about the possibility of religious beliefs being confused or mistaken we may ask again what is meant by referring to the absolute nature of religious beliefs. We have seen that they are referred to as requiring no external justification or verification in the same way as hypotheses, yet we are told that external checks can be applied in order to determine whether they are confused or mistaken. Phillips cites mathematics as an example of what he means when he refers to the absolute nature of religious beliefs. We do not look outside the rules of mathematics to determine whether what is done in mathematics is correct or not. Similarly we do not have to look outside religious beliefs in order to determine whether they are true or not. This is a puzzling situation. On the one hand religious beliefs are regarded as absolute, yet on the other hand they can be checked by what we know to be true in other circumstances to determine whether or not they are confused. Phillips defends his position by drawing a distinction between a 'check' and a 'criterion of verification or falsification'. The former he relates to the concept of a unity of language-games; the latter he relates to the notion that a single paradigm of rationality operates whereby the meaning a term has in one context is elevated to become the norm of intelligibility for all contexts. He rejects the view that a criterion of verification operates between language-games and prefers to use the term check. There is a difference, in his view, between criticising religious beliefs on the grounds that they do not fit in with facts as we know them, that is showing them to be mistaken or confused, and verifying religious beliefs by means of an external norm of meaningfulness or criterion of truth. If the distinction is not accepted then the enterprise which seeks to establish rational grounds for religious beliefs may be regarded as valid. The only problem that arises then is to determine what might constitute a universally applicable criterion of truth.

If we insist that there has to be an independent criterion of truth we would then have to make sense of the declaration

'These truths we hold to be self-evident'. We would also have to make sense of such statements as 'Jesus is the only begotten son of God' and 'Krishna is God incarnate'. For the majority of Christians only the former statement is true, while for Hindus the latter statement is a self-evident truth. When adherents of these religions claim the truths embodied in their religions to be self-evident, what independent criterion of truth can we produce to determine which religion is true? Phillips's view is that the search for an independent criterion of truth is mistaken and that the truth of a religion is the confession of the specific content of that religion and that we are concerned with intelligibility when we try to bring out the meaning of the content of a religion.

The question of an independent criterion of truth might be pursued further by enquiring whether morality plays any part in determining the truth or otherwise of religious beliefs. What if immoral activity belies my confession of faith in God? Could it not be argued that the false nature of my belief is made evident by an appeal to the external criterion of moral intelligibility? One possible reply to this question might be that the kind of immoral activity envisaged could not possibly follow from the confession 'I believe in God' given what is claimed to be the nature of the reality of God, and that the external criterion of morality appealed to is really internal to and bound up with religious beliefs. The claim Phillips makes is that religious beliefs are internally related to a believer's conduct and that it is in terms of religious language that a believer's conduct is to be understood.[19] But there have been those who have claimed to believe in God and whose immoral activities seem to falsify their belief claims. Does not morality in this case constitute a criterion of the truth or otherwise of religious belief? (The question whether it can be regarded as an external criterion, however, would depend on whether or not one accepts that religious beliefs and morality are internally related.) It might be pointed out in reply that some of the practices of the early Hebrews could be construed as barbaric and yet make more sense to them than the 'stumbling block' of the passion of Christ. The problem here is one of determining whether the kind of account that is given of religious belief, whether in words or activities, is indicative of the truth or otherwise of the belief concerned. It might be said that what these accounts indicate is the nature of the God one claims to believe in, and the kind of activities one has been taught to regard as right and proper. That is, one is first and foremost a participant in a form of life and not simply a neutral observer who first learns to identify actions as right and wrong under some kind of neutral description.[20]

The Wittgensteinian position is that morality cannot constitute an external criterion of the truth of religious beliefs. If the truth of a religion is the confession of the content of that religion, it is difficult to see from this viewpoint how morality can be regarded as a principle of verification. It is not clear either how morality can act as a check on whether religious beliefs are confused or mistaken. But Phillips does speak of the passion of Christ as reflecting 'true' religion more accurately than the barbaric practices of the early Hebrews. If the use of 'true' in this context is a philosophical judgement then it suggests the existence of an external criterion of truth, but in point of fact Phillips is making a religious judgement and indicating that what he knows of the passion of Christ makes him want to call it divine.[21] What is being suggested here is that there are competing moralities and competing religions grounded in different forms of life. But what if the truth claims of a particular religion are put forward as exclusive? If Christians believe Jesus to be the only begotten son of God are they not justified in seeking to lead others to Christ? The Wittgensteinian reply is that there can be no philosophical justification for speaking as if there is only one religion and one morality and that certain notions of mission may well reveal conceptual confusion in this respect. Could there be any justification for the use of force, for example, to lead men to what we believe to be the truth? Would not this amount to a denial of the Christian concept of love and show a greater love of dogma than of mankind?[22]

I have indicated hitherto what the Wittgensteinian approach to the philosophy of religion finds inadequate in the traditional approach, the most important aspect of which is the concept of the reality of God. From the Wittgensteinian standpoint the reality of God is not akin to the reality of physical objects: God is not a being among beings. As Winch points out, we cannot distinguish between what is real and unreal without understanding what the distinction is in the linguistic context where the distinction is made, because reality shows itself in the sense a language has.[23] When the philosophical problem of prayer, for instance, is regarded as the problem of ascertaining whether the believer is actually talking to someone or not, then the meaningfulness of prayer, and the question whether it makes sense or not, is made contingent upon verification of the existence of God. But we may ask whether this is not a reasonable approach. Is it not reasonable to enquire whether there is a God to pray to in the first place before we start to examine the concept of prayer? Phillips's reply is that to understand prayer is to understand what talking to God means and that it is a mistake to assume that in order to discuss prayer we must first determine whether God exists or not. If we ask why it is a mistake to seek to determine the existence of God we are told that we are presupposing that we already know what it is we are looking for, that is, that we know what is meant by divine reality.[24] But in fact the question as to what kind of reality divine reality is, is really akin to the question of the nature of the reality of physical objects. The latter question is logically prior to any kind of empirical investigation. Similarly, the question of the reality of God is a question of conceptual elucidation rather than a question of empirical investigation. It is a question about a kind of reality. And the question of the kind of reality divine reality is, like the question concerning the kind of reality physical objects possess, is a philosophical question, not to be confused with practical questions concerning the reality of physical objects.[25]

If to understand prayer is to understand what talking to God means, we may ask, if it is not an exercise in autosuggestion, whether some form of dialogue is involved. But does not the concept of dialogue lead us back again to the necessity to posit some kind of divine reality akin to the reality of physical objects, and is it not simply another way of pointing to the necessity to determine the existence of God in the first place? On the other hand, the concept of dialogue could be construed as an indication of some of the problems involved in the claim that religious language is not necessarily referential.

Phillips's argument is that the reality of God is absolute not relative and what he means by this is that belief in God is not synonymous with accepting an hypothesis, or holding an opinion which might be revised in the light of further evidence.

We can say of things that exist that it is possible to conceive of them ceasing to exist. But believers cannot conceive of God ceasing to exist: such a thought would make no sense. Neither would believers ask of God questions they might reasonably ask of a thing, such as how it originated and how long it had existed. According to Wittgenstein, the term 'God' is among the earliest terms we learn and we understand the meaning of the term through stories and pictures, but we do not see what is in the picture. That is, we do not see what is depicted by the picture of God in the same way as we see what is depicted by a picture of an aunt. Religious stories and pictures introduce us to the reality of God and when we understand the one we grasp the other. The fact that we do not see what the picture of God represents does not detract from the reality of God, because it is not the purpose of the picture to refer to external facts nor does it depend upon external facts. What the picture does is reveal the reality of God which in turn determines the attitude of believers to external facts. As Wittgenstein maintains, 'The whole *weight* may be in the picture'.[26]

From the Wittgensteinian standpoint the attempt of theologians like Mascall to seek external, rational grounds for belief in the existence of God is mistaken.[27] Wittgenstein himself is impatient with the proofs of God's existence since for him the importance of religious beliefs lie in the way they regulate our life. Attempts to prove the existence of God by means of cosmological arguments are also rejected by Phillips, since such arguments assume that the God whose existence is arrived at by the use of reason, the God of natural theology, is the same as the God who reveals himself through faith. Cosmological arguments, however, do have a certain value in that they make explicit the implicit grammar of religious belief, namely, that God is the source of the world. As Phillips points out:

> The attempts of cosmological arguments to move from the fact that *anything* exists to the reality of God has within it the seeds of the religious beliefs we have been grappling with – namely, the insistence that it is by contemplating the existence of human beings and natural events *as such* that one comes to see what is meant by God's being other than the world.[28]

But he argues that cosmological arguments cannot be taken seriously as proofs of the existence of God. Nature is alien and occasionally diabolical, with living beings hostile and destructive to one another; its testimony is not unequivocal. Proofs of God's existence are not necessary, however, for religious belief, nor do they necessarily reflect the faith of the believer. The believer does not argue from the world to God; his attitude to the world is religious from the beginning.[29]

Of the objections that can be levelled against the Wittgensteinian approach is the fact that no argument has been produced in favour of accepting the elucidative or clarifying role of philosophy. If the assumptions on which the approach is based are not to be regarded as *a priori*, then they stand in need of verification. The traditional philosopher of religion might argue, for example, that the criteria of logic arising out of one mode of social life and applicable to one mode of discourse, may equally apply within another mode of social life and within another mode of discourse provided relevant parallels can be drawn between the contexts concerned. He may also ask whether it is possible to draw a hard and fast distinction between intelligibility and rationality. If something is logical, then it could be argued that it is both rational and intelligible, and it follows that rationality cannot be denied in the name of intelligibility, So if we say that we are concerned with intelligibility when we seek to bring out the content of a religion, does it not follow that we are also concerned with its rationality? Is it permissible then to criticise those philosophers of religion who seek to establish the rationality of religious belief while we concern ourselves with the intelligibility of those beliefs? If the Wittgensteinian philosopher points to a confusion in the argument here by noting that there is a difference between showing the intelligibility of beliefs on the one hand, and seeking to establish rational grounds for those beliefs on the other, the traditional philosopher might claim that he sees no distinction and remain unconvinced.[30]

Another objection that can be levelled against the Wittgensteinian approach is that the rejection of natural theology implicit in the approach involves the rejection of a great deal of philosophical speculation on religion which has regarded the rational justification of religious belief as a viable option. While it may be true to say that some of the traditional philosophers concerned may have been affected by Hume's legacy, that would not be true of some of the more distinguished natural theologians and philosophers of the past.

Reference to the non-referential nature of religious language raises similar kinds of objections. The orthodox Christian tradition as we have indicated would uphold the referential nature of religious language. Believers may not necessarily conceive of the reality of God as akin to the reality of physical objects but they would still want to maintain that the term God has an objective referent. They might claim also that to conceive of dialogue with God without some kind of objective referent would be difficult if not impossible. 'Belief in' implies an object of belief even though it might be difficult to define precisely the object of that belief. But it is the question of how we define the object of our belief which is the point at issue between the traditional and the Wittgensteinian approaches to the philosophy of religion.

The reinterpretations of traditional accounts of religious beliefs offered by Phillips reveal the influence of Simone Weil and Kierkegaard but generally speaking they are not acceptable to orthodox Christian believers. His reinterpretation of belief in immortality is a case in point. He maintains that if it is construed as survival of death it is unsatisfactory since its logical status can be shown to be mistaken. The reason for this is that man is not immortal by nature and that eternal life cannot, therefore, be explained along the lines of earthly existence. Eternal life is here and now: it is life in God. Eternity for the believer can be construed as participation in the life of God and contemplation of divine love.[31] We may think that our moral life entitles us to heaven and happiness, such is the deep desire for recompense in human nature, but true religious belief seeks no recompense. Again belief in immortality as survival of death, whether as a non-material body or as a disembodied spirit, rests on a dualistic view of man which claims that the soul survives the death of the body. From the Wittgensteinian standpoint one of the difficulties posed by this view concerns the question of personal identity and whether or not 'an inner life depends on there being activities and a language which people have in common'. If so, 'any attempt to identify the essence of the self with an inner substance divorced from such connections is radically confused'.[32] But belief in immortality does not necessarily mean acceptance of the notion of survival, nor does it have to be construed as a future state of affairs. When this is recognised many philosophical objections to belief in immortality prove to be irrelevant.[33]

It has to be acknowledged, however, that many religious believers hold fast to traditional accounts of immortality which rest on a dualistic view of man. The *advaita* tradition of India which conceives of the essence of man, the *ātman*, as being at one with the essence of the universe, *Brahman*, is a case in point. The same applies to much Christian teaching which refers to the resurrection of the body or the immortality of the soul. It follows that from the Wittgensteinian standpoint the accounts given by different religious traditions of the immortality of the soul would have to be rejected as radically confused. Traditional religious believers might counter with the objection that the reinterpretations of belief in immortality on offer detract from and attenuate what they consider to be the faith of the fathers. This leads to the accusation that traditional belief is being undermined, and prompts the ironic comment that 'the beliefs of past and present men, in other cultures and in our own, make up a mountain of superstition supporting a tiny cairn of Wittgensteinian wisdom'.[34]

Phillips counters these accusations by distinguishing between faith and the accounts believers give of their faith. He clarifies this point in an analysis of the Welsh play *Byd y Saer Doliau* (*The World of the Doll Maker*) by Gwenlyn Parry. The setting is the work room, the world of the doll maker Ifans, whose belief in God and the Devil is graphically depicted by the telephone on the wall by means of which he speaks to the 'Gaffer', God, and the door of the cellar, behind which 'He', the Devil, is presumed to dwell. Two young people constantly taunt Ifans with arguments to show that his beliefs are naïve and incapable of substantiation. The analysis concludes with the remark that Ifans failed to realise that the arguments of the young people did not really affect his faith which remained unscathed and intact. Similarly, religious believers fail to realise that many of the scientific and philosophical arguments directed against their beliefs do not really touch their faith. Unfortunately, when the account they give of their faith is shown to be inadequate, they assume that their faith is also inadequate.[35] But that is not the case, for philosophy, as Wittgenstein claims, leaves everything as it is.[36]

3 Paul Tillich and the Historical Jesus

The problem of the relation of history to faith and the effect of historical criticism on Christian belief has proved to be a matter of continuing concern to a generation of theologians and Paul Tillich is no exception. He paid tribute to Ernst Troeltsch for first drawing his attention from the theology of mediation with which he was engaged at the time to the problems of historical research into the biblical writings, and he acknowledged his debt to Schweitzer's *The Quest of the Historical Jesus* and Bultmann's *The Synoptic Tradition* for providing him with historical insights into the New Testament.[1] In a set of propositions presented to a group of theological friends as early as 1911 he attempted to answer the question how it might be possible to interpret Christian doctrine if the non-existence of Jesus as a historical person were to become a probability.[2] In his *Systematic Theology* he could still raise the question of the historical Jesus in a most radical way and, without consciously evading difficulties, attempt to deal with the problems created by an uncompromising insistence on the historical basis of Christianity.[3]

Tillich claims that Christian belief is founded on the biblical picture of Jesus as the Christ and not on the historical Jesus. This picture is 'rooted in ecclesiastical belief and human experience, not the shifting and artificial construct of historical research'.[4] The paradoxical nature of this claim led to Tillich being misunderstood and misinterpreted. In America he was sometimes classified as a Barthian, while in his native Germany he was looked upon as a radical theologian. Tillich himself rejected these interpretations of his position claiming that acceptance of the Barthian paradox did not reflect agreement with Barthian supernaturalism, nor did his approval of the achievements of liberal theology imply the wholesale acceptance of liberal dogmatics.[5] This essay will seek to elucidate his views about the historical Jesus and to examine critically the implications of his position.

Tillich's attention was focused on the problem of the

historical Jesus by the work of Martin Kähler, one of his theological teachers.[6] The latter sought to solve the problem how one could be sure of the truth of the Christian message by equating the Jesus of history with the Christ of faith and making the Christ of faith independent of the uncertainties of historical research. Since he regarded any attempt to construct a life of Jesus as doomed to failure because of the uncertainties relating to historical research and the unreliability and inadequacies of the historical sources, he was able to maintain that the certainty of the Christian message had to be grounded in the Christ of faith. For him faith guarantees what historical research cannot determine.[7] The historical problem emerged later with Bultmann and his school so that Kähler was, as Tillich points out, 'the prophetic forerunner of what developed more fully only in the twentieth century.'[8]

This radical historical sceptical school with its doubts about the possibility of reaching the historical Jesus by the use of historical methods of investigation constitutes the background of Tillich's attempt to answer the question 'how can we say that Jesus is the Christ if historical research can never reach a sure image of the historical Jesus?'[9] Tillich refers to the second volume of his *Systematic Theology* as an attempt to look at the theological implications of radical scepticism concerning the New Testament in general and the historical Jesus in particular.[10] He sets out his position on the question of the historical Jesus in the chapter on 'The Reality of Christ'.[11] He argues there that the birth of Christianity does not coincide with the birth of the man called Jesus but with that moment when he was called the Christ by his disciples. 'For the event on which Christianity is based' he claims, 'has two sides: the fact which is called "Jesus of Nazareth" and the reception of this fact by those who received him as the Christ.'[12]

The historical nature of the fact to which the name Jesus of Nazareth points is, for Tillich, a theological necessity since without it, as he characteristically puts it, the fundamental Christian assertion that the estrangement of human existence has been overcome by essential God–Manhood is denied. What is insisted upon here is the historicity of the fact to which the name Jesus of Nazareth refers: 'If there were no personal life in which existential estrangement had been overcome, the New Being would have remained a quest and an expectation and would not be a reality in time and space. Only if the existence is conquered in *one* point – a personal life, representing exist-ence as a whole – is it conquered in principle, which means "in beginning and in power".'[13]

This stress on the historicity of the personal life referred to by the name Jesus and expressed in the biblical picture of Jesus as the Christ indicates that it would be a mistake to accuse Tillich of docetism. Yet charges of Gnosticism have been levelled against him which he himself attributes to a prema-ture judgement based on an incomplete analysis of his work.[14] Doubtless he underestimates the difficulties and apparent ambiguities students experience in interpreting his thought, but even so it has to be admitted that his insistence on the factual, historical, personal element behind the biblical pic-ture of Jesus as the Christ does prohibit any kind of docetic interpretation of his views.[15]

However, the receptive side of the event on which Christian-ity is founded is as important as the factual side, in Tillich's view, and calls for equal emphasis. Without the reception of Jesus as the Christ there would never have been the manifes-tation of the New Being in the personal life referred to by the name Jesus. The factual and receptive sides are of equal im-portance and the foundation of Christian theology is under-mined if either is ignored.[16]

The question that concerns us now is what can we know of the fact or the personal life to which the name Jesus refers and to what extent is it open to critical historical investigation? Tillich's answer to this question necessitates drawing a distinc-tion between the factual element of the Christ event and the historical Jesus. He describes the quest for the latter as a cou-rageous and significant endeavour, but concludes that if it is judged by its primary intention of seeking the empirical truth about Jesus of Nazareth it must be deemed a failure. The historical Jesus recedes from view as the quest progresses. This lack of success characterises both the old and the new quests since the methodological situation remains the same in both. As Tillich says: 'the result of the new (and very old) question-ing is not a picture of the so-called historical Jesus but the insight that there is no picture behind the biblical one which could be made scientifically probable'.[17]

The reason for the failure in Tillich's view lies not in the methods of historical research but in the nature of the sources. To find the historical Jesus behind the picture of Jesus as the Christ it is necessary in the first instance to distinguish between the elements on the factual side of the Christ event and the elements on the receiving side. With the material we are able to discover on the factual side we can then attempt to construct a life of Jesus but this biography is at best only probable and in Tillich's view cannot constitute the basis for accepting or rejecting the Christian faith. 'Historical research has made it obvious that there is no way to get at the historical events which have produced the Biblical picture of Jesus who is called the Christ with more than a degree of probability.'[18] The same applies to the attempt to formulate a *Gestalt* of Jesus by reducing the picture of the historical Jesus to the essentials and leaving particular details open to doubt because the shape of the *Gestalt* is dependent on the details.[19]

If the quest of the historical Jesus is a failure and if historical investigation produces nothing but probability does the same apply to the factual element of the Christ event or to the personal life witnessed to in the biblical picture of Jesus as the Christ? Tillich does not think so. Scepticism concerning the results of historical investigation into the life of Jesus does not apply to the factual element of the Christ event which is the *sine qua non* of Jesus as the Christ. We are not dealing here with the question of historical research but with a matter of faith which guarantees its own foundation. It guarantees the occurrence of 'an event in history which has transformed history for the faithful.'[20] It may not be able to provide historical information about the event or guarantee that the name of the person is Jesus, but it does guarantee 'the factual transformation of reality in that personal life which the New Testament expresses in its picture of Jesus as the Christ.'[21] Put in another way, what is being maintained is that the historical Jesus is elusive but not necessary anyway, because the factual element of the Christ event is guaranteed by faith and as a result history has been transformed for the faithful.

This is the crux of the historical problem for Tillich's theology. He maintains that faith provides certainty about its own foundation and that it is immune to critical investigation and unaffected by historical research.[22] The influence of Kähler, who emphasised the necessity of making faith independent of

'the unavoidable incertitudes of historical research'[23] is acknowledged. It may not be possible to guarantee the existence of
Jesus of Nazareth or the essentials of the biblical picture,[24] but
the appearance of that reality which created faith, namely the
New Being, is guaranteed by faith. Tillich justifies his claim on
the grounds that immediate awareness of, and participation
in, the New Being guarantees the reality of that personal life
in which the New Being has conquered the old being and
overcome existential estrangement.[25] That is, faith rather than
historical investigation grounds the historicity of the factual
element of the Christ event. Faith may not be able to guarantee that the name of the person is Jesus, but it does guarantee
that whatever his name was, 'the New Being was and is actually
in this man.'[26]

The validity of this argument is open to serious question as
we shall see, but at this stage it is necessary to point out that
Tillich insists on facing the historical problem. He refuses to
retreat from it by means of an existential acceptance of the
kerygmatic Christ. Historical criticism may well question the
characteristics and traits of the biblical picture of Jesus as
the Christ but it cannot deny 'that through this picture the
New Being has power to transform those who are transformed
by it.'[27] He rejects as unrealistic Kierkegaard's proposition that
it is enough to know one thing, namely, that in the year AD 30
God sent Christ for our salvation.[28] He rejects also the notion
that the biblical picture of Christ is an existential creation; it
represents rather a victory over existential estrangement that
has already taken place.[29] In answer to a question put to him
by one of his students concerning the possibility of the non-
existence of Jesus he said: 'I want to say that if we were able
to read the original police registers of Nazareth, and found
that there was neither a couple called Mary and Joseph nor a
man called Jesus, we should then go to some other city. The
personal reality behind the gospel story is convincing. It shines
through.'[30]

An extension of the argument for the fiducial guarantee of
the historical basis of Christianity is to be found in Tillich's
concept of *analogia imaginis*. He claims that there is an analogy
between the biblical picture of Jesus as the Christ which expresses the reality of the New Being and the historical personal life in which the New Being appeared and which lies

behind the biblical picture. On the basis of this analogy it can be concluded that while the empirical factualness of the biblical material cannot be guaranteed, it can be guaranteed 'as an adequate expression of the transforming power of the New Being in Jesus as the Christ.'[31]

Tillich anticipates the objection that the picture may have been an imaginary one in the first place.[32] His answer to the objection is that such a picture would have been the creation of those who had not experienced the transforming power of the New Being and would have been an expression of their search *for* the New Being rather than their actual transformation *by* the New Being. The biblical picture has transforming power precisely because it expresses the transforming power of the New Being; it creates the Church and individual Christians and is not created by them.[33]

The distinction Tillich draws between the probability of our knowledge of the historical Jesus and the certainty of our knowledge of that personal life which finds expression in the biblical picture of Jesus as the Christ needs to be critically assessed. The question that arises at the outset is why the historical Jesus should be subjected to critical, historical investigation while the factual element of the Christ event should be immune from it. On the face of it, it is difficult to understand why the personal life behind the biblical picture should not be subject to the same kind of historical research and investigation as the historical Jesus. Should not the same criteria apply to both quests? Tillich appears to be applying one criterion of historical truth to the historical Jesus and another criterion to the factual element of the Christ event. But should not the same norm of truth apply to both? The personal life which finds expression in the biblical picture of Jesus as the Christ is in no way less historical than the historical Jesus. To assert that there is a factual element behind the biblical picture is to make an historical judgement and such a judgement cannot be declared to be immune from historical investigation on the grounds of a fiducial guarantee. It does seem that Tillich wants to have it both ways.[34] On the one hand he accepts the most radical, historical investigation into the life of the historical Jesus, while on the other hand he guarantees on the basis of faith the historical existence of a personal life in which the New Being appeared and which is expressed in the biblical picture of Jesus as the Christ. But can a Christology which takes its historical basis seriously free itself in this way from radical, historical investigation?[35]

It has to be said that the validity of Tillich's argument for the fiducial guarantee of the historical basis of Christianity is logically questionable. What he is doing in fact is making religious truth the criterion of historical truth, a point that can be clarified by means of a philosophical analogy. The insistence of some philosophers on ordinary language as normative and the paradigm of rationality implies that words have a definite meaning in all contexts. When they are used in any other sense, as they are for example in religious language, their meaning is 'stretched' to the point of absurdity or 'eroded' by a thousand qualifications on the part of the believer.[36] But to insist on ordinary language as paradigmatic, or as the norm of meaningfulness, is to elevate the rules of ordinary language to the status of an evaluating standard for all other uses of language. It means taking the criterion of meaning applicable to one context and extending it to all other contexts. To say that a word *must* have a particular meaning in all contexts is to use language in an arbitrary fashion. The *must* here is in no way logical; it is a matter of preference. So to make ordinary language the paradigm for religious language is to make it normative rather than descriptive and the criterion of religious truth.

Tillich can be accused of a similar kind of arbitrariness in the use of language. His starting point is the New Being. The reality of the New Being in Jesus as the Christ is beyond question for the believer because he participates in it. The norm of meaningfulness and the criterion of religious truth for the believer is his immediate awareness of the New Being as expressed in the biblical picture of Jesus as the Christ. To say that this experience of the reality of the New Being *must* have a factual, historical element is to make a criterion of religious truth normative in an historical context. A measure of arbitrariness is involved in making religious truth the criterion of historical truth and it is an illegitimate use of religious language.[37]

A similar criticism, though in a different form, can be made of the claim that historical facts are verified by means of a dogmatic confession.[38] This amounts to a neo-orthodox solution of the historical problem and the difference between Barth and Tillich on this point is really minimal. For Tillich faith guarantees the historical basis of Christianity; for Barth acceptance of the biblical picture of Jesus in faith is the epistemological foundation for regarding him as the royal man.[39] The question that poses itself is why Tillich should be so concerned with guaranteeing the historical basis of the Christian faith free from the uncertainties of historical research?[40] The most probable explanation is that his whole interpretation of the meaning of history rests on a Christological foundation. The central concept in his interpretation of history is the *kairos*, by which he means that moment when history had matured to such a degree as to be able to receive the revelation of the Kingdom of God.[41] The unique *kairos* is the appearance of Christ as the centre of history and the source of unconditioned meaning. His appearance affirms the historical dimension and overcomes the threat of estrangement and meaninglessness.[42]

This Christological interpretation of history means that Christianity for Tillich cannot be divorced from its historical foundations. But its historical basis cannot be made independent of the uncertainties of historical research either, and if the appearance of Jesus as the Christ could be proved not to have occurred at all then faith would be threatened. Hence Tillich's solution that faith guarantees its own foundation.

My conclusion is that Tillich offers no real solution to the historical problem that concerned him throughout his career. To root the factual element of the Christ event in 'ecclesiastic belief and human experience'[43] and to make it independent of historical investigation is to protect the historical basis of Christianity with a dogmatic confession and an illegitimate use of religious language. Why should the historical basis of the Christian faith be so protected? To say that the risk of faith is existential and that a wrong faith destroys the meaning of a man's life is no justification for making faith guarantee an historical act. The value of faith, the historical basis of which is sheltered from the critical methods of historical investigation is questionable to say the least. The fact to which the name Jesus of Nazareth points should be open to the same methods of historical research as other events in history. There is no justification for constructing a sheltered zone for the historical basis of the Christian faith.

4 Truth, Religion and Non-Violence

This paper is divided into three sections. The first examines what Gandhi means by the term Truth; the second looks at the relationship between Truth and Religion; and the third notes the inextricable relationship he conceives to exist between Truth and non-violence. Comparisons with western thought are implicit in the first section and explicit in sections two and three.

THE CONCEPT OF TRUTH

When Gandhi gave his autobiography the sub-title *The Story of my Experiments with Truth,* he was indicating that the concept of Truth was fundamental to any understanding of his thought since it was the focus of his way of life. That being the case it is inevitable that we should enquire what he meant by the term Truth and what kind of connotation it had for him. The fact that his life has been referred to as an attempt to live in accordance with Truth, or as an existential quest for Truth, suggests that the key to the understanding of his life and thought lies in determining what he meant by the term. His followers consistently maintain that he was essentially a practical man with little inclination for or interest in philosophical speculation. While that may well have been the case, it can be argued that the basic unity of his thought and the interrelatedness and interdependence of various aspects of his teaching spring from certain metaphysical beliefs the nature of which become apparent when we try to explain what he means by Truth.

It is not my contention that Gandhi arrives at the meaning of Truth as the result of a process of linguistic analysis of philosophical reasoning; he is not a person who first defines Truth and then seeks to apply it to different aspects of life. What I am suggesting rather is that he is a participant in a form of life and that the meaning of the term Truth becomes apparent for him from the way the term is used in that

particular form of life. To say that his life can be viewed as an
existential quest for Truth is to imply that certain religious
and ethical beliefs acquired within the Hindu way of life inform his teaching and determine his actions. To maintain that
his 'criteria of truth' lie in the meeting of human need and
that his non-violent methods are not dependent on his metaphysical presuppositions is, to my mind, fundamentally mistaken.[1] Such a view misunderstands completely the importance
of the religious traditions in which he was nurtured and the
significance of the religious and ethical ideals which formed
an integral part of the Hindu way of life. It amounts to rejecting, or at least ignoring, the importance of metaphysical beliefs in his subsequent growth to religious and ethical maturity
which finds expression in his commitment to Truth and non-
violence, and in his deep-seated desire to meet human need.
It confuses the *motive* for seeking the welfare of all with the
expression of human concern. What I am saying is that 'the
meeting of human need', while it doubtless has a theonomous
nature in itself, actually springs from and is a consequence of
Gandhi's commitment to Truth. In my view his concern for
sarvodaya and his commitment to *ahimsa* are based on metaphysical presuppositions acquired within the Hindu way of life.

An analysis of the concept of Truth in Gandhi's writings
illustrates this point. He is faithful to the traditions of Hinduism when he affirms the isomorphism of *Satya* and *Sat*, Truth
and Reality. Within the Hindu way of life reality is variously
described as *Brahman* (the substratum of existence), *Ātman*
(Self), *Ekamevadvityam* (One without a Second), and *Neti Neti*
(Not this, not that). By his use of *Satya* Gandhi preserves the
metaphysical and ethical significance of terms like *dharma*
(eternal law) and *ṛta* (moral law). He maintains, for example,
that for him nothing exists except Truth,[2] and that where Truth
is there also is true knowledge (*cit*) and bliss (*ānanda*). Truth
is *saccidānanda* (being, consciousness, bliss), a description applied to Brahman in the Upanishads. This is one of the reasons why Gandhi has no difficulty in describing himself as an
Advaitin though to what extent and in what sense it is true to
refer to him as an *Advaitin* is another matter and beyond the
scope of this paper. (See the essay 'Gandhi's Concept of Truth
and the *Advaita* Tradition' – Chapter 5 in this volume.)

Truth is referred to also as the most correct and significant term that could possibly be used for God. On the face of it the statement God is Truth would seem to imply that Truth is simply an attribute of God and in the first instance Gandhi was content for the phrase to used in this way. Later, however, he realised that it did not accurately reflect his position and that it was more accurate for him to say that Truth is God rather than God is Truth. This is not inconsistent with his description of Truth as Being itself, as eternal, as that which alone is all else being momentary. Yet he is not averse to the view that Truth might assume shape or form sometimes in order to meet specific human needs and when it does so it is called *Īśvara*, and acquires a personal connotation.[3]

Gandhi's preference, however, is for the impersonal connotation. He refers to God as the essence of life, as pure, undefiled consciousness, as goodness, love, light, truth, and as the atheism of the atheist since the latter also seeks truth. The *dharma* of the Buddhists, he claims, is really their God so they cannot be considered atheistic.[4] These descriptions present us with the concept of an impersonal Absolute which is in accordance with Gandhi's expressed preference for the concept of God as formless Truth.[5] Yet he recognises that God is personal to those who need to feel his presence and embodied for those who need to feel his touch.[6] While his preference is for the *Advaita* or non-dualistic position, he accepts that others might prefer the *Viśiṣṭādvaita*, qualified non-dualistic position, or the *Dvaita*, dualistic position. He accepts what he calls, the doctrine of the non unitary nature of reality or the 'manyness of reality',[7] which makes it possible for him to approve of the non-creative aspects of God as propounded by the Jains as well as the creative aspects of God as propounded by Ramanuja the foremost exponent of the *Viśiṣṭādvaita* position. That such a tolerant attitude should lead to him being called a supporter of *anekāntavāda*, or one who believes in many doctrines, did not disturb him in the least.[8] But his position is such that it does produce the paradox of God being described both as an impersonal force and as omniscient, omnipotent and benevolent.[9] In point of fact Gandhi moves from impersonal to personal descriptions of God without difficulty and this might be interpreted as an indication that it was never his intention to present a systematic and coherent account of the concept of Truth or God after the fashion of Śankara, the principal

exponent of *Advaita*. On the other hand it could be argued
that when he moves from impersonal to personal concepts of
God he is distinguishing in *Advaita* fashion between higher
and lower levels of truth or reality. But acceptance of this
argument involves accepting the superiority of the higher,
impersonal level of truth over the lower, personal level and
acknowledging two levels of knowledge. Gandhi, however, acknowledges no superiority in conceiving God in impersonal
rather than personal terms so it is difficult to see how the
traditional distinction between higher and lower levels of truth
can be applied to him. Yet it has to be recognised that he does
not conceive of God as an entity or being in the form of an
extra-mundane person when he uses the term in a personal
sense. He insists that 'you labour under a limitation when you
think of a being or entity who is beyond the power of man to
grasp',[10] so it could be maintained that he is aware of the
problems involved in his personal–impersonal uses of the term
God.

He claims to be simple a seeker after Truth, ceaselessly searching for it, occasionally having glimpses of it, yet never finding
it.[11] It is as if he glimpses absolute Truth in and through particular instances of truth. He does not equate absolute Truth
with particular instances of truth, but it does not prevent him
from recognising that particular instances of truth are necessary to convey the meaning of absolute Truth. His existential
quest for Truth is in fact the key to his understanding and
interpretation of the Bhagavad-Gītā, the main aim of which he
believes to be a call to action. But since actions of themselves
bind man to the samsaric world and the endless cycle of birth,
death and rebirth, there is need of disciplined or desireless
action if liberation is to be achieved. Gandhi describes such
action as selfless, detached, sacrificial and non-violent or action on behalf of others and in the service of others. It is
action that derives from devotion to Truth and also enables us
to see Truth more clearly.

When asked on one occasion what he considered Truth
to be Gandhi replied 'What the voice within tells you'.[12] It is
tempting to interpret this statement as a self-authenticating,
subjective, absolute principle, namely, the voice of conscience.
But conscience is not self-authenticating in an absolute sense.
There are criteria which determine the way a man thinks and

acts, and in Gandhi's case they are the religious and ethical ideals of his own form of life. When conscience is defined in this way then we are brought face to face with the problem of the relativity of truth and whether under the circumstances we are justified in talking about absolute Truth at all. There may be criteria which determine the way others think and act conscientiously which may be completely contrary to those of Gandhi and what may be truth for one may be untruth for another. Gandhi recognises the problem of relativity and his solution is that before someone claims to speak of the inner voice he should recognise his limitations and discipline himself to cultivate truthfulness, humility, purity and non-violence, and embrace the twin ideals of poverty and non-possession. That is, he proposes that a man should try to understand the criteria which determine his thoughts and actions. He speaks of the need for *abhyāsa* (single-minded devotion), and *vairāgya* (indifference to worldly life) for 'If you would swim on the bosom of the ocean of Truth you must reduce yourself to zero'.[13] But the question arises whether this can really be regarded as a solution to the problem of the relativity of truth. Even a human cypher has to be able to listen to the inner voice and is subject to the failings of all human beings. It follows that his apprehension of Truth will of necessity be partial and relative and that absolute Truth will be forever beyond his grasp. Gandhi acknowledges this fact and as a practical idealist he accepts that it is impossible for mortal man to possess absolute Truth. He points out that:

> We can only visualise it in our imagination. We cannot, through the instrumentality of this ephemeral body, see face to face Truth which is eternal. That is why in the last resort one must depend on faith.[14]

So the concept of absolute Truth is an affirmation of faith and beyond our empirical grasp. This means that we must act in the knowledge that we hold on to such truths as we are able to apprehend in this world. Gandhi points out

> That relative truth must, meanwhile, be my beacon, my shield and buckler ... Even my Himalayan blunders have seemed trifling to me because I have kept strictly to this path ... I have gone forward according to my light. Often in my

progress I have had faint glimpses of the Absolute Truth,
God, and daily the conviction is growing on me that He
alone is real and all else is unreal.[15]

Without relative truth to hold on to it could be argued that
absolute truth would be nothing but empty utopianism. Since
we have no abiding city here particular truths cannot be identified with absolute Truth, yet it is through our awareness of
particular truths that we understand what it means to speak of
absolute Truth. When Gandhi claims to have had glimpses of
absolute Truth it may be reasonable to assume not that he has
glimpsed an extra-mundane entity or hypostatised Ultimate –
that would be to labour under a limitation – but that by holding on to particular truths he is made aware of the need to live
in accordance with certain religious and ethical criteria, and is
informed by the spirit of *dharma* or *ṛta* which he equates with
Satya (Truth). That is, he acquires his understanding of Truth
as a participant in the Hindu way of life.

TRUTH AND RELIGION

Gandhi's concept of Religion corresponds to his concept of
Truth. As particular instances of truth are necessary in order
to understand what it means to speak of absolute Truth so
particular religions are necessary in order to understand what
it means to speak of Religion. Religion, he claims, underlies all
religions. It cannot be equated with particular religions: it
transcends Hinduism, Islam, Christianity, and all other religions, yet it harmonises them and gives them reality.[16] It binds
man indissolubly to the Truth; it is that permanent element in
human nature which makes the soul restless until it is at one
with Truth or God.[17]
    It is because of the inherited beliefs and practices of the
Hindu way of life then that Gandhi is able to claim that he is
bound indissolubly to Truth. He understands what it means to
talk of Truth from his participation in the Hindu way of life.
Similarly he understands what it means to talk of Religion
from his awareness of the religious and ethical ideals of his
own way of life. The one true and perfect Religion that he
refers to is beyond predication and incapable of being realised
within finite existence. No particular religion can ever embody

the perfection of Religion or lay claim to a monopoly of Truth. Yet particular historical religions are necessary to convey the meaning of Religion in the same way as particular truths are necessary to convey the meaning of Truth. Gandhi defines particular religions as human constructs and expressions of that which underlies them and gives them reality. While all religions possess truth, all are to some extent erroneous. Even so the heart of one religion is identical with the heart of another.

> Even as a tree has a single trunk, but many branches and leaves, so there is one true and perfect Religion, but it becomes many, as it passes through the human medium.[18]

If, as seems likely, Gandhi is referring here to an essence common to all religions, then it is possible to draw comparisons between him and Schleiermacher. The latter speaks of Religion as pre-existing particular historical manifestations which are grounded in a fundamental unity of religion, an *a priori* condition.[19] This transcendental unity of Religion is necessary for the existence of positive religions which are historical expressions of a primordial form, the immediate religious consciousness, or 'the sense and taste for the Infinite'. Positive religions cannot encapsulate the universality or infinitude of Religion,[20] yet they are necessary for its complete manifestation since they contain something of its true nature. Positive religions are true in so far as they succeed in expressing the primordial form of Religion which in turn is comprehended in the depths of those particular religions.[21]

All religions for Gandhi are different roads to the same goal and his contention is that there will always be a wide variety of religions corresponding to different human outlooks and temperaments.[22] In this respect he echoes the teaching of the Hindu reformer Vivekānanda who claims that there are as many religions as there are individuals, and that even within particular religions there are different viewpoints manifesting different facets of the truth.[23] Unlike Vivekānanda, however, he rejects the claim that some religions are superior to others. Different religions may have different symbols but they should not become fetishes to enable one religion to claim superiority over another. Gandhi is unable to harbour the thought, even secretly, that another man's faith is inferior to his own because of his belief that all faiths are God's creation and therefore equally holy.[24] In view of this he is able to advocate the open and sincere study of all religions since in his view they all contain an element of truth. He rejects as mistaken the view that the study of other religions could undermine a believer's faith in his own religion. He insists rather that it could lead a believer to a better understanding of his own faith.[25]

Gandhi's openness to the plurality of religious traditions indicates that he is not content to confine himself to the small island of his own tradition and culture and that he is fully aware of the significance of the spiritual insights of other religions. His rejection of the right of one religion to claim superiority over another simply underlines his belief that a particular religion cannot fully embody the perfection of Religion. In this respect he echoes the views of Tillich for whom the holy or unconditional – what he calls Ultimate Concern – finds expression in a variety of different forms: in painting, which may have no religious content in the traditional sense; in philosophy, when attempts are made to understand the nature of ultimate reality; in ideologies which might normally be regarded as secular, such as nationalism, socialism and humanism; and in traditional religions.[26] When adherents of particular religions regard them as embodiments of the Ultimate then, in Tillich's view, the particular has been elevated to the status of ultimacy. This is a form of idolatry; it is the particularisation of the Ultimate and a form of demonisation.[27] Gandhi, as we have seen, uses different terminology when he speaks of religious symbols becoming fetishes which in his view are idolatrous and fit only to be discarded.[28] Differences in terminology, however, cannot disguise the similarity of views expressed by Gandhi and Tillich concerning the status of particular religions. For both, Religion or Ultimate Concern is that ideal by which we live and act, and although it is not embodied in particular religions since all religions are necessarily imperfect, it is nevertheless to be found in the depths of particular religions[29] and communicated to us through them.

TRUTH AND AHIMSA

These two concepts are so inextricably related in Gandhi's view that it is difficult to separate them. He maintains that they are 'like the two sides of a coin, or rather a smooth unstamped metallic disc'.[30] So *Ahiṁsa* is the means leading to the realisation of Truth. But since means and ends are convertible terms in his philosophy, to practice *ahiṁsa* is to realise Truth and to realise Truth is to practice *ahiṁsa*. The attainment of the one involves the realisation of the other.

> Ahimsa is my God and Truth is my God. When I look for Ahimsa, Truth says, 'Find it through me'. When I look for Truth, Ahimsa says 'Find it through me'.[31]

The convertibility of these terms indicates that religious and ethical ideals not only inform our ends but also the means we use to reach them. The same moral demands apply to means as well as ends in the quest for Truth. That is they 'impose a limit on our purposes and their execution which the distinction between means and ends cannot account for, since means and ends alike come under moral scrutiny'.[32]

So the Machiavellian view that a leader 'must not mind incurring the scandal of those vices without which it would be difficult to save the state'[33] must be regarded as completely contrary to Gandhi's view, as is the separation of politics and morality implicit in Machiavelli's argument. Whenever attempts were made to distinguish between means and ends, Gandhi could point to the crimes committed in the name of religion on the grounds that the end justifies the means. Given the misery and suffering caused by holy wars, crusades against infidels and inquisitions, the strength of Gandhi's argument becomes patently obvious. 'Your reasoning', he says, 'is the same as saying that we can get a rose through planting a noxious weed. . . . The means may be likened to a seed, the end to a tree; and there is just the same inviolable connexion between the means and the end as there is between the seed and the tree. . . . We reap exactly as we sow'.[34] Aldous Huxley echoes Gandhi's views when he claims that the means whereby we attain something are as important as the end if not more so.[35]

Gandhi refers to *ahiṁsa* as his eternal creed and as the law of the human species. Nature may be full of *hiṁsa* but man is superior to nature and has a duty to practice *ahiṁsa* in a world where *hiṁsa* abounds. His essential Self or *Ātman* is imperishable and eternal and at one with Truth or God. For one man to inflict deliberate violence on another, according to Gandhi, is a violation of the Self and a rejection of Truth. Hence the importance of *ahiṁsa*, but as Gandhi shows it is not an easy matter to practice it. Man may be distinguished from the animals with his capacity for non-violence but it does not mean that he has shed all vestiges of the animal within him. He may well be a child of the spirit but he remains a child of nature and the practice of non-violence requires both discipline and courage on his part. It is impossible to be truly non-violent without being utterly fearless in Gandhi's view, which explains his consternation on hearing that the men of the village of Bettiah ran away when police raided their homes and attacked their womenfolk. They explained their actions as an attempt to adhere to the principle of non-violence, but as Gandhi pointed out it could equally be interpreted as cowardice and given the choice between cowardice and violence he would himself choose violence.[36]

It will be evident from this that *ahiṁsa* poses real problems for Gandhi. He recognises for instance that we are 'caught up in the conflagration of Himsa'[37] and that our life on earth involves the destruction of certain forms of life. No matter how careful and compassionate and self-restrained a person may be he cannot entirely escape committing *hiṁsa*: 'It is impossible to sustain one's body without the destruction of other bodies to some extent'.[38] Man's existence seems to require some form of *hiṁsa*, and since no man is an island it is impossible for him not to 'participate in the Himsa that the very existence of society involves'.[39] To destroy a madman, for example, may be necessary in order to protect other members of society. So killing may be regarded as a moral duty in certain circumstances in spite of the instinctive horror we might feel about the destruction of a living being. To allow *ahiṁsa* to become a fetish would be a mistake and not to kill in certain circumstances could be regarded as a form of *hiṁsa* rather than *ahiṁsa*.[40] Peter Winch gives an example of this dilemma when he cites an incident from the film *Violent Saturday* in which a gang of robbers hide from the police on a farm belonging to a strict religious community which upheld the principle of non-violence. He points out that 'At the climax of the film one of the gangsters is about to shoot a young girl member of the community in the presence of the community's elder. With horror and doubt on his face, the elder seizes a pitchfork and hurls it into the gangster's back'.[41] Winch's argument is that the elder knows he has done wrong in killing the gangster, but that nevertheless he had not 'abandoned or qualified his commitment to the principle of non-violence'.[42] It is simply that in that particular situation he had to act as he did, and to have acted differently would have meant that he would have been in the wrong. He acted out of moral considerations which were involved in the perspective of the action.[43] It was a matter of situational ethics.

What emerges from this example is that there are situations of moral dilemma which impose limits on what it is possible for someone to do. We may be forced to act in a certain way out of moral considerations which still involve us in feelings of guilt and remorse. What must be done in certain circumstances cannot be said to be good without qualification. The elder acted morally in the situation in which he found himself even though he failed to adhere to the sect's fundamental principle of non-violence. That is, he did not make a fetish of the principle of *ahiṁsa*. As Gandhi points out:

> Perfect non-violence is impossible as long as we exist physically ... Perfect non-violence whilst you are inhabiting the body is only a theory like Euclid's point or straight line, but we have to endeavour every moment of our lives.[44]

But if perfect non-violence is impossible and if what must be done in certain circumstances cannot be said to be good without qualification, is it not necessary to go to war against those who oppress mankind in the same way as it is necessary and unavoidable to kill a homicidal lunatic who threatens society? Gandhi's reply is that no man is so evil as to be beyond redemption and no man so perfect as to be justified in killing those whom he regards as evil.[45] So his attitude to war is unequivocal: he regards it as wholly wrong since it degrades, demoralises and brutalises men trained for it. Yet his adherence to the principle of non-violence does not mean that he fails to recognise that different moral considerations apply for different people in different situations.[46] He does not seek to prevent those who feel compelled to engage in warfare from doing so, yet he still maintains that those who participate in it should strive to free the world from it. It is interesting that he felt compelled himself to recruit men for ambulance work during the war in South Africa, and referring to his actions on that occasion he states:

> There is no defence for my conduct weighted only in the scales of _ahiṁsa_. I draw no distinction between those who wield the weapons of destruction and those who do red-cross work. Both participate in war and advance its cause. Both are guilty of the crime of war ... Life is governed by a multitude of forces. It would be smooth sailing, if one could determine the course of one's actions only by one general principle whose application at a given moment was too obvious to need even a moment's reflection. But I cannot recall a single act which could be so easily determined.[47]

He recognises that in the ordinary circumstances of life we are confronted by situations that make clear-cut decisions or a choice between black and white well nigh impossible. Yet like the community elder he does not abandon his commitment to _ahiṁsa_. He still maintains that non-violence is the nobler way and that the prevention of the brutalization of human nature is preferable to its promotion. He also continues to regard _ahiṁsa_ as a more effective means of liberation than revolution since in his view the self sacrifice of one innocent man is a more potent force than the sacrifice of a million men who might die while killing others.[48]

One of the implications of the interrelation of Truth and _ahiṁsa_ for Gandhi is that he sees it as involving _sarvodaya_, the uplift of all men. The utilitarian formula of the greatest happiness of the greatest number is, in his view, completely at odds with _sarvodaya_. The votary of _ahiṁsa_ strives for the greatest good of all rather than the greatest good of the greatest number. Furthermore, the methods employed by the utilitarian would always be considered justified if they succeeded in producing the desired end, whereas _sarvodaya_ could never be produced by dubious means since means and ends are convertible terms. The utilitarian approach would have justified the forcible ejection of the British on the grounds that the greatest good of the greatest number would have resulted from it. Such an approach would not have been countenanced by Gandhi because it would have involved rejecting _ahiṁsa_ and relinquishing _sarvodaya_.[49] Compared with _sarvodaya_ utilitarianism shows a distinct lack of humanity and in Gandhi's view is less dignified also.[50] If it is argued that *sarvodaya* is really an unattainable ideal and that in the end it is better to settle for the greatest good of the greatest number, the reply might be that an unattainable ideal is a better goal than a limited attainable goal when it comes to the welfare of all men. At least it can be said that the former shows a more commendable motivation.

The interrelation of *Satya* (Truth), *ahimsa* (non-violence), and *sarvodaya* (the welfare of all), has political, economic and social implications but, fascinating as they are, they lie beyond the scope of this essay.

5 Gandhi's Concept of Truth and the *Advaita* Tradition

It is difficult to understand Gandhi's philosophy without some kind of idea of what he means by Truth. When I asked some of his followers in India what they thought he meant by Truth their replies showed quite clearly that in their view his concept of Truth was linked to the Hindu concepts of *dharma* and *ṛta*. What this seems to indicate is that his understanding of Truth is something that he acquired within his own form of life and that his experiments with Truth are ultimately determined by his understanding of the Hindu tradition. This is not to say that insights from other religious traditions did not inform his apprehension of Truth: his acknowledgment of those influences is sufficient in itself to substantiate that claim. But it is also clear that it is not possible for us to understand what he means by Truth without some prior knowledge of the religious tradition in which he was nurtured and which determined his way of life.

In the Indian religious tradition the concept of God is not the primary concept and it is interesting to note that it is conspicuously absent from some important streams of thought. This might account for Gandhi's dissatisfaction with the statement 'God is Truth', which he was content to accept in the first instance but later came to realise did not accurately reflect his position. His preference for the statement 'Truth is God' not only reflects his position more accurately but also indicates that he regards the term God to be an appellation for Truth rather than the term Truth to be a description or an attribute of God. When he says 'Truth is God' it is not inconsistent with his claim that Truth is Being itself, or that which is eternal. It is consistent also with his rejection of the suggestion that Buddhism is atheistic since, in his view, God is really the *dharma* of the Buddhists. It also sheds light on the fact that the primary connotation of the term God is impersonal rather than personal for him, and why he is able to describe God as the essence of life, pure undefiled consciousness, the unseen power that pervades all things, and as that which is indefinable and formless. If we were to use classical Hindu terminology we might say that Gandhi is propounding the notion of the isomorphism of *satya* and *sat* when he describes Truth as Being itself because these terms are two forms of the same concept, though *satya* evidently preserves the ethical connotation of such terms as *dharma* and *ṛta*.

Gandhi's expressed preference for the impersonal concept of God does not prevent him from recognising that God is personal to those who need to feel his presence. While he may not consider it necessary for himself for Truth to assume shape or form at any time, he is aware that for some it has to be given a personal connotation in order to meet specific human needs, and when it does so it acquires the name *Īśvara*. This enables him to maintain that it makes no difference whether a devotee conceives of God in personal or impersonal terms since the one position is not inferior in any way to the other. His readiness to acknowledge that God is all things to all men enables him to accept the *Dvaita* and *Viśiṣṭādvaita* positions as well as maintaining his own preference for *Advaita*. Two issues are raised here both of which are worthy of discussion. The first concerns Gandhi's claim to be an Advaitin and the other his acceptance of the Jain doctrine of *anekāntavāda* or what is sometimes referred to as the doctrine of the manyness of reality. I am concerned in this essay with the first of the issues though it has to be acknowledged that the second issue is not unrelated to it.

Gandhi's claim to be an Advaitin clearly does not prevent him from recognising the possibility of *Dvaita* and *Viśiṣṭādvaita* interpretations of the nature of ultimate reality. That being so we might ask: in what sense can he be called an Advaitin? It can be said that he is clearly an Advaitin to the extent that he believes in the essential oneness of all that exists. He states explicitly:

> I believe in *advaita*. I believe in the essential unity of man and for that matter of all that lives. Therefore I believe that if one man gains spiritually, the whole world gains with him and, if one man falls, the whole world falls to that extent.[1]

His belief in the oneness of humanity and the unitary nature of the soul is also explicitly expressed:

> I believe in the absolute oneness of God and therefore of humanity. What though we have many bodies? We have but one soul. The rays of the sun are many through refraction. But they have the same source.[2]

That man has to become aware of this oneness is evident, but the emphasis with Gandhi is on the method of *karma* (action) rather than *jñāna* (knowledge) and this fact, coupled with his recognition of alternative interpretations of the nature of reality, raises the question of the relationship between the *Advaita* position he claims to hold and the classical *Advaita* of Śankara. Is he using the term *advaita* in a distinctive way or are there comparisons to be drawn between his position and the philosophical school of *Advaita Vedānta?*

Śankara's *Vivekachūdāmani* and his commentary on the Vedānta sūtras provide us with his own expression of *Advaita*. His basic view is that the inner Self, *Ātman*, is identical with the substratum of the universe, Brahman.

> Because there is nothing else whatever but Brahman, and That is the only self-existent Reality, our very Self, therefore art thou that serene, pure, Supreme Brahman, the One without a second.[3]

When we fail to discriminate between the Self and the non-self and through ignorance falsely identify ourselves with the body we are bound to the realm of *samsāra*. We need to recognise the oneness of the Self and Brahman and see the Self as indivisible, infinite and free from all limiting adjuncts such as body, mind and ego.[4] Perfect discrimination, however, is brought about by immediate, intuitive apprehension achieved in the *samādhi* state wherein all relative ideas are transcended.[5]

If Brahman-Ātman is the only self-existent reality it follows that apart from Brahman the world has no existence. To maintain otherwise would be to acknowledge a reality other than Brahman and the Advaitic view is that the world is simply a phenomenal appearance of Brahman. This is Śankara's *vivartavāda* doctrine. The rudiments of phenomenal existence belong to Brahman and are variously described as the *māyā* (appearance), *śakti* power, or *prakṛti* (nature) of Brahman. The world is the *lilā* (sport) of Brahman which is a natural activity analogous to breathing and has no other purpose than to fulfil the nature of Brahman.[6] As the sun or moon reflected in the water becomes manifold, so the one Self or Brahman abiding in all individual beings appears one and many at the same time.[7] This is not to say that the world is unreal or illusory. It is not unreal because it is the common collective experience of individuals, yet it is not ultimately real because ultimate reality is Brahman, the one without a second. To mistake the empirical for the ultimately real is the consequence of *avidyā* (ignorance) which binds man to the world of *saṁsāra.* Śankara's acceptance of two levels of truth enables him to determine whether something is true or false by taking into consideration the sphere of reality concerned. It would be true to say that the empirical is real when compared with dreams or hallucinations, but it would not be true to say that the empirical is real when what we have in mind is ultimate reality. On the lower level of truth it would be appropriate to refer to Brahman as *Īśvara* and to the world as the creation of *Īśvara*, but on the higher level of truth Brahman alone is real and *Īśvara* and the world merely apparent. To confuse these two levels of truth would be to engage in what is called *adhyasā* or illegitimate transference. So according to Śankara it would be appropriate to refer to the world as real on the lower level of truth, but since man's final goal is to experience ultimate reality and the identity of the Self and Brahman, he seeks to see the world as it is from the higher level of truth.

A close comparison between Śankara's view and that of Meister Eckhart has been admirably demonstrated by Rudolf Otto who shows that for Eckhart that which is, is Being itself, which is logically prior to the notion of a Supreme Being or God. Pure Being is indefinable; it is neither this nor that; it is the pure Godhead beyond predication. As one needs to go beyond God into the silent void (*Wüste*) of the Godhead, according to Eckhart's mystical teaching, so it is with Śankara that we need to ascend from the lower level of *Īśvara* to the higher level of *nirguṇa* Brahman.[8]

The way of liberation for both these thinkers is the way of knowledge (*jñāna*), which is not to be confused with intellectual apprehension or discursive reasoning. It is rather intuitive knowledge or the insight of the self within the self. Śankara speaks of knowing the self in the self through the self (*ātmani, ātmānam, ātmanā*). That is to say, we realise the identity of Ātman-Brahman in the depth of the *ātman*. It is the way in which Śankara and Eckhart emphasise the importance of intuitive knowledge as the means of liberation which, according to Otto, colours their metaphysical concepts with mysticism.[9]

If this is a reasonably accurate though admittedly inadequate account of the classical *Advaita* of Śankara we may now ask to what extent Gandhi was justified in describing himself as a believer in *Advaita* and whether he is an Advaitin only to the extent that he believes in the essential oneness of all that exists. We have already noted the isomorphism of *satya* and *sat* in Gandhi's thought when he describes Truth as Being itself so it is reasonable to assume that what he has in mind when he uses the term Truth is not far removed from the traditional concept of Brahman including the concepts of *dharma* and *ṛta*. He clarifies this point when he states:

> This Truth is not merely the truth we are expected to speak.
> It is That which alone is, which constitutes the stuff of which
> all things are made, which subsists by virtue of its own power,
> which is not supported by anything else but supports every
> thing that exists. Truth alone is eternal, everything else if
> momentary. It need not assume shape or form, it is pure
> intelligence as well as pure bliss.[10]

Since Truth is *sat-cit-ānanda*, or being, consciousness, bliss, a description ascribed to Brahman in the *Advaita* tradition, then we may well be justified in claiming that so far as his understanding of ultimate reality is concerned Gandhi is an Advaitin. But as we have seen, he links the concept of the absolute oneness of Truth to the concept of the unity of humanity. He also claims that whoever recognises the Ātman inhabiting the body to be part of the Supreme Ātman will dedicate everything to him.[11] That is, Gandhi equates the Self with Truth or God and goes so far as to insist that prayer is the worship of the Self, an invoking of the divinity within, a petitioning of 'my Higher self, the real self, with which I have not yet achieved complete identification'.[12] This fact was pointed out to me in a conversation I had with Ācharya Kripalani on the subject. The Rāma invoked by Gandhi with his dying breath on the

occasion of his assassination was not the historical or mythological Rāma but the Self within which in turn is identical with
Truth. For Gandhi, therefore, as for Śankara, to know the Self
is to know the Truth and to identify with the Self is to identify
with Brahman the substratum of the universe. When man is
released from the bonds of *avidyā,* he is at one with Truth and
when that unity is realised *bhakti* or devotion is transformed
into knowledge. Śankara insists that the reality underlying the
phenomenal world is in no way different from the Self and
Gandhi may be expressing the same idea when he maintains:
'If I exist God exists' and 'If He is not we are nowhere'.[13]

When we turn to the Advaitic view of the phenomenal world
we may be tempted in the first instance, given Gandhi's total
involvement in social activity and his reluctance to divorce
religion and politics, to maintain that his attitude is totally
opposed to that of Śankara. On the face of it, it would be
difficult to attribute a dual theory of truth to Gandhi. Yet
there are explicit references in his writings to the world as
māyā and as the *lilā* of God.[14] He refers also as we have seen
to Truth as that which alone is real and everything else unreal:
'He alone is, nothing and no one else is. Everything else is
illusion.'[15] However we interpret these references to the ultimate unreality of the phenomenal world it would not be possible to credit Gandhi with Śankara's two-level theory of truth
that would make the higher level superior to the lower level.
He recognises as we have shown the validity of *Dvaita* interpretations of the nature of reality and the basic equality of personal and impersonal conceptions of God. It would be a mistake
to assume that his view of the empirical world as unreal pre-
cludes in any way social and political involvement in human
affairs since he equates the service of God with the service of
humanity.[16] He goes even further when in a stark phrase he
refers to God as the belly of a starving man and as the bread
of life.

> I may as well place before the dog over there the message
> of God as before those hungry millions who have no lustre
> in their eyes and whose only God is their bread.[17]

In what sense then is the world unreal for Gandhi we may ask?
Is it illusory in the same way as dreams are illusory? Hardly: yet
he insists that it has no permanence.

The world is changing every moment and is therefore unreal, it has no permanent existence.[18]

Can it be that what Gandhi is trying to convey is the relative
reality of the phenomenal world compared with the absolute
reality of Truth? He speaks, for example, of having glimpses of
absolute Truth in the empirical realm and insists that man's
apprehension of Truth here and now must necessarily be partial
and relative. In this respect he reflects the views of Kierkegaard
for whom no single, external form of man's *telos* or perfection
exists, and who believes that no outward expression of goodness can embody absolute goodness. For Kierkegaard particular expressions of goodness in the finite, temporal world must
inevitably assume limited forms and are thereby necessarily
relative. Yet particular expressions of goodness convey the
meaning of absolute goodness which is incognito and consists
in having an appearance which is not distinctive.[19] Similarly
for Gandhi particular instances of truth within finite existence
are necessary to convey the meaning of absolute Truth and to
give him glimpses of it, but it is not possible for him to equate
absolute Truth with these particular instances of truth. If it is
the relative reality of the phenomenal world that Gandhi is
seeking to convey in the statements we have quoted, then to
that extent his position is similar to that of the classical *Advaita*
of Śankara, for whom the world is the phenomenal appearance of Brahman and has a relative, dependent reality only.
Yet as we have shown it is not possible to attribute to Gandhi
the concept of two levels of truth. He could not accept the
notion of a superior higher level of truth and at the same time
claim no special merit for being able to conceive of God in
impersonal rather than personal terms. While the worship of
Īśvara is appropriate only on the lower level of truth for Śankara,
it makes no difference to Gandhi whether God is conceived of
in personal or impersonal terms. His preference is for the
impersonal concept but no superior higher level of truth is
implied.

Further comparisons between classical *Advaita* and Gandhi's
thought relates to acceptance of the oneness of the Self and
Brahman. Śankara stresses *jñāna,* knowledge, as the way of
liberation from the bonds of nescience and the realm of
transitoriness. This is intuitive knowledge rather than that which

is acquired through the process of reasoning, and if this fact gives Śankara's metaphysics a mystical flavour we may ask whether the same mystical approach characterises Gandhi's apprehension of Truth. He speaks of knowing the Truth by listening to the inner voice for when asked on one occasion what he considered Truth to be he replied: 'What the voice within tells you.'[20] This has firm roots in the Indian tradition, and Manu, for example, refers to intuition as one of the four or five authorities on the *dharma*. If Gandhi's inner voice can be equated with the higher Self then it could be said that he knows the Truth in the Self, through the Self, which is the *ātmani, ātmānam, ātmanā* approach of Śankara, and which corresponds to what Eckhart refers to as hearing inwardly the affirmation of Truth as if one is struck by lightening. This is what Otto calls the 'mysticism of introspection' which stresses the need to look within in order to arrive at an intuitive apprehension of Truth or Brahman.[21] The problem is that different people claim to hear different voices within, which results in different and sometimes contradictory concepts of truth being propounded. Gandhi recognises that since the human mind works through different media and that the evolution of the human mind is not the same for all, it must follow that what may be truth for one person will be untruth for another. He concludes that it would not be appropriate for anyone to claim to hear the inner voice without showing in the first place a measure of self-discipline, single-mind devotion and indifference to worldly interests.[22] It is because of lack of self-discipline that untruth abounds in the world, hence his claim:

> All that I can in true humility present to you is that Truth is not to be found by anybody who has not got an abundant sense of humility. If you would swim on the bosom of the ocean of Truth you must reduce yourself to a zero.[23]

This might be interpreted as a recognition of the need to remove all hindrances of the empirical self in order that Truth which is at one with the real Self might be realised. If so then the same kind of mystical quality found in Śankara is present in Gandhi's apprehension of Truth. He does in fact speak of seeking the Truth within.

> Truth resides in every human heart, and one has to search for it there, and to be guided by truth as one sees it. But no

one has the right to coerce others to act according to his own view of truth.[24]

The possible similarity between Śankara and Gandhi in their apprehension of Truth does not in itself, as Gandhi acknowledges, resolve the problem of different truth claims. The fact is that the ideals which determine the way a man thinks and acts are those which derive from his own form of life. Even if he reduces himself to a zero his apprehension of truth will still be determined by his awareness of the need to think and act in accordance with certain religious and ethical criteria, so it has to be recognised that what is truth for one person would not necessarily be truth for another. Gandhi acknowledges this fact when he states that perfect Truth is beyond man's grasp.

> We cannot through the instrumentality of this ephemeral body see face to face Truth which is eternal. That is why in the last resort one must depend on faith.[25]

Does his reference to faith here explain how it is that he is able to conceive of absolute Truth? Is this his mystical apprehension of the nature of Truth? He speaks of an indefinable mysterious Power pervading everything which though he does not see he senses. It is a changeless living power that underlies all change and holds all together; it is the 'Spirit of God ... [and] He alone is.'[26]

If it is correct to maintain that there is a mysticism of introspection, to use Otto's term, in both Śankara and Gandhi where the stress is on the need to turn within in order to attain a true understanding of the nature of the Self and its relation to Truth or Brahman, it is equally true so far as Gandhi is concerned to display a mysticism of unifying vision. This further phrase of Otto is taken to mean that in contemplating the multiplicity of the world one sees the whole in each particular. The distinction between the two types of mysticism, however, is one of analysis only since in actual fact they interpenetrate one another forming the warp and woof of the fabric of mystical experience.[27] That is, the mystical vision of unity that sees the manifold world as one can be said to be inextricably bound up with the intuitive apprehension of the nature of Truth. It is certainly possible to show that Gandhi's teaching concerning the unity of existence is related to his concept of the oneness of God or Truth. There may be manifold bodies but there is only one soul even as the rays of the sun become many through refraction, and the One which is the ground of the many is the mysterious power that pervades everything and underlies all change.[28] The manifold things of the world are seen not in their multiplicity but in their unity and as changing modes of the One. It is this fact that leads one to claim that Gandhi is an Advaitin only to the extent that he believes in the essential oneness of all that exists.[29] The same point could be expressed differently, namely, that both Gandhi and Śankara conceive of the relation between the many and the one as a relation of dependence even though their views may differ as to the nature of the reality of the manifold.[30]

Hitherto I have pointed to comparisons that can be drawn between Gandhi's views and classical *Advaita* and the extent to which his claim to be an Advaitin might be justified. But that there are contrasts to be drawn between his views and those of Śankara is evident. The latter, for example, insists on knowledge as the sole means of liberation and refers to moral and religious activities as aids to the attainment of *jñāna*.[31] They are regarded as necessary but not sufficient conditions for the realisation of the identity of Ātman and the attainment of *mokṣa*. The experience of liberation, of course, could result in a life of social activity and the promotion of love, but it would be because the *jīvan mukta* or liberated soul sees all beings in himself and himself in all beings. He promotes love and does good to others because he knows that he is at one with them. His morality rests on metaphysical foundations. Gandhi stresses *karma* rather than *jñāna* as the way of liberation. For example, he speaks of *ahimsa* and *satya* thus:

> They are like two sides of the same coin, or rather a smooth unstamped metallic disc. Who can say which is the obverse, and which the reverse?[32]

He regards the practice of *ahimsā* as the means for the realisation of the goal of Truth. But since means and ends are convertible terms in his philosophy he can say not only that *ahimsā* leads to the realisation of Truth but that to realise Truth is to practice *ahimsā*. It is a two-fold movement as Gandhi explains:

> Ahimsa is my God and Truth is my God. When I look for Ahimsa, Truth says, 'Find it through me' When I look for Truth, Ahimsa says 'Find it through me'.[33]

In the same way Gandhi refers to the service of humanity as equivalent to the service of God. In order to see the Truth one must be able to love the meanest creature as oneself.[34] His emphasis on *sarvodaya* bears witness to the fact that he recognises the theonomous nature of humanitarian activity. Through the service of humanity and the uplift of all we are brought to a better understanding of Truth. To help the helpless, to feed the hungry is to see God.

Our unity with our fellow men, in Gandhi's view, presents us with an inescapable moral obligation towards them. We have no right to possess anything while millions remain unclothed and unfed. We should adjust our wants and undergo voluntary privations if necessary in order that they may be cared for.[35] So religion is not an individualistic affair; it is not something that concerns man in isolation from his fellow man; it is not simply a matter of the individual soul seeking release from the endless cycle of *saṁsāra*. Rather it is bound up with all the activities of life whether they be social, political or economic.

> I am endeavouring to see God through the service of humanity, for I know that God is neither in heaven nor down below, but in everyone.[36]

Here Gandhi is reinterpreting the traditional doctrine of *mokṣa*. He is advocating renunciation *in* action, *karma yoga*, rather than renunciation *of* action. In this respect he is faithful to the teaching of the *Gītā* on the need for detached or selfless action and goes well beyond the kind of emphasis on activity that one finds in the teaching of Śankara.

While it has to be admitted that Gandhi's stress on social and moral activity is not present to the same extent in classical *Advaita* it could be asked whether his emphasis on *karma* is not matched by a similar emphasis on *jñāna*. Does not the practice of *ahiṁsā* and *sarvodaya* rest on metaphysical presuppositions concerning the indivisibility of Truth, the identity of the soul and God and the essential unity of all that exists? He claims that religion is to morality what water is to seeds in the soil and that a moral life without religion is like a house built on sand.[37] *Karma yoga* may lead to the realisation of Truth but does it not presuppose that there is a Truth to be realised? What we might say is that the principles of identity and participation are so closely intertwined that it is difficult sometimes to distinguish between them. His sense of identity with his fellow men is a primary reason for his participation in the social and political affairs. On the other hand through participation in the service of others he comes to realise his true self and his identity with all that lives. Identity and participation are two sides of the same coin; it is difficult to say which is the obverse and which the reverse. In Hindu terminology we might say that while *jñāna* leads to *karma* it is equally true that *karma* leads to *jñāna*. As a true *karma yogin* Gandhi insists that detached, selfless action is action in the service of humanity and that *sarvodaya* springs from and leads to the realisation of Truth.[38]

I have tried to show to what extent Gandhi might be considered an Advaitin in the traditional mould. Similarities between his position and that of Śankara can be drawn but they are perhaps not as evident as contrasting views and differences of emphasis. In many ways Gandhi's thought bears a closer resemblance to the teaching of Vivekānanda. He certainly echoes the teaching of the latter when he claims that there as many religions as there are individuals, and that even within particular, historical religions there are different viewpoints manifesting different facets of the truth.[39] Both thinkers distinguish between personal and impersonal conceptions of God and the highest concept for Vivekānanda is the Vedāntic concept of Being, Consciousness, Bliss. The essence of religion, he maintains, is to see God as 'the Soul of our souls, the Reality in us'.[40] All that exists is in effect a manifestation of Being itself which is the impersonal God, the One through whom we know, see, think and exist.

> He is the essence of our own Self. He is the essence of this ego, this I and we cannot know anything excepting in and through that I. Therefore you have to know everything in and through Brahman.[41]

Thus the impersonal God is the only reality for Vivekānanda. All else is unreal and manifested by the power of *māyā*. Brahman is Truth, the Self of man, and the purpose of life is to know the Truth. We attain knowledge of Truth when we come to know that we are at one with the Universal Being.[42]

Like Vivekānanda, Gandhi expresses preference for the impersonal concept of God and his claim that Truth and Reality are one corresponds to Vivekānanda's view that the impersonal God is Being itself. But comparisons between the two go

even further. As Gandhi refers to personifications of the ultimate as an indication of man's desire for symbols, so does
Vivekānanda refer to forms and images as symbols manifesting
man's attempt to realise the ultimate.

> The Hindus have discovered that the absolute can only be
> realized, or thought of, or stated, through the relative, and
> the images, crosses, and crescents are simply so many sym-
> bols – so many pegs to hang spiritual ideas on. It is not that
> this help is necessary for everyone, but those that do need
> it have no right to say that it is wrong.[43]

Gandhi's reference to symbols as manifestations of man's craving for the unseen and intangible corresponds to Vivekānanda's
claim that they are pegs for spiritual ideas. Both recognise the
need for symbolic representations of the ultimate and that
they are necessary for the religious life of some people. Both
agree that image worship is an indication of man's need for
symbols and ought not to be construed as idol worship. Both
express preference for the impersonal concept of God as Being
itself or Truth and both would agree that there is nothing
wrong in conceiving God in personal terms. Gandhi, however,
goes one step further on the question of the superiority and
inferiority of impersonal and personal concepts of God. He
draws no distinction between the two concepts. It makes no
difference to him whether God is conceived in one way or the
other since the personal concept of God is not inferior to the
impersonal concept. His readiness to acknowledge that God is
all things to all men enables his to accept the validity of the
Dvaita and *Viśiṣṭādvaita* positions while at the same time maintaining his preference for *Advaita*. Vivekānanda on the other
hand sees the concept of a personal God as characteristic of
the religion of the masses. He recognises that those who do
not need such a concept have no right to condemn it and
should acknowledge that it has its rightful place in the social
structure, nevertheless in their view it represents an inferior
position and a lower form of truth. His view is that *Dvaita* is
fulfilled by *Viśiṣṭādvaita* which in turn finds complete fulfilment in *Advaita*.

> Now, as society exists at the present time. All these three
> stages are necessary; the one does not deny the other, one

is simply the fulfilment of the other. The Advaitist or qualified Advaitist does not say that dualism is wrong; it is a right
view, but a lower one. It is on the way to truth; therefore let
everybody work out his own vision of this universe, according to his own ideas.[44]

If Gandhi is at odds with Vivekānanda on the question of
the superiority of the *Advaita* position, he is at one with him
on the question of the unity of existence which, according to
Vivekānanda, is the main lesson man needs to learn.[45] The
difference between man and the animal kingdom is one of
degree and not of kind for man is at one with the universe.[46]
The test of spirituality is the ability to recognise the oneness of
life and this occurs when the veil of ignorance falls from man's
eyes and he achieves the state of *jivan-mukti* or self-liberation.[47]
He sees that there is but one Self, one reality, and that the
empirical world is a manifestation of the One.[48] The unity of
the individual self with the universal Self means that an individual cannot inflict an injury on another without injuring
himself. So *ahimsā* for Vivekānanda as for Gandhi is the inescapable corollary of belief in the essential unity of mankind.

Thou art with this Universal Being, and, as such, every soul
that exists is your soul; and every body that exists is your
body; and in hurting anyone, you hurt yourself, in loving
anyone, you love yourself.[49]

The similarities between the views of Gandhi and Vivekānanda on the question of the non-violent implications of
the unity of mankind are evident. The same is true of the
social implications of the doctrine. Vivekānanda saw clearly
that it involved a change in the orthodox treatment of outcastes
and in the traditional Hindu attitude to privilege and wealth.
He recognised as Gandhi did that religion applied not just to
one dimension of a man's life but to every aspect of his existence. Both rejected the attempt to compartmentalise religion
and at the same time removed the demarcation line between
the sacred and the secular. Both saw God in the face of the
poor: Vivekānanda refers to him as *Daridrānāryan*, God of
the poor, while Gandhi speaks of finding God in the hearts of
the needy and seeing him as the bread of life for starving
men. Vivekānanda's enthusiasm for social reform is prompted
by the plight of the poor.

The poor and the miserable are for our salvation, so that we may serve the Lord, coming in the shape of the diseases, coming in the shape of the lunatic, the leper, and the sinner! Bold are my words; and let me repeat that it is the greatest privilege in our life that we are allowed to serve the Lord in all these shapes.[50]

He saw that the crying need of India was not religion but bread. He considered it an insult to offer starving people religion or to teach them metaphysics when what they needed was to be saved from starvation.[51] Poverty was the root evil of India and one of the solutions to the problem was education for the masses.[52]

Gandhi echoes Vivekānanda's teaching on social matters and works out in thought and action the far-reaching implication of those metaphysical beliefs common to them both. His depth of feeling on the question of untouchability is such that if it were regarded as an essential part of the Hindu way of life then, as he says, he would rather that Hinduism died than that untouchability should live. The immorality, injustice and inhumanity of the practice of untouchability is implicit and explicit in everything he says and does, and he is right to maintain that the passion of his life was to be of service to the Harijans of India. His life-long fight on their behalf is matched by his enlightened attitude to women, whose basic human rights he sought to restore with the provision of equality of opportunity in the field of education.

The similarity between Gandhi's view of religion and that of Vivekānanda is also evident. For the latter religion is in essence one and its goal is the realisation of God in the soul.[53] Nevertheless it takes different forms in accordance with the various circumstances of people. So far as externals are concerned there may be as many sects or religions as there are human beings. Truth can be expressed in a variety of different ways embodying different philosophies, mythologies and rituals, but in essence it is one. The ideal universal religion is that which produces a harmonious balance of the elements of philosophy, mysticism and emotion.

And this religion is attained by what we . . . call Yoga-union. To the worker, it is union between men and the whole of humanity; to the mystic, between his lower and Higher Self;

to the lover, union between himself and the God of Love; and to the philosopher, it is union of all existence.[54]

Gandhi speaks of religion as one which becomes many as it passes through the human medium. Religions for him, as for Vivekānanda, correspond to the variety of environments and temperaments that exist in the world. There are as many religions as there are individuals but they are simply different roads leading to the same goal. Religion is that which underlies all religions; it harmonises them and gives them reality; it is that element in human nature which seeks to realise the oneness of the Soul and Truth or God.[55]

We return to the question posed at the outset, namely, in what sense can Gandhi be called an Advaitin? Does his claim to be a believer in *Advaita* relate only to the concept of the essential unity of existence? I have tried to show that certain comparisons can be drawn between his position and that of classical *Advaita* but that the differences are too basic to enable us to call him ad Advaitin in that sense. The similarities between his views and the views of Vivekānanda, however, are sufficiently clear to enable us to say that he is closer to the neo-Vedāntic position that to classical Vedānta and that the similarities extend beyond the concept of the essential oneness of existence. While differences between them exist, it is still evident that Gandhi is much more in tune with Vivekānanda's basic position and with the way he develops the moral, social and political implications of his metaphysical beliefs. So it is possible to conclude that he *is* an Advaitin, but in the neo-Vedāntic sense of the term, and for that reason he is also a reformer in the modern Hindu tradition.

6 Gandhi's Philosophy of Education

In order to understand Gandhi's thought it is important in my view to be aware of what he means by Truth. It is no accident or coincidence that he should have given his autobiography the subtitle *The Story of my Experiments with Truth*, because his whole life could well be regarded as a quest for Truth, or an attempt to live in accordance with Truth. His followers are in all probability right when they maintain that he was essentially a practical man with little or no interest in philosophical or metaphysical speculation as such. My discussions with Morarji Desai, former Prime Minister of India, and Acharya Kripalani, one of Gandhi's foremost disciples, were sufficiently detailed to convince me of that fact. Yet while that may well have been the case, and while it may be wrong to describe him as a philosopher in the generally accepted sense of the term, there can be little doubt that his thoughts and actions spring from firmly held religious and metaphysical beliefs. The nature of those beliefs become evident when we understand what he means by Truth. It would be wrong to suggest that he arrives at the meaning of Truth as a result of a process of philosophical or metaphysical speculation undertaken in the abstract as it were. He is not a neutral observer, or a speculative philosopher in the traditional sense of the term, who first seeks to define Truth and then applies it to different aspects of life; rather he is one who participates in the Hindu way of life and who comes to understand what Truth means from the way in which the term is used in that particular form of life.

From his writings we are able to discern that he equates Truth (*Satya*) with Reality (*Sat*) and he asserts unequivocally that nothing exists except Truth since for him Truth is Reality.[1] In true Advaitin fashion, therefore, he is able to state that where there is Truth there also is Reality, Knowledge and Bliss, or *Saccidānanda*. Students of Indian philosophy are well aware that this is one of the Upanishadic descriptions of *Brahman*, the Ultimate.[2] Truth then is Being itself or Ultimate Reality, but when it assumes shape or form at any time in order to meet specific human needs for the concrete and tangible, it is called God or *Īśvara*. Gandhi recognises that while the concept of formless Truth might be sufficient for some, it has to assume the personal form of God for those who feel the need for a tangible representation of the Ultimate and who need to be aware of his presence and to experience his touch.[3] His own preference is for the formless concept of Truth, but he does not consider those devotees who desire a more personal concept of God to be in any way inferior to those who prefer the formless concept of Truth.[4]

In the tradition of Advaita Vedānta Gandhi is able to maintain that no hard and fast distinction can be drawn between the Self within or *Ātman*, and Truth or *Satya*. His reference to the soul (*Ātman*), and the Ultimate (*Brahman*), as knowers rather than objects of knowledge, and his claim that it is not possible for mortal beings to know the knower of knowing, bears this out.[5] It is consistent also with the teaching of the Upanishads concerning the identity of *Ātman-Brahman*, a position Gandhi maintains when he says that the Self within is at one with the essence of reality. He conceives the purpose of life to be knowing the Self which is equivalent in his view to knowing the Truth or realising God. The Self released from the bonds of darkness and ignorance is at one with God and identical with Truth, for Self-realisation is Truth-realisation which is the realisation of God. The basic presupposition here is that the existential quest for Truth is the same as seeking to know the true nature of the Self. This in turn involves accepting the concept of the indivisibility of Truth and the essential unity of life, a view Gandhi espouses when he says: 'I believe in Advaita, I believe in the essential unity of man and, for that matter, of all that lives'.[6] He did not conceive it possible to realise Truth, or accept the concept of the absolute oneness of God, without at the same time recognising the essential unity of existence. 'What though we have many bodies?' he says, 'We have but one soul. The rays of the sun are many through refraction. But they have the same source. I cannot, therefore, detach myself from the wickedest soul nor may I be denied identity with the most virtuous.'[7] All men are brothers, therefore, because they share the same *Ātman* and partake of the same reality or Truth source.

Gandhi's understanding of Truth coupled with his belief in

the essential unity of life has profound social, economic and political implications and affects his view of the relationship that should exist between man and his fellow man. This is well illustrated in his teaching on *sarvodaya*, the uplift or welfare of all mankind. His concern for the welfare of all is revealed most clearly in his treatment of the untouchables, or Harijans (children of God) as he calls them. Since they partake of the nature of God, or derive from the same Truth source, then they have to be regarded as at one with other (caste) members of Hindu society and with the whole of mankind. His life-long fight on behalf of the untouchables is matched by his enlightened attitude towards women. Nothing was so shocking, in his view, as man's abuse of the female sex. *Sarvodaya* had as much to do with the status of women as with the treatment of the untouchables in Hindu society and was concerned with the restoration of the basic human rights of both groups. One of the primary ways in which their rights could be restored so far as he was concerned was by the provision of equality of opportunity in the field of education. It is my contention, therefore, that Gandhi's philosophy of education is related to, if not determined by, his belief in *sarvodaya* which in turn is rooted in his belief in the essential unity of mankind and his understanding of the indivisibility of Truth.

In some respects Gandhi's attitude to education is reminiscent of Plato. In his theory of education Plato refers to the cultivation of the soul as the ultimate goal and points to gymnastics and music as the necessary prerequisites of a well-balanced education for the cultivation of man's body and soul. Similarly Gandhi speaks of the need for a form of education that would develop the whole man, body, mind and spirit, and considers this to be the ultimate ideal. It would be a mistake, he insists, to seek to cultivate the mind in isolation from the body and the spirit. Referring to the Gujarati word for education *kelavani* he points out that it has the same connotation as the English term 'education', namely, 'drawing out'; it implies the development of latent talents, or as Plato would describe it, the cultivation of the inherent qualities of the soul. The Welsh word for culture, *diwylliant*, has a similar connotation since its literal meaning is 'to make less wild', and its purpose is to remove all harmful tendencies and to cultivate man's latent, beneficent qualities. True education for Gandhi, as for

Plato, is that which cultivates the soul or the spirit and which leads ultimately to the full and complete development of man's body, mind and spirit. He recognises that our contemporary educational system may be able to develop the mind and body without difficulty but not necessarily the spirit. The fact that we may fill a person's mind with a lot of information, however valuable, does not mean that he is thereby educated. A literate mind, Gandhi claims, can be like a wild horse pulling us hither and thither. So in order for the intellect to develop effectively it is necessary for the spirit to be properly cultivated. This may explain the reason why Gandhi sees music as an integral part of the school curriculum since it involves the concepts of rhythm and order and has a soothing effect on the minds and hearts of students. Used judiciously, he claims, it could lead a man to a vision of God. It was with regret that he noted the neglect of the study of music in India because without it the educational system of the country was in his view incomplete. The haste with which Universities in the United Kingdom sought to close down music departments in the 1980s in response to philistine, utilitarian legislation, might elicit a similar feeling of regret in the hearts of those who share the ideals of Plato and Gandhi and are only too well aware of the uplifting character of music. The latter refers to the pacifying and tranquillising effect of music in his own life: 'I can remember occasions when music instantly tranquillized my mind when I was greatly agitated over something. Music has helped me to overcome anger'.[8] It is clearly Gandhi's view that it would not be appropriate for educationalists today to concentrate on the development of the mind, or the intellectual faculties of a person, to the exclusion of his physical and spiritual faculties, since together they constitute an indivisible whole. It would be a mistake also, he believes, to regard literacy as the be-all and end-all of education, or even as the best way to begin to educate a child. It is this attitude to literacy which constitutes the starting point of his theory of education.[9]

It is interesting to note at the outset that in Gandhi's view the teaching of handicrafts should be given pride of place in the education of children. In propounding this view he was influenced by two considerations. In the first place he had a high regard for the creative skills involved in producing artistic objects, and secondly, he believed that the sale of such

objects produced by students might enable a school to become economically self-supporting.[10] Developing his theory
of basic education he goes on to suggest that it would not
be impossible to communicate the rudiments of history, geo-
graphy and mathematics alongside the teaching of crafts, and
that the basic skills of reading and writing would also follow.
He is not convinced, for example, that it was to a child's advantage to be forced to learn the alphabet, or to read books,
at a tender age. Clearly he is attracted to the value of the oral
communication of knowledge, and as such he is lending his
support to the long established traditions relating to the literary heritage of India. 'Literary training by itself', he claims,
'adds not an inch to one's moral height and character build-
ing is independent of literary training.'[11]

This view of basic education may have derived from Gandhi's painful memories of his own early education. But his
attempt to relate education, in the generally accepted sense of
the term, to practical activity, especially in the primary stages,
shows that he is convinced of the need to combine the art of
acquiring knowledge with the acquisition of practical skills. It
would appear that this is the kind of approach some educationalists today consider to be necessary for a person to live an
effective and satisfying life. They believe that certain interdependent elements are the necessary prerequisites of a basic
educational programme, namely, a positive attitude to work on
the one hand, and the acquisition of the basic skills of literacy
and numeracy on the other. They recognise, however, that
there has long been what they describe as a tyranny of the
intellect because of the emphasis that has always been placed
on the importance of intellectual skills, but they also acknowledge that the love of working with one's hands is difficult to
suppress. It is involvement in skilled activity through the use of
his hands that gives a child great joy in the early period of his
life, and they argue that it ought not to be too difficult to
reinstate the concept of the dignity of this kind of creative
activity in modern educational programmes. Such a restruc-
turing of the educational curriculum, it is claimed, might well
result in the release of a great amount of creative energy.[12]
Gandhi, as we have seen, combines these two prerequisites of
a balanced educational programme when he suggests that the
acquisition of the basic skills of literacy and numeracy should

go hand in hand with the creative activity involved in the production of handicrafts.

It would be a mistake to assume that Gandhi, who never aspired to academic distinction, was in any way enthusiastic about propounding his views on education. The fact of the matter is that he was extremely hesitant about stating his theories for fear of being ridiculed. Who was he after all to lecture educational experts on the purpose of education? But his quest for Truth which is related to his firm belief in the unity of existence and finds practical expression in his concern for the uplift and service of all, *sarvodaya*, enabled him to overcome his initial fears. When he expressed his views on education and advocated a system of compulsory primary education for everyone, he had in the forefront of his mind those unfortunate members of Hindu society whose basic human rights had been ignored. One of the ways in which their basic human rights could be restored was by the provision of equal opportunity in the field of education. This applied particularly to women who had hitherto been sadly neglected by those responsible for providing education in India. Gandhi was realistic enough, however, to see that no compulsory system of basic education was likely to succeed unless it included some form of vocational training coupled with the economic self-sufficiency that could be derived from the sale of crafts produced by students. Yet he advocated vocational training and the teaching of handicrafts not only because of the educational and economical benefits such an approach would provide, but also because it prepared a person for life by giving him the means to earn his living and thereby ensuring the economic survival of his family. It was impossible, in Gandhi's view, to exaggerate the harm done to the youth of India by the notion that somehow it was not fitting for them to labour with their hands in order to earn their living. He considered the craft of handspinning in particular as a sacrament. Nothing, he claims, is more ennobling because it symbolises one's identification with the poorest of the nation and by making the effort to learn the craft of spinning we add to the strength of the nation.[13]

What he has to say about primary education applies equally to his view of higher education. Asked on one occasion whether primary education should be for the villages, secondary education for the cities, and higher education for those who would take up work in the social services, he replied that he saw no reason why villagers should be satisfied with primary education and that they had as much right as anyone else to receive secondary and higher education. So he approves of the provision of higher education for all who desired it and who might benefit from it, but he does not agree that it should be paid for by the state or that it was the responsibility of the state to find the money to establish universities. His view is that university education should be in line with basic education; if people wanted it they would supply the funds for it. This attitude would doubtless meet with the approval of many today who feel that it is not the responsibility of the state to support financially those who wish to proceed to higher education and also those who would advocate the provision of loans rather than grants to enable students to study for degrees. Gandhi, however, goes further when he maintains that universities like schools and colleges should be self-supporting. That is, he extends to higher education the principle of self-sufficiency that he claims should operate in primary education, and by so doing he is proposing a form of university education which he believes is consistent with the needs of India. When he suggests that colleges and universities should be attached to industries which should pay for the training of the graduates they need, he is almost contemporary in his approach.[14] What this implies is that there should be careful monitoring of curricula by Universities' authorities who should ensure that their teaching programmes are vocationally oriented and produce the type of graduates both industry and society need.[15] Gandhi in fact acknowledges this point though whether he envisaged that the link between industry and higher education should apply even in conditions of economic recession which would automatically adversely affect a student's educational programme is not at all clear. What is clear is that he regarded education in art subjects, though with the exception of music it would seem, as a 'sheer waste' which 'has resulted in unemployment among the educated classes'.[16] This is a sentiment in line with that expressed by certain United Kingdom politicians who view the study of art subjects, such as history and music, as a luxury. Gandhi's view may well have been a reflection on the non-vocational nature of art subjects in general and, if so, it could be said that like his modern political counterparts he

had a limited understanding of the nature and purpose of
higher education in the arts, hence his opposition to the idea
of education for its own sake. On the other hand, it could be
argued that what he was proposing was a system of education
that in his view best fitted the needs of his country. Education
would perform a disservice to Indian society as a whole in his
view if it produced graduates who were contemptuous of
manual labour and disinclined to soil their hands, or who
considered it beneath their dignity to engage in tasks that
other less able people could do quite effectively.[17] It is ironic
to say the least that the British educational system in India
succeeded in creating an educated elite inclined to despise
those of their fellow countrymen who cut wood and carried
water, and who were content to be what the system intended
them to be, namely, clerks and interpreters in the Indian Civil
Service.[18]

An important strand in Gandhi's philosophy of education is
his view of the significance and importance of the language
used as the medium of instruction in schools and colleges. He
insisted that the use of English as the medium of instruction
in the education of the youth of India had done incalculable
damage to the nation both intellectually and morally. It had
broken the concordance that ought to exist between home
and school by undermining the importance of the mother
tongue of those involved in the educational process. He recalls
with misgiving his own school experience of the priority given
to the mastery of English before learning could begin, and of
the punishment inflicted on those caught speaking their mother
tongue in class, in his case Gujarati. This policy seems to have
been the accepted English practice since it was not confined
to India. A similar educational system was imposed on Wales
in the nineteenth century when English was made the medium of instruction in Welsh schools and the use of the mother
tongue was discouraged by the infliction of mental and physical punishments. Gandhi's argument is that it would have been
much easier for him to grasp the rudiments of subjects taught
at school had he been able to learn them through the medium of his mother tongue. Furthermore the vocabulary of
Gujarati would have been enriched in the process.[19] He is
firmly of the view that real education for the people of India
was impossible through the medium of a foreign language

since it led to the neglect of the indigenous culture of the nation. It estranged students from their mother tongue and sought to cut them off from their roots in the cultural traditions of their country. In his view the only reason why they were not totally alienated from their cultural heritage, which was often depicted as barbarous and superstitious, was because they were too firmly rooted in the ancient traditions of their country.[20] The sooner the educated people of India freed themselves from what he calls the hypnotic spell of a foreign medium the better it would be for India as a whole. But his indictment of the alien education system that fostered what he called 'the tyranny of English', was not simply that it had inflicted a moral and intellectual injury on the Indian nation by undermining its literary foundations and damaging its cultural heritage, but that it was also a violation of Truth, an affront to Indian self-respect, and a grievous blow to the self identity and national identity of the Indian people.

As we have seen the primary aim and purpose of education for Gandhi, as for Plato, was the development of the mind and character of people, that is, the development of the whole man, body, mind and spirit. This raises the interesting question whether he saw a place for religious education in the school curriculum. It is significant that he shows a remarkable openness to the study of world religions and is favourably disposed to what is referred to today as religious pluralism. He commends the teaching of ethics and the main tenets of other faiths because, as he claims, understanding and appreciating the different beliefs and doctrines of the great religions of the world in a spirit of reverence and tolerance can lead to a better appreciation of one's own faith.[21] Not for Gandhi, therefore, the narrow, exclusivist, dogmatic approach to religious education, or what he calls the religion of the prison house. He has no desire to confine religious education to instruction in the principles of the Hindu faith any more than he wishes the teaching of literature to be confined to the cultural heritage of India. In this respect he claims an affinity with Ram Mohan Roy and Rabindranath Tagore, both of whom desired the windows of India to be opened wide to the winds of culture from other lands though not of course to the neglect of its own culture.[22]

It is possible to see in Gandhi's theory of education echoes of the teachings of other Hindu reformers. Ram Mohan Roy, who has been described as one of the most creative of nineteenth century thinkers in India, sought to harmonise Western science and technology with the spirituality of the East for the benefit of mankind as a whole. This meant that in the field of education he desired above all that the native population might be provided with instruction in 'mathematics, natural philosophy, chemistry and anatomy and other useful sciences' by the British Raj rather than instruction in Sanskrit through the establishment of a Sanskrit school in Calcutta.[23] Unlike Roy, Dayananda Sarasvati, one of the most influential figures in the history of modern India, was fully aware of the intimate connection between language, culture and national identity. He fully supported the teaching of Hindi and Sanskrit as national languages and advocated that they should be the medium of instruction in schools. He deplored the neglect of these languages to such an extent that he was reluctant to allow an English translation of his *Vedabhashya* to appear lest Sanskrit and Hindi should suffer as a consequence.[24] Gandhi, as we have seen, supports Roy's endeavour to broaden the intellectual horizons of his fellow countrymen, but he would not have approved of his campaign against the teaching of Sanskrit which he considered to be the linguistic basis of Hindu culture.[25] Gandhi's reference to 'the tyranny of English', and his awareness that real education was not possible for the people of India if the indigenous languages and culture of the nation were neglected, meant that he was in sympathy with the general thrust of the arguments put forward by Dayananda about the importance of language in relation to both self identity and national identity.

Tagore's pursuit of his religious, cultural and educational ideals led him to establish the Vishva Bharati University at Shantiniketan where, in a residential setting in close proximity with nature, he sought to show that the purpose of education should be the emancipation of the soul and the liberation of the human spirit. To achieve this end he saw that it was not enough to be concerned with imparting information or cultivating the mind or the intellect alone, rather it was necessary to cultivate the whole man, body mind and spirit. To achieve this goal it was important to pay particular attention to the atmosphere and environment in which education was to be imparted, and also to the languages that were to be used in the development of the whole man. Tagore's emphasis on the importance of the mother tongue in the cultivation of man's soul and the need for the harmonious development of all man's faculties and not just the mind in isolation from the body and spirit, bears a close resemblance to the educational ideals of Gandhi. Like Gandhi also he states clearly that he has no fear or distrust of other cultures simply because of their alien character. They should be welcomed rather than resisted and in due course assimilated into the Hindu way of life in order to become a source of strength and nourishment to the culture of the nation.[26]

It is possible to show that Gandhi's theory of education echoes also the teachings of Vivekānanda and that they are further developed in the writing and labours of his ardent disciple Vinoba Bhave. In fact his relation to other reformers in the Hindu tradition, which has been touched upon only briefly here, might be considered a fruitful area of further research. Suffice it to say that his views on education are in many ways similar to those of other modern Hindu reformers.

We may be justified in drawing the conclusion that Gandhi's philosophy of education can hardly be regarded as ideal. He could be criticised, for example, for being too vocationally oriented or for failing to see the value of education for its own sake. Gandhi might well agree with these criticisms, but he could still maintain that in the prevailing circumstances what he was proposing was the best system of education for the people of India as a whole, and that it was preferable to a system which simply served the needs of the Indian civil service. At least it was a system which preserved the cultural heritage of the nation, produced no crisis of self-identity or national identity, and was not a violation of Truth.

7 Religion and Religions: Gandhi and Tillich

This essay seeks to analyse the views of Gandhi and Tillich on the subject of religion. It seeks to show that Gandhi's view of religion is inextricably bound up with the Hindu way of life and has implications for his attitude to religious symbols, the secular, missionary activity and other historical religions. Comparisons with Tillich's views on religion will show that similar implications apply for those who belong to the western tradition and that the mystical–prophetic distinction sometimes drawn between eastern and western religious traditions may well be too sweeping a generalisation.

It is a well-documented fact that Gandhi's concept of religion corresponds to his concept of Truth. The subtitle of his autobiography, *The story of my experiments with Truth,* indicates that throughout his life he tried to live in accordance with those ethical and religious beliefs which were an integral part of the Hindu tradition. His concept of Truth may in fact be viewed as that which determined the spirit in which he lived his life and which permeated the religious and ethical criteria governing his thoughts and actions. He understands what it means to talk about Truth from the way in which the term is used in the Hindu context. Similarly, it is as a participant in the Hindu way of life that he understands what it means to talk about Religion. He has glimpses of absolute Truth, he maintains, through his acquaintance with particular instances of relative truth. In the same way he has glimpses of Religion through the existence of particular, historical religions. He claims that what he understands by the term Religion is not to be equated with particular religions. It transcends Hinduism, Islam, Christianity and all other religions, for example, yet at the same time it harmonises them and endues them with reality.[1] It is that which binds man to Truth; it is synonymous with belief in *ṛta*, an ordered, moral government of the universe; it is that permanent element in human nature which makes the soul restless until it rests in God.[2]

The true and perfect Religion Gandhi refers to is beyond

predication and not capable of being realised within finite existence. No particular, historical religion, in his view, can ever embody the perfection of Religion or lay claim to a monopoly of Truth. Even so, particular religions are necessary to convey the meaning of Religion in the same way as particular truths are necessary to reveal the meaning of Truth. But as particular truths fail to embody the fullness of Truth so particular religions fail to embody the fullness of Religion. They are simply human constructs or expressions of that which underlies them and gives them reality, and the heart of one religion is identical with the heart of another.

> Even as a tree has a single trunk, but many branches and leaves so there is one true and perfect Religion, but it becomes many, as it passes through the human medium. The one Religion is beyond all speech.[3]

The question that arises is whether Gandhi is referring to an 'essence' or 'primordial element' when he speaks of the heart of one religion being identical with the heart of another. If so then it is quite possible to draw a comparison between his teaching and that of both Tillich and Schleiermacher. The latter conceives of religion as pre-existing particular historical manifestations and grounded in the fundamental unity of religion as an *a priori* condition.[4] The transcendental unity of religion for Schleiermacher is necessary for the existence of positive religions which are simply concrete expressions of the primordial form, namely, the immediate religious consciousness or 'the sense and taste for the Infinite'. No finite, positive form of religion, however, can encapsulate the universality or infinitude of religion. The notion that a finite form of religion can be universally valid is inappropriate.[5] Yet it does not follow that finite forms are superfluous in any way because religion has to find expression in concrete forms and the plurality of particular religions is necessary for the complete manifestation of religion. Every positive religion, according to Schleiermacher, contains something of the true nature of religion, and the primordial form, or essence, of religion is apprehended not by deducing it from the common elements of particular religions as a kind of abstraction, but in and through the language and traditions of particular religions. The latter are true in so far as they express the primordial form of religion which in turn is comprehended only in the depths of particular, historical religions.[6]

The same emphasis is to be found in Tillich's definition of religion as Ultimate Concern, which refers not only to man's subjective concern but also to that which is the source of his concern. That is, Ultimate Concern has an objective as well as a subjective connotation since it is possible for man to be grasped by an Ultimate Concern. This concern manifests itself in what Tillich quaintly calls the Religion of the Concrete Spirit which occurs in fragmentary form in the depths of particular religions. So for Tillich, as for Schleiermacher and Gandhi, religion as Ultimate Concern finds expression in positive, historical religions. The concept of Ultimate Concern is really not far removed from Schleiermacher's 'feeling of absolute dependence' which has both a subjective and objective connotation, or from Gandhi's true and perfect religion which is beyond predication but which finds expression, albeit imperfectly, in particular, historical religions.

One criticism that can be levelled against idealistic philosophy is that the problem with maintaining the existence of a 'primordial element' is determining how to go about isolating it and how to determine the relative truth of particular religions by means of it. Is there an element of truth in Cantwell Smith's claim that there are problems in seeking to postulate 'a transcendental ideal of which historical actualities are a succession of mundane and therefore imperfect, compromised manifestations',[7] and that the term religion is not one 'that can be formulated and externalised into an observable pattern theoretically abstractible from the persons who live it'?[8]

We have noted that for Gandhi no particular religion can embody the fullness of truth and that all historical religions contain errors because they are human constructs. Yet he is convinced that they are different roads to the same goal and he believes that there will always exist a variety of religions corresponding to different human temperaments.[9] He echoes the teaching of the Hindu reformer Vivekānanda when he maintains that there are as many religions as there are individuals, and that even within particular religions there will be different viewpoints reflecting different facets of the truth.[10] When he suggests that it is of no consequence which road one takes to achieve the ultimate goal of liberation he seems to be implying that the end justifies the means. But we have to point out that such a view would be contrary to what he has to say about the convertibility of means and ends, so it is hardly likely that he would be unconcerned with the kind of religion a person professes. He would be very concerned, for example, if the content of a particular religion proved to be at odds with the ethical criteria he would normally associate with the concept of Truth. In his view it is inconceivable for religion to exist without morality and should a religion deny the virtues of truth, mercy and goodness, then it forfeits the right to be called a religion. To lose our basis in morality, he claims, is to cease to be religious, for religion and morality are inescapably bound up with one another.[11] His emphasis on *sarvodaya* (the welfare of all) as an expression of Truth and as a means of realising Truth illustrates this very point. He is fully aware of the theonomous nature of humanitarian activity. Through the service of humanity and by means of action in the cause of brotherhood we are brought to a better understanding of Truth, for to help the helpless and feed the hungry is to see God.[12] Truth and *sarvodaya* are so interrelated in Gandhi's thought that they are like two sides of the same coin. So what he may be suggesting by the statement that it is of no consequence which road one takes to attain the ultimate goal of liberation is that too much importance can be attached to a particular religion when it results in exclusivist claims being made on behalf of that religion.

The reference to *sarvodaya* as an expression of Truth and as a means of realising Truth points to a further comparison that can be drawn with the views of Tillich. The theonomous nature of humanitarian activity is evident in Tillich's writings. He classifies humanism, together with nationalism and socialism, as quasi-religions, and as expressions of ultimate concern. The term 'quasi' has no pejorative connotation for him; it simply means that movements such as humanism, which have their origin in the secular sphere, have some of the characteristics of religions. To the extent they do so they are real expressions of Ultimate Concern.[13] Neither Gandhi nor Tillich would wish to draw a hard and fast line of demarcation between the sacred and the secular; they concur in referring to the religious significance of the secular dimension. For Tillich the secular is never 'essentially and inescapably secular' but always 'potentially sacred and open to consecration' because the infinite has to express itself through finite forms.[14] For Gandhi existence is a unity and the secular is pervaded by the spirit of Truth or God.[15] The secular often exercises a liberating function for Tillich in the sense that it saves the holy in its traditional religious form from irrational activities, and when it does so it displays a theonomous element. It is possible for religion to be so ritualised as to ignore or deny the claims of justice, goodness, truth and beauty, but Tillich argues that the secular, or the world of rational structures, can point to the irrationality of those denials of morality and aesthetics, thereby showing something of the prophetic spirit and theonomy that we normally associate with religion.[16] Gandhi, as we have seen, believes religion to be inconceivable without morality, and when it denies the virtues of truth, mercy and goodness then it does not deserve to be classified as religion because religion and morality are inescapably bound up with one another.[17] Gandhi may not express himself in the systematic way Tillich does yet he clearly indicates that morality in the secular sphere, or in the world of rational structures, has all the characteristics of true religion. Similarly, because of the interrelation of Truth and beauty, art might be regarded as an expression of the soul; it is theonomous in the sense that it an aid to self-realisation, which in turn is the realisation of Truth.[18]

Exclusivist claims made on behalf of particular religions is rejected outright by Gandhi who found it difficult to accept that one religion could be considered superior to another. Since all religions are diverse, finite expressions of religion in its essence, it is not possible for adherents of particular religions to claim possession of absolute truth. Different religions may have different symbols, but no symbol should become a fetish to enable a particular religion to claim superiority over another. Tillich makes a similar point when he notes the difficulty involved in seeking to express one's faith in terms of concrete symbols. Yet he still expresses the view that every great religion hopes to provide 'the all-embracing symbol in which the faith of men universally will express itself' while upholding at the same time 'the conditional and non-ultimate character of its own symbols'.[19] All religions in Gandhi's view are equally holy, hence his desire to promote the study of faiths other than his own.[20] He advocates respect and reverence for all religions on the grounds that they possess an element of truth, and he rejects as mistaken the view that the study of other religions might undermine a believer's faith in his own religion. He maintains rather that the study of other religions could extend one's regard for one's own religion to the faith of other men and provide at the same time a better understanding of one's own faith.[21]

The openness Gandhi shows to the plurality of religious traditions indicates that he is not content to confine himself to the small island of his own tradition and culture, or to ignore the spiritual insights of other religious traditions. His rejection of the right of a particular religion to claim superiority for itself underlines his view that it is not possible for particular religions to embody what he calls the 'one true and perfect religion.' In this respect he propounds views similar to Tillich for whom Ultimate Concern expresses itself in a variety of forms: in painting, which may have no religious content in the traditional sense; in philosophy, when attempts are made to understand the nature of ultimate reality; in ideologies which might normally be regarded as secular, such as nationalism, socialism and humanism; and also in traditional religions.[22] When particular religions regard themselves as complete embodiments of the Ultimate, however, and accord themselves the status of ultimacy, they are guilty of idolatry and what Tillich calls demonisation, namely, the particularisation or objectification of the Ultimate.[23] Gandhi uses different terminology when he speaks of religious symbols becoming fetishes which are idolatrous and fit only to be discarded.[24] Differences in terminology, however, cannot disguise the similarity of views expressed by Tillich and Gandhi on the status of particular religions. Both maintain that when a particular religion claims ultimate status for itself it denies the fact that all religions are imperfect and consequently incapable of embodying absolute truth. For both, particular religions are necessary to convey what it means to speak of the one true and perfect religion, which is beyond predication and not capable of being realised within finite existence, or Ultimate Concern which occurs in fragmentary form in the religion of the concrete spirit. So that ideal by which we live, though not embodied in particular religions, nevertheless is communicated to us through those religions.[25]

A further consequence of Gandhi's insistence on the imperfect nature of particular religions is his antipathy to certain forms of missionary activity and the methods employed in proselytising.[26] What becomes evident through his strictures on the attitudes of Christian missionaries is that it is possible for religious zeal and enthusiasm to lead to activities inconsistent with the religious and ethical ideals being promoted. For example, Christians might regard it as an expression of Christian love and a moral duty to convert others to Christ, but would the use of force be justified? Would that not indicate a greater love of dogma than of man? If conversion involves the use of inquisitorial means is not the concept of love distorted? Do not means come under the same moral scrutiny as ends?[27] What Gandhi objects to is the presupposition of superiority that accompanies missionary activity and the implicit if not explicit assumption that the end justifies the means.

It would be wrong to conclude from this, however, that Gandhi is opposed to conversion from one religion to another.[28] On the contrary, he defends the right of those who wished to change their religious affiliation to follow their inclinations in this matter. In his view it is a personal matter between an individual and God. The right of conversion is not questioned, rather the methods employed to effect it. He approved of the humanitarian activity of Christian missionaries especially in the field of health and education, but he disapproved of some of the methods used to proselytise. A patient should not be expected to change his religious beliefs simply because the doctor who cured him happened to be a Christian. Healing ought to be its own reward, but when a missionary report refers to the cost *per capita* of converting people to Christianity, and budgets for the next harvest of souls, then conversion had become something of a business venture. There is an element of justification in Gandhi's injunction to those who would convert India by such questionable means: 'Physician heal thyself'.[29] He regarded many conversions with suspicion and misgiving. He viewed the conversion of his son Harilal to Islam, for example, as one that was prompted by monetary considerations, and in the case of such converts he believed that they should be readmitted to the Hindu faith without hesitation if they so desired. The unacceptability of certain conversion methods is heightened for Gandhi because of his belief that all religions have an element of truth and that none can claim to monopolise it. He believed the scriptures of all faiths to be equally inspired and his respect for other faiths was as strong as it was for his own. His response to Christians who wished to convert to the Hindu way of life was to urge them to be good Christians since the Gītā could not offer them more than the Bible.[30]

Gandhi's antipathy to missionary activity was coupled with a dislike of preaching. He believed that a man's life was a more effective testimony to the truth of his religion than his words. 'A rose does not need to preach', he claims, 'It simply spreads its fragrance ... The fragrance of a religious and spiritual life is much finer and subtler than that of the rose.'[31] The silent witness of a man's life, of course, is more in accord with the meditative and contemplative tradition Gandhi was accustomed to than the more vocal and prophetic approach of the Christian tradition, but his objection to preaching goes deeper than that. He speaks of predication as a limitation of truth. For him language circumscribes and limits truth which ultimately is best represented by the way a man lives his life. This is an affirmation of the effectiveness of silence in the communication of truth, a fact fully understood by the Buddha and his followers. Should a man's way of life succeed in influencing and converting others then that might well be regarded as a valid form of evangelism.[32]

There is a clear suggestion in Gandhi's writings that he considered Christians to be lacking in receptiveness. What he means by this is that he believed them to be unprepared to accept with open minds whatever good India might be able to offer them. He urged them to recognise that by not seeking to understand the philosophic tradition of India they were depriving themselves of the opportunity of serving India.[33] This mild rebuke of the attitude of missionaries to the religious traditions of India corresponds to his criticism of orthodox Christianity which in his view had distorted the message of Jesus. Since it was true that all religions were imperfect and that Hinduism was no different from Christianity in this respect, the Christian claim to possess the final revelation of God in the person of Christ could not be universally accepted. Gandhi could not accept the claim that Jesus was the only begotten son of God; the phrase Son of God should be taken figuratively and not literally. Jesus was divine, but in the same way as Krishna or Rama or Mohammad or Zoroaster were divine,[34] and they, like Jesus, were begotten sons of God.[35] While Christianity was doubtless a noble religion it still had a greater contribution to make to the welfare of humanity. Gandhi's implicit suggestion here is that Christianity had yet to offer whole-hearted support for the principle of non-violence for example, because as he points out, bishops still felt able to support slaughter in the name of Christianity.[36]

Gandhi's attitude to mission finds an echo in Tillich's rejection of *missionwissenschaft*, an approach to religions which regards the main purpose of religious dialogue as a means of conversion from one religion to another. It is reflected also in Tillich's rejection of the superficial approach to religion which sees value in every religious tradition other than one's own, and in the kind of approach that seeks a synthesis of individual religions into an all-embracing whole. Like Gandhi, Tillich does not attempt to underestimate the significance or detract from the importance of particular religions. He recognises that each religion has in its depth a clue to the meaning of ultimate reality,[37] and that without the particular there would be no way of understanding the universal or the ultimate. That is, particular religions, while not embodying Ultimate Concern, or the fullness of truth, are necessary to convey what it means to speak of absolute truth.

Similar views on conversion are to be found in the writings of Simone Weil who maintains that much missionary activity is mistaken and dangerous. Her position is that those who call upon Osiris or Krishna or Buddha with a pure heart receive the holy spirit within their own traditions and have no need to abandon them for another.[38] This is analogous to the claim Gandhi makes in an address to Christian missionaries that 'many men who have never heard the name of Jesus Christ or have even rejected the official interpretation of Christianity *would* probably, if Jesus came into our midst today . . . be owned by him more than many of us . . .'[39]

Another consequence of Gandhi's insistence on the imperfect nature of particular forms of religion is his plea for toleration on the grounds that it increases spiritual insight and gives a better understanding of one's own faith. Not that he likes the term tolerance because he recognises that it might be given a pejorative connotation and indicate a readiness to compromise and accept something inferior. He uses the term for the want of a better word, however, and tries to give it a connotation which incorporates an element of respect.[40] He accepts as a basic premise the truth of all religions and acknowledges the benefits that could be derived from a sympathetic understanding of the scriptures of different faiths. Since all faiths are imperfect the question of comparative merit does not arise and what tolerance does is impart insight into one's own faith as well as breaking down those barriers that might exist between one faith and another.

> My respectful study of other religions has not abated my reverence for or my faith in the Hindu scriptures. They have indeed left their deep mark upon my understanding of the Hindu scriptures. They have broadened my view of life.[41]

Tolerance then does not blind a man to the imperfections of religion or blur the distinction that exists between religion and irreligion, but it does deliver him from fanaticism in respect of his own faith. The golden rule for Gandhi is mutual toleration since we will never all think alike because 'we shall always see Truth in fragment (*sic*) and from different angles of vision'.[42] The goal of tolerance and mutual respect is not the creation of one all-embracing religion, but rather the acceptance of unity in diversity. Gandhi claims to be a Sanati Hindu himself, but as he points out his religion is not exclusive nor is it missionary in the generally accepted sense of the term.

> Hinduism tells everyone to worship God according to his own faith or Dharma, and so it lives at peace with all religions.[43]

He is not blind to the imperfections of Hinduism however. Its cardinal sin is its acceptance of the practice of untouchability which stunts the growth of forty million people. Only when this poison is removed from the Hindu way of life will exploitation cease and co-operation prevail.[44] Gandhi's attitude to untouchability is indicative of the social implications of his quest for Truth and he firmly believes that as an institution it has no place within Hinduism.[45]

Tillich expresses views similar to Gandhi when he points to the need for Christianity to exercise self-criticism. Christianity should be judged by the criteria derived from the event of

Jesus as the Christ[46] which involves rejection of the tendency to demonise Christianity by elevating it to a status of ultimacy. He also advocates tolerance since a tolerant attitude to other religions widens a man's horizons and enables him to take a more accurate view of his own religion. He speaks of his re-awakened interest in world religions after a visit to Japan which prompted the proposal for a joint seminar with Mircea Eliade on the relation between the history of religions and systematic theology.[47] Tillich's initial attraction to world religions was prompted by his teacher Martin Kähler who showed him the dangers of exclusivism and dogmatism with the inevitable loss of openness and spiritual freedom that would follow.[48] Schelling also taught him that religion could not be assigned to a particular human function but had to be regarded as 'the all embracing function of man's spiritual life'.[49] And Ernst Troeltsch was influential in pointing out the value of that freedom which delivers man from the narrowness of biblicism and traditional theology and accepts the need for the cross-fertilisation of religious ideas. The *Religiongeschichliche Schule* helped him to recognise the many saviour symbols that existed in the history of religions and the possibility of understanding them in relation to their social matrix.[50]

Like Gandhi, Tillich takes religious plurality seriously, but he goes beyond Gandhi's plea for toleration and mutual respect when he speaks of the need for greater interpenetration between systematic theology and the history of religions. In his view future theological enquiry had to consider not only the existential problem of modern man in a predominantly secular, technological society, but also the variety of religious experiences as exemplified in the different religious traditions of the world. The theologian who confines himself to the small island of his own tradition and refuses to acknowledge the significance of other religious insights or to engage in dialogue with them is in danger of remaining provincial and missing the world historical occasion.[51]

The type of inter-religious dialogue Tillich propounds recognises the basic unity of all religions in virtue of the interdependence and interrelatedness of the type-determining elements of sacramental, mystical and prophetic. The sacramental element manifests the holy; the mystical element resists all attempts to particularise the holy; and the prophetic element opposes demonic forms of the holy which deny the virtues of love and justice. While Tillich recognises that talk of types of religion refers only to abstractions he still points to mystical types as being more prevalent in the Indian religious traditions.[52] Yet the basic unity of religions is reaffirmed when he speaks of the inner *telos* or aim of all religions as the harmonious relation of these three elements.

The goal of tolerance and mutual respect for Gandhi is not, as we have seen, one all-embracing religion but unity in diversity. Tillich's dialogical approach is similar in that it emphasises the basic unity of all religions while not undermining the importance of particular religions. He recognises that every religion has in its depth a clue to the meaning of ultimate reality and a universality which, when liberated through dialogue, points to what he calls the Religion of the Concrete Spirit. This is a religious experience that harmonises the sacramental, mystical and prophetic elements of the holy and enables us to acquire the spiritual freedom necessary to ascertain different manifestations of the Spiritual Presence or the New Being in different expressions of man's Ultimate Concern. In this respect Tillich's lack of exclusivism echoes that of Gandhi and it could be said that both are seekers after Truth, each in his own way and in the context of his own culture and tradition.

8 Liberation Theology: Bonhoeffer and Gandhi

The purpose of this essay is to examine critically the relation between faith and action in liberation theology as expressed in the writings of Gustavo Gutierrez and Juan Luis Segundo; to show how this reflects some of the fundamental concerns of Dietrich Bonhoeffer; and to illustrate how the issues of liberation exemplified in the work of these western theologians find a parallel in the life and work of Gandhi who was nurtured in the Indian religious tradition and informed by the Hindu way of life.

It is difficult to give a precise answer to the question what liberation theology means. It could be argued that all theology is concerned with liberation and that it not easy to understand why one form of theology should claim the description more than another. One explanation offered by liberation theologians is that they are not concerned with 'deducing' forms of political action from a pre-fashioned theology, but with committing themselves to the process of liberating the oppressed and exploited in the countries of Latin America, and then bringing theological reflection to bear on their attempts to remove injustice and create a better society. They see their goal as a reconsideration of the great themes of Christian Theology in the light of a prior commitment to social action, because in their view the Gospel can only be made meaningful when there is commitment to the liberation of the oppressed and exploited. As Gutierrez maintains: 'Only by participating in their struggle can we understand the implications of the Gospel message and make it have an impact on history'.[1] We might question whether this commitment to social action on the part of liberation theologians would have been engaged in initially had it not been motivated by metaphysical assumptions and ethical ideals, but perhaps to raise such a question is to prejudge the issue. It could be argued equally well that commitment to liberation of the oppressed can be undertaken also from a humanitarian standpoint which would necessarily preclude theological presuppositions.

When Gutierrez speaks of the meaning of liberation theology he refers to it as a question '*about the very meaning of Christianity and about the mission of the Church*'.[2] He suggests that traditional methods of theological reflection are no longer adequate if Christianity is to have any significance or relevance to present-day needs, and he conceives the proper function of theology to be critical reflection on social action.[3] Christian faith is manifested through love, action and commitment to the service of mankind, and theology is reflection on such activity rather than its motivation. It follows that such a theology is far from static and sterile; it is vital, radical, prophetic and concerned with making the world a better place in which to live.[4] It is a theology which not only reflects on historical events but seeks to transform the world, restore human dignity, and build a new and just society; it is active and dynamic in the sense that it 'tries to be part of the process through which the world is transformed'.[5]

Liberation theology for Gutierrez is clearly both reflective and dynamic. In it dynamic aspect it is concerned with 'the aspirations of oppressed people and social classes'.[6] It is also concerned with man's acceptance of his responsibility for his own life and the lives of others in society as well as the need to seek to liberate man from injustice and oppression in accordance with the example of Christ. If one is tempted to claim that this is precisely the concern of a genuine faith, the reply might be that liberation theology is the working out of such a faith in intellectual and practical terms. This appears to be Gutierrez' view when he says: 'From the viewpoint of faith, the motive which in the first instance moves Christians to participate in the liberation of oppressed people and exploited social classes is the conviction of the radical incompatibility of evangelical demands with an unjust and alienating society'.[7]

One of the consequences of the social and political concerns of liberation theology is that the autonomy of the world is accepted. Here Gutierrez recognises that he reflects Bonhoeffer's concept of a world come of age,[8] and although he does not explicitly mention the fact it is clear that the elimination of the hard and fast distinction between the sacred and the secular characteristic of liberation theology parallels

Bonhoeffer's thinking about 'religionless Christianity' and the 'beyond' in the midst of life. The elimination of the natural–supernatural distinction means that sin is not simply a private matter between man and God but a social matter, a historical reality, evidenced by the absence of love between men and manifested in oppressive social structures, exploitation, and the domination and enslavement of people.[9] Similarly, liberation is not simply an individual matter, but has political and social overtones and is viewed as a movement in society from injustice to justice, from oppression to freedom, and from subhuman to human existence.[10] To reduce the concept of liberation to the 'religious' sphere is to limit its effectiveness and at the same time to betray a lack of awareness of the comprehensive nature of liberation in a world come of age.[11] To be truly liberated and thus truly human implies seeking to create a just and equitable society.[12]

A further consequence of the concern of liberation theology for man's needs is that he is considered to be of inestimable value in the sight of God. The incarnation makes this evident, because if God became man then humanity as a whole can be regarded as God's temple, and it follows that we encounter God in our dealings with our fellow men.[13] To do justly, love mercy, feed the hungry, and uplift the oppressed, is to love God for the love of God 'is unavoidably expressed *through* love of one's neighbour'.[14] If these considerations bring to mind what Bonhoeffer has to say about grace and discipleship and what is involved in Gandhi's concept of *ātman* (self) and *sarvodaya* (the uplift of all), it simply points to the parallels that can be drawn between thinkers of different religious traditions. The spiritual life for these three thinkers then is one that is lived in solidarity with all men and not as a personal private affair in isolation from the everyday world of secular society. Liberation theology involves 'de-privatisation' and social commitment.[15]

Segundo shares the basic premises of Gutierrez. He accepts that liberation theology must necessarily have social and political implications and he rejects the accusation of meddling in politics levelled against him by some academic theologians as stemming from their own involvement with the political *status quo*.[16] He affirms that the first step in the process of liberation is commitment to the socially oppressed to be followed by theological reflection. But he raises the question posed earlier in this essay, namely, whether such commitment presupposes metaphysical beliefs or whether the liberation message of the Gospel precedes theological assumptions.[17] People with prior theological assumptions, he claims, tend to have closed minds; nevertheless Christians do have a specific contribution to make to the liberation process, but they understand what that commitment is only when they involve themselves in the problems of social and political liberation in the everyday world.[18] What this means is, that according to Segundo, it is political and social action that gives the Gospel message meaning rather than *vice versa*.[19] But what specific form does the Christian contribution to liberation take, and in what way, if any, is it different from other commitments to the process of liberation derived from other ideologies or beliefs? Segundo's reply is that we should not begin by asking what the Christian contribution is: the more the mind is free from ideological trappings or pre-fabricated theological assumptions, the better we shall be able to recognise human need and become involved in an authentic process of liberation. If, as is being suggested here, theology is the second step as it were, then 'any preliminary consideration of the possible nature of some specifically Christian contribution to liberation – a process in which people of many different beliefs and ideologies participate – is senseless and hence unanswerable'.[20] What Segundo is saying here, and he claims that Gutierrez shares his views, is that a Christian interpretation of the Gospel message is not possible without prior political commitment. He wants theology to be an instrument of human liberation and not simply an academic discipline. The first step is commitment: theological reflection follows.

Stress on the need for existential commitment on the part of Christians in the political and social realm is to be applauded. Not for liberation theologians, it would seem, the pietistic approach on the one hand, or the approach of the armchair theologian on the other. The question is whether action in the political and social realm springs from commitment to Christian ideals, or whether, as Segundo claims, the authentic process of liberation is prior to a true understanding of the Gospel message. It may be a mistake to draw such a hard and fast line between religion and morality here. Social and political commitment could be regarded as concomitant with belief in the

Gospel message. Gandhi makes a similar point when he claims that religion 'cannot be divorced from morality without becoming like "sounding brass"'.[21] What might be said in this context is that commitment to political and social action in the cause of human liberation is the necessary condition of true religion. Put in this way the danger of divorcing morality and religion is avoided. Such a danger is implicit if not explicit in what Gutierrez and Segundo say about the priority of commitment to social action, though Gutierrez would seem to be aware of this danger when he points to the motive behind Christian involvement in social amelioration and liberation of the oppressed as recognition of the incompatibility of religious ideals and social injustice.[22] If it were to be argued that commitment to political and social action is both the necessary and sufficient condition of liberation, then there would be little to distinguish liberation theology from humanism since both are concerned with the meeting of human need. If liberation theology is *theology* in the ordinary sense of the word, then metaphysical assumption would seem to be inevitable despite the fears expressed by liberation theologians about pre-fabricated theological assumptions. Their fears might be allayed if it were pointed out that the difference between a moral sacrifice and a religious sacrifice is that the former is an occasion. The moral man may be ready to sacrifice on specific occasions, but the religious man *must* sacrifice because the essence of the spiritual life is dying to the self. Sacrificial actions follow inevitably from the religious and ethical ideals that determine the way he thinks and acts and inform the spirit in which he lives his life. Put in the terminology of liberation theology we might say that commitment to political and social action is the inevitable concomitant of a man's faith and ideals and not the 'deduction' of a pre-fashioned theology.

The question that may now be asked is to what extent liberation theology reflects the basic concerns of Dietrich Bonhoeffer. Gutierrez himself recognised that he echoed Bonhoeffer's concept of secularisation and of a world come of age. The latter believed that the movement towards man's autonomy which began in the thirteenth century reached its climax in our time. It took the form of a confidence that man was able to solve the problems of life without having recourse to a

Divine Being. The Christian response to this confidence is to
deny that man can live without God and that God alone can
provide an answer to the ultimate questions of life and death.
Bonhoeffer regards this response in the first place as pointless,
since it deprives man of his adulthood and tries to reduce him
to a state of adolescence; secondly as ignoble, since it seeks to
exploit man's weakness for purposes alien to him; and thirdly
as un-Christian, because a particular stage in man's religious-
ness is being substituted for Christ himself.[23] This last remark
points to the Christocentric nature of Bonhoeffer's theology
which we shall return to. At this stage, however, it is sufficient
to note that secularisation is not a defection from the Christian message for Bonhoeffer. Rather it corroborates the view
that Christianity far from being other worldly, or a way of
avoiding the problems of the world, is a religion deeply concerned with secular events. The Christian is not a *homo religiosus*
but a human being and, in Bonhoeffer's view, it is only by
living completely in this world that man truly learns how to
believe.[24] God is to be found at the centre of life and not on
the frontiers of knowledge; he is not a stop gap for man's
defective understanding.[25] The 'beyond' of God is not the
'beyond' of our perceptive faculties but the 'beyond' in the
midst of life.[26]

It could be argued that little distinguishes Bonhoeffer's
emphasis on worldliness and his insistence that we learn what
it means to believe through complete involvement in the world,
from the stress Gutierrez and Segundo place on commitment
to political and social action as prerequisites of a true understanding of the implications of the Gospel message. Julio de
Santa Ana supports this view when he suggests that the concept of a world come of age has overcome the traditional
separation of the church and the world, and that no other
western theologian has influenced more profoundly discussions about the relation between church and society in Latin
America than Bonhoeffer.[27] Clearly no theologian is less pietistic than Bonhoeffer as his advocacy of 'religionless Christianity' shows, but commitment to political and social action is not
a substitute for religion for him nor the sufficient condition of
human liberation. When he speaks of religion in the context
of 'religionless Christianity' he refers to an individualism that
would abandon the world; a form of other worldliness that

would preserve the dualism of the natural and supernatural and relegate God to a diminishing role on the periphery of life; a concept of God as *deus ex machina* who, while providing man with answers to life's many problems, deprives him of his adulthood.[28] His criticism of this concept of religion leads him to claim that we are moving towards a time of no religion and to the recognition of Jesus as 'the man for others'. So while 'religious' interpretations remove God from the world Christianity seeks to establish Christ at the centre of existence.

This approach is exemplified further in Bonhoeffer's interpretation of discipleship. He views it as a recovery of the true meaning of faith because faith is real only when obedience is involved.[29] Liberation theologians make a similar claim when they say: 'obedience is not a consequence of our knowledge of God . . . (it) *is* our knowledge of God'.[30] Discipleship then confirms the social essence of the Gospel for Bonhoeffer. His attempt to form an order known as Bruderhaus was a practical application of his study of discipleship and may have been a response to Gandhi's emphasis on the value of the ashram. In May 1934, he wrote to his grandmother expressing his desire to visit India.

> Sometimes it even seems to me that there is more Christianity in their 'paganism' than in the whole of our Reich Church . . . I might go to Rabindranath Tagore's university. But I'd much rather go to Gandhi and already have some very good introductions from close friends of his. I might be able to stay there for six months or more as a guest.[31]

For Bonhoeffer, as for Gandhi, living together in a communal life of discipleship produces a better understanding of the religious life than more traditional methods. If critics were to construe such an experiment in communal living as a retreat from the world it would have to be pointed out that no one was more aware of the dangers of pietism and religiosity than Bonhoeffer.[32] He refers to cheap grace as grace without discipleship, without involvement in the sufferings and rejection of Christ. Costly grace, on the other hand, means acceptance of the need to be concerned with human suffering and oppression. To be a Christian one has to combine prayer and action, for the spiritual life is one that is lived in solidarity with all men.[33] So for Bonhoeffer, as for Gutierrez, discipleship involves 'de-privatisation' and social commitment.

To return to the Christocentric nature of Bonhoeffer's theology which is referred to as its unifying element.[34] For him there is no God other than the God incarnate in Christ and he rejects what he calls Barth's neo-Kantian transcendentalism which is based on the premise that *finitum incapax infiniti*. The ontological, transcendental approach gives way to the sociological emphasis that *finitum capax infiniti* and that 'God is not free *of* man but *for* man'.[35] The incarnate Christ is the centre of human existence, of history and of nature and we find in him our true humanity for he is above all 'the man for others'. Gutierrez reflects this aspect of Bonhoeffer's thought when he argues that liberation involves the whole man:

> the liberating action of Christ – made man in this history and not in a history marginal to the real life of man – is at the heart of the historical current of humanity; the struggle for a just society is in its own right very much a part of salvation history.[36]

Because divine and cosmic history are one in Christ, says Bonhoeffer, it should be recognised that the whole world is bound together in him.[37] The concepts of Christian worldliness and 'religionless Christianity',[38] therefore, are Christological judgements stemming from a true understanding of the incarnation.[39] It follows that salvation for Bonhoeffer, as for Gutierrez, means the transformation of social structures, man's liberation from political and social exploitation, and his deliverance from injustice and oppression.[40]

Given the centrality of Christology in Bonhoeffer's theology there can be little doubt that he sees the need for moral action arising not from the recognition of human need, or from an acknowledgement of the inherent value of man, but from the reality of God in Christ. Divine and cosmic reality are one because God became man in Christ. Commitment to social action is necessary because Christ is 'the pioneer for others'.[41] Gutierrez lays a similar stress on the importance of the incarnation. Humanity is the temple of God because God became man and we encounter God in our dealings with our fellow men. To do justly and to love mercy is to love God.[42]

Gandhi's motive for moral action differs from that of Bonhoeffer. Not that he denies the reality of God; on the contrary, for him Truth is God and the essence of reality. When he says that his life can be viewed as an existential quest for Truth, or as an attempt to live in accordance with Truth, he is implying that certain religious and ethical beliefs acquired within the Hindu way of life inform his teaching and determine his actions. To maintain as some scholars do that his understanding of Truth lies in the meeting of human need is to reduce him to a humanist. It misunderstands the importance of the religious tradition in which he was nurtured and the significance of the ethical ideals which governed his life. It is a rejection of those metaphysical beliefs which find expression in his commitment to Truth. Gandhi's concern for non-violence (*ahiṁsā*) and the welfare of all men (*sarvodaya*) is based on metaphysical assumptions acquired within Hinduism. His experiments with Truth involved him in the practice of *bhakti yoga*, the discipline of prayer, and *karma yoga*, the discipline of action, which are disciplines that Bonhoeffer also considered to be necessary for the Christian life. Gandhi's insistence on self-discipline in his quest for Truth is linked to his stress on the need to realise Truth through the service of others. Like Bonhoeffer he recognises the importance of human solidarity, but his starting point is not the incarnation of God in Christ since Jesus is not the only begotten Son of God and is only as divine as 'Krishna or Rama or Mohammad or Zoroaster'.[43] The phrase 'Son of God' can be used only in a figurative sense so that in effect anyone 'who stands in the position of Jesus is a begotten son of God'.[44] Gandhi draws no distinction between Truth, God, the essence of reality and the highest Self or *Ātman*, for the highest Self is at one with the essence of reality and to know the Self is to know Truth and to realise God. Furthermore since all men partake of the same *Ātman* then all men are brothers.

> I believe in the absolute oneness of God and therefore of humanity. What though we have many bodies? We have but one soul ... I cannot, therefore, detach myself from the wickedest soul nor may I be denied identity with the most virtuous.[45]

Gandhi's basic metaphysical assumptions are the indivisibility of Truth and reality, the identity of the Self or *Ātman* and God, and the essential unity of existence. The social and political implications of these presuppositions are far-reaching and make commitment to human beings as inescapable for him as for Bonhoeffer and the liberation theologians.

Gutierrez speaks of finding God in the temple of humanity and in our dealings with our fellow men while Bonhoeffer emphasises the social implications of the doctrine of the incarnate Christ. Gandhi starts from his understanding of Truth and insists that religion cannot be an individualistic affair or something that concerns man in isolation from his fellow men. He sees it as bound up with the whole of life including social and political activities and claims 'to see God through the service of humanity'.[46] This is similar to the sentiment expressed by Gutierrez that to do justly, to love mercy, to feed the hungry and uplift the oppressed, is what loving God means. There is no doubt that Gandhi's concept of religion involved helping the helpless, alleviating poverty and starvation, and seeking the uplift of all men (*sarvodaya*). His passion to serve the underprivileged is such that he claims to find God in the hearts of the poor. In a stark and poignant phrase he refers to God as the belly of the starving man and views the gift of food to such a man as a gift to God: 'I may as well place before a dog over there the message of God as before those hungry millions who have no lustre in their eyes and whose only God is their bread'.[47] Our unity with our fellow men in the bonds of Truth presents us with an inescapable moral obligation towards them and shows clearly the inescapable relation that exists between morality and religion. We have to adjust our wants and needs and be prepared to suffer privation if necessary to provide for our brethren who are unclothed and unfed.[48]

A religion that shows no concern for man's welfare, in Gandhi's view does not deserve to be called a religion. *Sarvodaya* embodies and seeks to implement the belief that 'God pervades everything that is to be found in this universe down to the tiniest atom'.[49] Gandhi's concern for the welfare of mankind and his sense of kinship or identity with them, is exemplified in his treatment of the untouchables, whom he calls Harijans, children of God, and by his enlightened attitude towards women.[50] He points to the immorality, injustice, iniquity and

inhumanity of the practice of untouchability and to the inde-
fensibility of the treatment of women in Hindu society. Of all
the evils perpetrated by man none was worse than his abuse of
the female sex, the better half of humanity. By taking up the
cause of the untouchables Gandhi was challenging the traditional orthodox teaching on caste and flying in the face of
centuries of Brahmanic teaching. It is true that initially he
approved of a society which recognised functional distinctions
based on the different abilities of various member of society.
He saw *varṇāśramadharma*, as he called it, as a means of preserving the stability of social life. Later, however, he rejected
this practice that could lead to the preservation of caste distinctions and maintained that should untouchability be considered an integral part of the Hindu way of life then he would
have to stop calling himself a Hindu. It was better, in his view,
that Hinduism should die than that untouchability should live
because it was like arsenic in milk, a poison destroying the life
of Hindu society. The strength of his feelings on this issue led
him to seek to effect a change of attitude among his fellow
countrymen in order to restore the purity of the Hindu way of
life.

His life-long fight on behalf of the untouchables is matched
by his enlightened attitude towards women. In the traditional
Hindu system their lot was not an enviable one. Their domination by men had led to an unfortunate sense of inferiority
on their part and Gandhi's argument was that provided they
remained true to their nature they were capable of wielding
great power. They were the nobler sex, the personification of
self-sacrifice and the incarnation of *ahiṁsā*. They had greater
endurance than men and an infinite capacity for love. They
were capable also of doing much for the cause of Truth and
the art of peace in the world.

The social implications of Gandhi's concept of religion are
evident in his attitude to the Harijans and the status of women
in Hindu society, and also in his concern for *sarvodaya*. The
same applies to the importance he attaches to politics. He
refuses to draw a hard and fast line between religion and politics
on the grounds that religion should govern every form of
activity, and that to speak of leaving religion for politics or
politics for religion was nonsense. To be truly religious, he
claims, means taking an active part in political life. A politics

permeated by religion would be a politics dedicated to serving the needs of humanity, and the preservation of human rights and individual freedom.[51] These aims would not be inconsistent with the aims of the liberation theologians who are concerned with freeing man from the shackles of injustice, exploitation and oppression. What could be said is that the meta-politics of both these theologians and Gandhi is people-oriented; it is politics where people matter. Bonhoeffer's position is similar in that he too refuses to divorce religion and politics. Christianity for him is this-worldly not other-worldly. It is only when we take life in our stride, he claims, with all its problems, that we truly learn to believe.[52] So the Church has a duty, according to Bonhoeffer, to denounce and oppose those policies which militate against the Christian faith and to promote the establishment of a new order. Whenever the state fails in its function to preserve law and order in society then a Christian has the right to engage in activities directed towards that end.[53]

It is possible to maintain that Gandhi is closer to the liberation theologians than Bonhoeffer in respect of political activities in that he was not averse to effecting the transformation of social structures through non-violent means. Liberation in the Indian context meant for him *swarāj*, self-rule, which involved not only dedication to India but also commitment to the service of humanity.[54] He regarded the traditions, the language, and the cultural heritage of his country to be a great significance to India, and for that reason he resisted those forces of the British Raj that tended to undermine its traditions and deprive his fellow countrymen of their cultural roots. In his view it was a policy that inflicted a moral and intellectual injury on the Indian nation and was consequently a violation of Truth. So *swarāj* had a theological foundation; it had its roots in metaphysical beliefs about Truth and God. Nationalistic aspirations were entirely justified; self-determination, therefore, was a basic human right and people ought not to be deprived of the right to govern themselves.

If it is argued that the pursuit of nationalism is a retrograde step and a threat to internationalism, Gandhi's reply is that nationalism in fact is the prerequisite of internationalism since the latter implies that people of different cultures and countries come together to agree on a common policy. He seeks *swarāj* for India not that it might erect barriers against other nations but that it might express itself for the benefit of humanity as a whole. He distinguishes between nationalism and dogmatic exclusivism and insists on the preservation of national traditions in order to prevent the growth of what might be called the anxiety of meaninglessness and alienation. Nationalism and internationalism were not mutually exclusive. For Gandhi, patriotism and *sarvodaya* are two sides of the same coin. My love of nationalism, he says, 'is that my country may become free, that if needs be the whole country may die, so that the human race may live'.[55] Yet he seeks *swarāj* because he regards it as an expression of Truth, and he labours for India's freedom because having inherited its culture he recognises that it has a prior claim on his loyalty and efforts.[56]

It is evident that what Gandhi is advocating in the social and political sphere is a theology of liberation. His starting point may differ but his goal is the same as that of the liberation theologians and Bonhoeffer, namely, the creation of a just society where injustice gives way to justice, inhumanity to humanity, and exploitation to freedom.

9 Modern Hinduism

Any attempt to give an account of Hinduism in the nineteenth and twentieth centuries must of necessity be selective. What I propose to do in this essay is to select those thinkers who may be regarded as inheritors of the religious and social traditions of India and also contributors to the renewal of Hinduism and the development of modern India.

It is not without a measure of justification that Ram Mohan Roy (1772–1833) has been described as the father of modern India. His enthusiasm for reform may be attributed in part to the influence of Islamic thought and Western ideas, but as his *Vedanta grantha* shows, he is also indebted to Vedāntic teaching concerning the unity and supremacy of Brahman as the One without a second. His defence of Hinduism against the attacks of Christian missionaries is an indication of the influence of his Brahmanic upbringing and the part it played in moulding his desire to restore the religious purity of Hinduism. He endeavoured to do this through his journalistic and literary activities and through the formation of the Brahmo Samāj, a society he founded in 1828 to promote the worship of the one, eternal, immutable God and the rejection of image worship so characteristic of popular devotion. If the intellectual bent of the Brahmo Samāj deprived it of popular appeal it nevertheless succeeded in creating an atmosphere of liberalism and rationality in which a reinterpretation of the Hindu tradition could take place.

Roy's emphasis on logic and reason is reputed to have characterised his early Persian work entitled *Tuhfatul-ul-Muwahhiddin* (*Gift to Deists*), in which belief in a Creator, the existence of the soul, and life after death, are claimed to be the tenets of all religions (though it has to be said that such tenets could hardly be attributed to Buddhism). The same work dismisses as irrational, beliefs in miracles, anthropomorphic deities and the efficacy of rituals in man's salvation. It was Roy's earnest endeavour to convince his fellow countrymen and prove to his European friends that what he called superstitious and idolatrous practices had nothing to do with the pure spirit of the Hindu religion. He was unconvinced of the symbolic nature of

117

the images worshipped by his fellow countrymen and claimed that they believed in the existence of innumerable gods and goddesses.

His opposition to idolatry is matched by his rejection of some of the social customs of Hinduism, especially suttee, the practice of burning widows on the funeral pyres of their husbands. His advocacy of the provision of education for all his fellow countrymen, including mathematics, natural philosophy, chemistry, and what he called other 'useful' sciences, was aimed at the elimination of such practices, and the cultural improvement of the native population and the harmonisation of Western science and Eastern spirituality for the benefit of mankind as a whole. His pursuit of this goal justly earned him a place of eminence as one of the most creative personalities of nineteenth century India.

A fellow member of the Brahmo Samāj whose opposition to idolatry matched that of Roy was Devendranath Tagore (1817–1905). It was his firm belief that the ultimate good of India would derive from the rejection of Tantric and Puranic myths and legends and the acceptance of Brahma as revealed in the Upanishads. He showed great enthusiasm for the purification of the Hindu religion and joined in the campaign to provide free education for Hindu children. A man of sensitive spirit, Tagore in his later years inclined to mysticism and his piety earned him the title Maharishi, great sage. He attracted many able men to the Samāj including Keshab Chunder Sen (1838–1884) who became equally committed to religious and social reform.

Sen's enthusiasm for the propagation of the message of the Samāj led him to found the *Indian Mirror* and the *Dharmatattva*, journals of religion and philosophy, and to establish branches of the Samāj in many parts of India. Like Roy he rejected idolatry as erroneous and superstitious, but unlike his predecessor he recognised the popular need for visible and tangible expressions of the Divine and the intense love, reverence and faith manifested in the worship of images. Hence his claim that Hindus ought to be grateful for the gods and goddesses of India and the legends of Hindu mythology. His unbounded enthusiasm and vitality proved a mixed blessing to the society and schisms ensued which resulted in the founding of the Brahmo Samāj of India in 1865 and subsequently the setting up of the Sadaran Brahmo Samāj in 1878 by his disenchanted followers.

Sen's close acquaintance with Christian teaching provided him with the terminology he needed to express the principle of his New Dispensation. This he refers to as equivalent to the Jewish and Christian dispensations; as the fulfilment of Christ's prophecy; as the harmonisation of all scriptures and all religions; and as proclaiming that message of love which prohibits distinctions to be drawn between Brahmans and Shudras, Asiatics and Europeans. The uniqueness of the New Dispensation lay in its insistence on the direct, unmediated worship of God. His acceptance of the divinity of Jesus and his acceptance of the title Jesudas, servant of Jesus, suggests that he embraced the Christian faith completely, but in fact he refers to Christ as an Asiatic and his concept of the incarnation is far from traditional. The incarnation, in his view, was not 'once and for all' but the manifestation of God in history through great men and prophets. Christ, he claims, held the doctrine of the divinity of humanity which is essentially a Hindu doctrine and at one with the Vedāntic view of the *Ātman-Brahman* identity and man's unity with the Absolute.

Sen's belief in the providential nature of British rule in India would not have been shared by Dayananda Sarasvati (1824–1883) whose promotion of Hindi as a national language was not unrelated to his concern for the development of national self-consciousness. He was convinced that there was an intimate relation between language, religion and nationalism and believed that political independence was the natural corollary of the restoration of Vedic ideals. It was his firm belief that the Vedas contained the true revelation of God and constituted the authoritative source of the Hindu religion. Through the generosity of his followers he founded schools to teach the Vedas but the venture proved unsuccessful. More successful was his insistence on the place of morality in true religion and his denunciation of idol worship as a practice contrary to the teaching of the Vedas. In his view God, being formless yet omnipresent, could not be conceived as existing in particular objects, and that the evil practice of idol worship was responsible for the widespread ignorance and mendacity that existed in the country.

The Ārya Samāj founded by Dayananda in 1875 provided

him with the organisation necessary to propagate his religious and social ideals. Among the rules adopted by the society, belief in God, the authority of the Vedas, prohibition of idolatry, and the rejection of incarnational doctrines were paramount. The duty of all members of the Samāj was to promote spiritual monotheism, Vedic authority and social reform. Among the reforms he advocated were the prohibition of child marriages and allowing the remarriage of widows through the practice of *niyoga*. He was well aware of the problems relating to child marriages and early widowhood hence his advocacy of *niyoga*, the temporary legal union of widows and widowers, as an interim solution to the problem of early widowhood. He advocated also the education of both sexes insisting that it was the basis of mutual respect between husband and wife. The best form of marriage in his view was marriage by mutual choice and consent (*Swayamvara*) after the education of both parties had been completed. The educational process itself should involve both Hindi and Sanskrit and he sought to argue the case for making both languages the medium of instruction in schools.

Dayananda's aggressive nationalism and his deep desire to lead his fellow countrymen back to the Vedas earned him the title of the Luther of India, a description which it could be said is not entirely inappropriate.

Of the mystics of modern India pride of place must go to Ramakrishna (1836–1886) who, from an early age, is reputed to have experienced mystical trances. Though lacking formal education he possessed an abundance of native intelligence and for the greater part of his life served God at the Kali temple at Dakshineswar. Through his association with the followers of the Tantric and Vedānta schools he acquired an understanding of yoga techniques and the ways of devotion (*bhakti*) and knowledge (*jñāna*) as the means of union with the Divine. His personal experience of other religious traditions especially Islam and Christianity enabled him to make the claim that different religions are simply different paths to the same goal. As Kali, the Divine Mother, and *Brahman* are two aspects of the same reality so the mystical experience of Christ is at one with the mystical experience of Allah. God may be called by different names but he is one and the same ultimate reality. There is no need to choose between the form-less Absolute and the personal God because God with form is a real as God without form and the difference between them is no more than the difference between ice and water. The impediment to spiritual development is worldliness which is *māyā*. It is man's ignorance of his true self that causes him to become enmeshed in *māyā* in the first place and release is attained through discrimination which recognises God alone as real and eternal. Social reform, including the elimination of caste distinctions, should derive naturally from the love and worship of God.

Ramakrishna's disciples, of whom Vivekānanda was the most prominent, proclaimed his teaching throughout India, but they were more explicitly committed to social reform than their master and established schools, orphanages and hospitals in order to give practical expression to their religious ideals.

Another Indian mystic was Rabindranath Tagore (1861–1941) whose views concerning the interrelation of God, man and nature would enable us to classify him as a nature mystic. The Absolute, he claims, is manifested in creation and both man and nature are revelations of God. The same power that cre-ated the universe enlightens man's consciousness and the main goal of life is to realise the Absolute through the immediate apprehension of the Divine in the soul. Spiritual progress is achieved through a life lived in close proximity to nature hence the rural location of Visva Bharati University founded by Tagore in 1921 to promote his religious and cultural ideals.

Man's kinship with nature, according to Tagore, is similar to his kinship with his fellow man. God's immanence in creation means that man should be concerned with the needs of all God's creature and with social justice. Furthermore, in a world suffused with the spirit of God nothing should be deemed untouchable and the rigidity and exclusivism of the caste sys-tem should be rejected as contrary to the cultivation of spiritu-ality. Similarly the selfish pursuits of materialistic goals which intensifies the inequality between the haves and the have nots, undermines the social system and degrades man himself. The same applies on a national level when selfishness takes the form of patriotism devoid of concern for humanity as a whole and which resorts to force to achieve its ends. Concern for the nurture of the soul determines Tagore's attitude to every aspect of life and gives a marked distinctiveness to his social, cultural and religious ideals.

One of the foremost mystical philosophers of India is generally accepted to be Aurobindo Ghose (1872–1950) who, after a period of political activity in close association with Bal Ganghadhar Tilak (1856–1920) which resulted in his being jailed on a charge of advocating terrorism and violence, withdrew to the French settlement of Pondicherry where he spent forty years in study and contemplation. The fruit of those years is his philosophical system of integral yoga which he describes as Vedāntic. The essence of his system is that the Absolute by a process of involution and evolution manifests itself in, and expresses itself through, grades of reality or levels of being from matter to spirit. The Absolute is the starting point of the evolutionary ascent from lower forms of matter through mind to supermind and spirit, and the involutionary descent of the spirit through supermind to mind and matter. For Aurobindo every aspect of reality is permeated by the Absolute and the veil between mind and supermind is where the higher and lower levels of reality meet. The development of divine consciousness depends on rending the veil through involution and evolution and the divine life produced manifests that fullness of spirituality which can be described as gnostic being. Because of their divine cosmic consciousness gnostic beings are able to effect the transformation of levels of being and the whole of nature.

What Aurobindo seeks to do in what is called his philosophy of synthesis is to reconcile matter and mind, mind and spirit, finite and infinite, God and man. Though complex and highly esoteric in terminology his system is marked with spiritual insights which inspires enthusiasm among intellectuals in particular for the cultural heritage of India.

Two of the more systematic philosophers of India are Vivekānanda (1863–1902) and Radhakrishnan (1888–1975) who was an acknowledged academic and for a period President of his country. Both were interpreters of the philosophical school of Advaita Vedānta. A significant tenet in Vivekānanda's teaching is the Vedāntic doctrine of the divinity of man and this was one aspect of the message he proclaimed at the World Parliament of Religions held in Chicago in 1883. A further aspect of his message was the essential unity of all religions and the basic oneness of existence. For Vivekānanda there is but one life, one world and one existence. God permeates all that exists from stones and plants to human beings and it follows that the difference between one form of life and another is a difference of degree and not of kind. It would be contrary to Vedāntic teaching in his view to claim that animals were created simply in order to provide man with a source of food. Similarly he upholds the ideal of a universal religion, but not in the sense of a particular religious philosophy or a single ritual or mythology, rather in the sense that all particular religions reflect aspects of the universal truth embodied in the universal Form of religion. Particular religions are pearls on a string and no single historical form of religion will suffice for everyone. Religion is one in essence but diverse in manifestation and a spirit of toleration is needed to prevent us from looking for defects in religions other than our own. The Non-Dualist (Advaitist) or the qualified Non-Dualist (Visistadvaitist), for example, according to Vivekānanda, does not claim that Dualism (Dvaita) is wrong. It is the right view of reality for those on that level of understanding, but for Vivekānanda it is characteristic of a lower level of comprehension and therefore a stage on the way to a higher level of truth. This Vedāntic doctrine of two levels of truth might lead us to the conclusion that ultimately the finest pearl on the string for Vivekānanda is Advaita Vedānta. But that conclusion is only sustainable if it can be shown that non-dualism as a philosophical principle is inseparable from Advaita Vedānta as a particular, historical form of religion.

Radhakrishnan claims that in his philosophical writings he seeks above all to convey his insight into the meaning and purpose of life; to provide a coherent interpretation of the world; and to promote what he calls the religion of the spirit. He sees no discontinuity between animal life and human life, or between human life and spiritual life, since all forms of life are expressions of the Divine Spirit. Spiritual existence is the fulfilment of human life and the ultimate goal of the cosmic process. What this means is that the world is not illusory, as interpreters of Advaita Vedānta sometimes maintain, but a manifestation of the Divine Spirit. It depends on the creative activity of an immanent God without which it would cease to be. So the reality of the world is a dependent reality and not an ultimate reality, which is precisely what the doctrine of *māyā*, in Radhakrishnan's view, seeks to convey. Knowledge of the Divine Spirit is possible through rational analysis of empirical data, but most certainly through an immediate, intuitive apprehension of the nature of ultimate reality. This intuitive apprehension is sometimes referred to as gnosis (*jñāna*) or integral insight; it is a state of ecstasy, an experience of being at one with God. This is an experience common to all religions, according to Radhakrishnan, hence the need and importance of learning about the basic principles of the world religions and recognising the folly of missionary activity. No one historical religion can justifiably claim to be exclusive for religious traditions are simply imperfect expressions of the essence of religion which is truth. All men are bound together in one spirit, so a life of service and sacrifice in the cause of humanity and in defence of the ideals of justice and freedom is essential for those who would promote the religion of the spirit.

One of the most remarkable men of twentieth century India was Mohandas Karamchand Gandhi (1869–1948). Though he resented being called a saint since he thought it too sacred a term to be applied to a simple seeker after truth, there can be no doubt that he was a most remarkable man and worthy of being regarded as a Mahatma. Fundamental to his thought is the concept of Truth (*Satya*). His existential quest for Truth is the basis of his philosophy and he is faithful to the traditions of the Hindu way of life in which he was nurtured when he affirms the oneness of Truth (*Satya*) and Reality (*Sat*). He describes Truth as Saccidānanda – Being, Consciousness, Bliss – and as the most significant term that could be used for God. For him Truth is God rather than the reverse, namely, God is Truth. His preference is for the concept of formless Truth rather than the concept of a personal God, yet he recognised only too well that God has to be personal for those who need to feel his presence and that ultimate reality is revealed in different ways to people of different temperaments.

Gandhi acknowledges that perfect Truth is beyond man's

empirical grasp and that consequently he must hold on to such relative truth as he is able to apprehend. He acquires his own understanding of Truth through the essential teachings of his own religious tradition, but he is well aware that all religions possess Truth and that no single, historical religion can embody perfect truth since as a human construct it is necessarily imperfect. The implications of this view for much of the missionary activity and proselytising that took place in India is evident and explains why Gandhi stressed the need for toleration.

Truth and non-violence are two sides of the same coin so far as Gandhi is concerned and the realisation of the one involves the attainment of the other. Ends and means are convertible terms in his philosophy so the end never justifies the means. This does not imply that he is unable to conceive of situations when acts of violence might be justified. Like perfect Truth absolute non-violence is beyond man's grasp and in situations of moral dilemma one must do what it is morally possible for one to do while holding fast to Truth and continuing to be informed by the spirit of *ahiṁsā*. The same applies to satyāgraha, the technique of *ahiṁsā*. Its method is conversion rather than coercion and although it involves civil disobedience and non-cooperation it seeks to establish social justice by means of the power of love and gentle persuasion.

There is no distinction to be drawn between Truth (*Satya*) and Reality (*Sat*) in Gandhi's thought. Similarly no distinction can be made between Reality and the Self (*Ātman*) for in true Advaitin fashion Gandhi recognises the identity of *Ātman-Brahman*. The Self within is at one with the substratum of the universe, ultimate reality, *Brahman*, which in turn is at one with Truth. It follows that belief in the identity of *Ātman-Brahman* and the indivisibility of Truth involves belief in the unity of humanity. We may have many bodies but we have but one Soul or *Ātman*. These metaphysical presuppositions which inform Gandhi's thought and the Hindu way of life in which he was nurtured, point clearly to the interrelation of religion and morality and imply that as human beings we have an inescapable moral obligation to our fellow men. This is illustrated in Gandhi's emphasis on *sarvodaya*, the uplift or welfare of all, which is revealed in his abiding concern for the lowly status of the Harijans, the children of God, or outcastes, and the position of women in Indian society. He saw the need ultimately for the abolition of the caste system, the practice of child marriages, enforced widowhood, and the custom of purdah, all of which he believed to be harmful to the moral and spiritual growth of the nation. Radical social changes were required to improve the lot of the outcastes and the status of women in society and, in his view, only the restoration of the purity of the Hindu way of life would effect the necessary changes.

The social, economic and political implications of Gandhi's emphasis on *sarvodaya* are far-reaching. His economic policy is people-oriented and rejects those developments that dehumanise and degrade people's lives including unbridled industrialisation. His alternative educational programme fosters rather than undermines the cultural heritage of the nation. His political goal of *swarāj* or self-rule promotes self-respect and strengthens the determination of the Indian people to accept responsibility for managing their own affairs.

It is not without significance the Gandhi should have subtitled his autobiography *The story of my experiments with Truth* because it is clear that he sought to live his life in the spirit of Truth and in accordance with the religious and ethical ideals of the Hindu way of life.

An ardent admirer and enthusiastic follower of Gandhi's principles was Vinoba Bhave (1895–1983). He was impressed in particular by Gandhi's views on the importance and significance of the use of the indigenous languages in the field of education; on the plight of the poor and outcastes in Indian society; and on the need for purity in personal and public life. In the Ashram that he founded at Wardha, he laboured diligently to prove himself a true disciple of Gandhi and was one of the first satyagrahis to be chosen when the civil disobedience movement began. After Gandhi's death he inaugurated the bhudan movement designed to encourage wealthy landowners to denote land voluntarily to those less fortunate than themselves who had nothing. Over a period of six years, by means of persuasion in accordance with the principle of *ahimsā*, he succeeded in acquiring four million acres of land for distribution among the poor.

Another of his activities involved the decentralisation of

government and the development of self-governing, self-sufficient village units. *Gramrāj*, as village government came to be called, was regarded as an extension of *swarāj* with each village having the power to manage its own affairs. This meant the progressive abolition of central government control, *rāj-niti*, and the establishment of government by the people for the people, *lok-niti*. The best form of government so far as Bhave was concerned was freedom from central government, and this was what *sarvodaya* meant for him.

With the decentralisation of government and the development of *gramrāj*, however, goes the responsibility for educating people to manage their own affairs. Bhave's concept of *nai talim*, new education, involved setting up a programme directed towards establishing a *vidyapith*, a seat of knowledge or a university, in each village. It meant also the establishment of village industries to provide the economic support for such an educational programme and to ensure that social equality might prevail. In short his programme of *nai talim* was a programme designed for the whole of life.

The parallels that can be drawn between Vinoba Bhave and Gandhi are evident, but it will be seen that the former developed his own methods of *ahiṁsā* and *sarvodaya* and that the bhudan movement must be regarded as his distinctive contribution to the uplift of his fellow countrymen and the resolution of the poverty of the masses of India.[1]

10 Vivekānanda and Essentialism

A significant tenet in Vivekānanda's teaching is his belief in the unity of existence and the essential unity of all religions. It is his contention that God permeates all that exists from lower to higher forms of life, from stones and plants to human beings and higher spiritual beings. The differences between one form of life or existence and another is a difference of degree rather than of kind and in his view that it would be contrary to Vedāntic teaching to maintain, that the sole purpose of animal existence is that man should be provided with the means of daily sustenance. In the same way he upholds the concept of universal religion, but not in the sense of a single set of rituals, or a single mythology, or a single philosophy for the whole of mankind, rather, as he explains, in the sense of an universal truth, aspects of which every particular, historical religion proclaims according to its own insights. Each religion has to be regarded as one pearl on a string of pearls, and since they complement one another it has to be acknowledged that no single form of religion will do for everyone. So it would seem that Vivekānanda sees beauty as well as human necessity in variety and diversity.

> Just as we have recognised unity by our very nature, so we must also recognise variation. We must learn that truth may be expressed in a hundred thousand ways, and that each of these ways is true as far as it goes.[1]

This is an expression of the idealist philosophical position. It reflects the Platonic view that Forms or Ideas or universals exist in themselves; that they are timeless, real, unchanging, ideal, perfect, transcendental substances; that particulars reflect universals or participate in Forms or essences; and that particulars also are inadequate, imperfect manifestations of Forms or essences or universals. Like many idealists before and after him Vivekānanda upholds the essentialist position that religion is one in essence but diverse in manifestation, hence the need for toleration and the cultivation of an attitude

129

that would deter us from looking for defects in religions other than our own. The existence of so many different religions in the world is, in his view, a divine dispensation, and since they are all basically good and in essence the same, then they should be allowed to increase in number until every man has 'a religion unto himself!'[2] It is clear that as an essentialist he is predisposed to accept the concept of universal religion in the sense of a transcendental essence or primordial unity or universal truth, but this does undermine his position as a pluralist nor adversely affect his attitude to particular religions or detract from his belief that they should be encouraged to proliferate. On the contrary, since all religions are in essence one it would seem to him to be eminently desirable that diverse manifestations of this essence should be encouraged to multiply.

Vivekānanda shares with Radhakrishnan and other idealists his belief in the basic oneness of existence and the essential unity of religions. What Radhakrishnan refers to as the religion of the spirit is in point of fact akin to Vivekānanda's concept of universal religion. For both thinkers religion is one in essence, and both acknowledge that each particular religion follows its own path to the realisation of the goal of union with the Divine. In the same way Radhakrishnan's essentially spiritual interpretation of the universe which enables him to see the cosmic process as a movement with an inherent teleology and a specific goal where all forms of life are expressions of the Divine Spirit, is at one with Vivekānanda's belief that there is no discontinuity between animal life and human or spiritual forms of life, and that all forms of existence are manifestations or expressions of the spirit of God.

It is the Vedāntic philosophical tradition that inspires Vivekānanda. He explicitly acknowledges his indebtedness to it and it is implicit in all that he writes. The Vedāntic doctrine of the divinity of man was one aspect of the message he proclaimed at the World Parliament of Religions in Chicago in 1893 and it was the same message that permeated his subsequent writings.

One principle it (Vedanta) lays down – and that . . . is to be found in every religion in the world – that man is divine, that all this which we see around us is the outcome of the consciousness of the divine. Everything that is strong, and good, and powerful in human nature is the outcome of that divinity, and though potential in many, there is no difference between man and man essentially, all being alike divine.... So, potentially, each one of us has that infinite ocean of Existence, Knowledge, and Bliss as our birthright, our real nature; and the difference between us is caused by the greater or lesser power to manifest that divine.[3]

The Vedāntic notion of Brahman as *Sat Cit Ānanda* is echoed in Vivekānanda's insistence that God is pure spirit, 'the Soul of our souls, the Reality in us',[4] the heart of our hearts, the One through whom we know, see, think and exist.

> He is the Essence of our own Self. He is the essence of this ego, this I, and we cannot know anything excepting in and through that I. Therefore you have to know everything in and through the Brahman.[5]

This corresponds to what Śankara has to say about knowing the self in the self alone through the self (*ātmani, ātmānam, ātmanā*), or experiencing the *Brahman-Ātman* identity in the depth of the *ātman*. Vivekānanda's claim that the impersonal God is Being itself, the only reality, all else being manifested by the power of *māyā*,[6] corresponds also to Gandhi's insistence on the isomorphism of Truth and Reality or God and given the great measure of agreement between them on a variety of different issues it is difficult to believe that Gandhi was not thoroughly acquainted with the thought of Vivekānanda. Both distinguished between personal and impersonal concepts of God, for example, and both had significant things to say about the relation between Truth and God. For Vivekānanda, however, as for Gandhi, it is the impersonal concept of God that has the greater appeal since the impersonal concept is infinite while the personal concept is limited. God is beyond the limitations of space and time when we conceive of him as impersonal Being, but he is limited when we conceive of him in personal terms.[7] But the similarity between Gandhi and Vivekānanda goes even further than the distinction between personal and impersonal concepts of God. Gandhi points to personifications of the ultimate as an indication of man's desire for symbols. In the same way Vivekānanda, after the fashion of *Advaita*, refers to forms and images as external symbols manifesting man's endeavour to apprehend the absolute or the eternal.

> The Hindus have discovered that the absolute can only be realized, or thought of, or stated, through the relative, and the images, crosses, and crescents are simply so many symbols – so many pegs to hang the spiritual ideas on. It is not that this help is necessary for every one, but those that do not need it have no right to say that it is wrong.[8]

Both recognise the need for symbolic representations of the ultimate and both acknowledge that they are necessary in the spiritual life of some people. Both agree that image worship simply illustrates man's need for symbols and ought not to be construed as idol worship and both would express preference for the impersonal concept of God as Being itself (*Sat*) or Truth (*Satya*). Yet both would agree that there is nothing basically wrong in conceiving God in personalised terms. As Vivekānanda states:

> Those reformers who preach against image-worship, or what they denounce as idolatry – to them I say, 'Brothers, if you are fit to worship God-without-form discarding all external help, do so, but why do you condemn others who cannot do the same?'[9]

Radhakrishnan makes a similar point when he distinguishes between the Supreme as absolute spirit and the Supreme as personal God.

> It is a difference between God as He is and God as he seems to us. Personality is a symbol, and if we ignore its symbolic character it shuts us out from the truth.[10]

Vivekānanda's expressed preference for the impersonal concept of God as the fundamental ground or basis for any understanding of the personal concept of God meant that the type of religion that had the greatest appeal for him was that which propounded impersonal rather than personal concepts of the absolute. He was well aware that certain historical religions laid claim to universality, but he doubted whether it was possible for any historical religion to make such a claim which presumably included Advaita Vedānta.[11] That is, he is suggesting that it is not possible for universal religion to be equated with a particular, historical religion with its own brand of philosophies, rituals and mythologies. Yet in the same way as he professes preference for impersonal concepts of God, so he expresses his approval of those religions which embody impersonal concepts of the absolute. This prompts him to claim that dualism (*Dvaita*) is on a lower level of understanding than qualified non-dualism (*Viśiṣṭādvaita*) and perfect non-dualism (*Advaita*).

> Now as society exists at the present time, all these three stages are necessary; the one does not deny the other, one is simply the fulfilment of the other. The Advaitist or the qualified Advaitist does not say that dualism is wrong; it is a right view, but a lower one. It is on the way to truth; therefore let everyone work out his own vision of this universe, according to his own ideas.[12]

He expresses himself more forcibly when he criticises those religions that are based on historical data such as the historicity of a person, because if or when the historicity of a person is disproved the whole fabric of the religion concerned is undermined.[13] This criticism would not apply to Advaita Vedānta, he claims, since it does not depend on the life and teaching of an historical person but is based rather on principles that are common to all religions.

Vivekānanda's comments on this subject, which are perfectly in accord with the philosophical idealism that he supports and expounds, have elicited much criticism. He has been accused of adopting an exclusivist attitude to Advaita Vedānta and presenting it as the highest stage of religious awareness open to man in contrast to those dualistic forms of religion which, though necessary stages on the road to perfection, nevertheless manifest lower stages of spiritual development. He states, for example:

> Would to God that the whole world were Advaitists tomorrow, not only in theory, but in realisation. But if that cannot be, let us do the next best thing; let us take the ignorant by the hand, lead them always step by step just as they can go, and know that every step in all religious growth in India has been progressive.[14]

This reference to the 'next best thing' may be an indication that Vivekānanda regarded dualistic forms of religion as inferior to the monistic or non-dualistic forms and that, in his view, dualism would need to be transcended and culminate in non-dualism if the stage of perfection is to be attained or realised. The question is whether he equates non-dualism with Advaita Vedānta as a particular, historical religion or rather as a principle that ought to determine our understanding of ultimate reality and the absolute. His critics would accuse him of the former and *ipso facto* guilty of sectarianism.[15]

There can be no doubt, however, that he accepted the validity of all religions and not just Advaita Vedānta. He claimed, for example, that he accepted the validity of Islam, Christianity and Buddhism and that he would be able to 'worship God with every one of them'.[16] But it is equally clear that all dualistic forms of religion are, in his view, valid only on the lower level of truth and that attainment of the stage of perfection is the prerogative of non-dualism.

If we maintain that Vivekānanda accepts non-dualism, or *Advaita*, as a principle that ought to determine our understanding of the absolute or ultimate reality, it is possible also to maintain that his concept of universal religion is akin to Tillich's concept of the Religion of the Concrete Spirit. This religion of the spirit, we are told, harmonises the sacramental, mystical and prophetic elements of man's experience of the holy, and is the ultimate aim or *telos* of all religions. It is the type of religious awareness which is to be found in fragmentary form in the depths of all particular, historical, religious traditions. It is, according to Tillich, the type of religious experience, or one might say the religious principle, which determines our rejection of the demonisation of the holy in whatever form it occurs, whether it be the particularisation of the holy, or the objectification of the ultimate, i.e. those attempts to limit or circumscribe the holy or the ultimate, or to reject the operation of love and justice. It is described as 'a fight of God against religion within religion', i.e. against arid and fossilized forms of religion within historical, religious structures, and it finds expression in the depths of 'concrete', i.e. particular, historical religions. But while it occurs in the depths of particular religions it should not to be identified with the outward forms of those religions.[17]

There is a strong case for maintaining that Vivekānanda's view of *Advaita* is not sectarian in the sense that he puts forward Advaita Vedānta as the most acceptable particular historical religion available, but rather that he regards non-dualism as a principle that ought to determine our attitude to the nature of ultimate reality. This would be totally in accord with the philosophical idealistic view he upholds and expounds in his writings. As we have seen he applauds the variety of religious traditions that exists and claims that Vedānta has nothing to say against any one of them:

> whether you are a Christian, or a Buddhist, or a Jew, or a Hindu, whatever mythology you believe, whether you owe allegiance to the prophet of Nazareth, or of Mecca, or of India, or of anywhere else, whether you yourself are a prophet – it has nothing to say. It only preaches the principle which is the background of every religion and of which all the prophets and saints and seers are but illustrations and manifestations.[18]

It is Vivekānanda's conviction that man has religion in his soul and that the aim of all religions is to realise God in the soul. That is the one universal religion.

> The greatest name man ever gave to God is Truth. Truth is the fruit of realisation; therefore seek it within the soul. Get away from all books and forms and let your soul see its Self. . . . Religion is one, but its application must be various. Let each one, therefore, give his message; but not find defects in other religions. You must come out from all form if you would see the Light.[19]

The escape from form referred to here would presumably include escape from any constricting sectarian form of Advaita Vedānta, or from what Tillich would call the demonisation or particularisation of the holy or the objectification of the ultimate. From what he has written it is difficult to accept that Vivekānanda sought to limit or circumscribe in any way our experience of Truth or God. His universal religion is in the depth, and constitutes the background, of all religions.

The essentialist view of religion which Vivekānanda, like Radhakrishnan, exemplifies is characteristic of an idealist philosophical outlook. It may well be that Hegel as an absolute idealist was one of the foremost thinkers to regard religion as a self-subsisting essence, or a transcendental entity, underlying all particular historical manifestations. But it was Schleiermacher, the theologian of romanticism, the school that owed its origin to Goethe and was a protest against the tyranny of rationalism, who gave significant expression to the religious programme of romanticism with his speeches on religion addressed to its cultured despisers. Both were preceded by Plato, of course, with his theory of Forms and Ideas which insisted on the ontological and epistemological requirement of universals for the existence of particulars. What Schleiermacher endeavoured to do in his speeches on religion was to show that religion was not simply a theological system or a set of theories, doctrines, principles or ideas, or even an analysis of the nature of an incomprehensible being, but something that had to do with man's soul. To discover what religion really is, he maintains you have to turn away from what is usually called religion by cultured despisers and look within at the 'pious' soul. The primordial form of religion is the 'soul dissolved in the immediate feeling of the Infinite and the Eternal'.[20]

For Schleiermacher the starting point of religion is man. It originates in the soul's response and surrender to the Universe, the One, the Whole, the Godhead, the Infinite. True religion is the 'sense and taste for the Infinite'.[21] It cannot be equated with its outward forms, though according to Schleiermacher it has to be acknowledged that its primordial essence does find expression in the sorry form of earthly religions. Each historical religion is a distinct though impure form of religion in its essence yet the multiplicity of earthly religions is necessary for the complete manifestation of the essence of religion.[22] It is interesting to note that this view is reflected in the teaching of Kierkegaard for whom limited outward expressions of goodness succeed in conveying the meaning of absolute goodness.[23] The impure form of historical religions means that, for Schleiermacher as for other idealists, it is not possible to nominate a particular historical religion as the perfect embodiment of the essence of religion. Yet the essentialist position is that without religious diversity and multiplicity the transcendental unity, or primordial form, or essence of religion is not revealed. This is not to say of course that essences or universals do not exist in themselves;

they do according to Plato, because they are perfect, ideal, transcendental substances which exist *ante rem*.

It will be seen that Vivekānanda from an idealistic standpoint propounds an essentialist view of religion not dissimilar to that of Schleiermacher. He lays stress on the realisation of God in the soul in the same way as Schleiermacher refers to looking within at the pious soul. Both are wary of outward forms yet both see the need for diversity and variety or multiplicity. The universal religion of Vivekānanda is not far removed from the primordial essence of religion found in the writings of Schleiermacher. For both, religion is one in essence and diverse in manifestation, and both regard the transcendental unity of religion as a necessary prerequisite for the existence of historical religions through which the essence of religion is manifested. A similar essentialist approach is to be found in Otto's concept of the numinous and Hocking's reconception theory, both of which seek a better understanding of the essence that underlies all forms of religious life. What is characteristic of essentialism is that it believes it possible for God to be contemplated and worshipped in a variety of different ways and that it would be wrong of us to insist on religious uniformity. As Radhakrishnan correctly pointed out 'The world has bled and suffered from the disease of dogmatism, of conformity',[24] a sentiment echoed in Tillich's writings and forcefully expressed by Vivekānanda when he referred, as we have seen, to truth being expressed 'in a hundred thousand ways, and that each of these ways is true as far as it goes'.[25]

The essentialist approach as exemplified by Vivekānanda is in stark contrast to the relativist approach of a thinker like Ernst Troeltsch. His mature position is that all religions are culturally determined. For him the principle of development is so fundamental that we have to acknowledge the same kind of development in religious, ethical and philosophical ideas as we find in the spheres of legislation and economics.[26] All religions contain an element of truth and although they move in the direction of unity they manifest individual differences which are likely to remain. Hence

so far as the eye can penetrate into the future, it would seem probable that the great revelations of the various civilizations will remain distinct . . .[27]

Troeltsch points out that the modern view of history knows of no universal principle governing historical realities and no law determining the essence of religion. It follows that he views with disquiet those theological works which regard the principle or essence of religion as some kind of power or entity underlying individual religions. From the standpoint of the modern approach to history any attempt to present a particular religion as the embodiment of, or the most perfect expression of, the essence or underlying principle of religion must, in his view, be considered untenable.[28] It will be seen that he is in accord with Vivekānanda on the question of the diversity and multiplicity of religions, but not because they are manifestations of a primordial essence, a view which he rejects as untenable because of its inaccessibility to historical investigation, rather because they are culturally determined.

Troeltsch's implicit criticism of the essentialist position from the standpoint of an historian raises a number of critical questions. Is Hans Küng right, for example, to maintain that the notion of a transcendental unity underlying all historical religions, or a primordial essence which is experienced as a 'sense and taste for the Infinite' to use Schleiermacher's terminology, or the sense of the numinous according to Otto, is simply an affirmation of faith? Much would depend on the connotation he gives to the word faith here presumably, and whether it ignores the philosophical idealism of a person like Plato, who, as we have seen, considered universals or essences to be the ontological and epistemological requirement of particulars. Again, if it is, as Radhakrishnan claims, the result of intuitive awareness, which as a way of knowing might possibly be regarded as distinguishable from a simple affirmation of faith, how do we go about isolating it and apprehending it as a primordial essence or transcendental unity? In other words, what does intuitive awareness, or to use Platonic terminology 'anamnesis', recollection, pre-natal knowledge, mean? Is Cantwell Smith as a historian who is not so far removed from Troeltsch right to maintain that the quest for the essence of religion simply leads us further away from a true understanding of particular religious traditions? Again is there a measure of justification for Troeltsch's claim that historical investigation can point to no such universal principle underlying the appearance of historical realities, and that those who would elevate the concept of the essence of religion to the position of a norm inevitably assign an inferior status to the discipline of historical investigation? Is it the case that what we have here is an illustration of the perennial battle between empiricism and idealism? Or can it be that what we have in the case of essentialism as presented by Śankara, Vivekānanda, Radhakrishnan, Schleiermacher, Otto, Tillich, and Plato is an affirmation of faith, as Küng claims, or the presentation of the traditional idealist philosophical viewpoint based on what is referred to as immediate self-consciousness, or intuitive aware-ness (Radhakrishnan), or the sense and taste of the infinite (Schleiermacher), or anamnesis (Plato) concerning the na-ture of ultimate reality.

It may not be possible to establish to everyone's satisfaction, certainly not to the satisfaction of someone like Troeltsch, or critics of traditional expressions of philosophical idealism, that historical, religious traditions are relative expressions of a pri-mordial form of religion, or finite forms of the transcendental essence of religion, which is intuitively apprehended or mysti-cally experienced. But whether or not the attempt to postulate the concept of a transcendental essence or primordial form of religion accessible to intuitive awareness, or immediate self-consciousness, or anamnesis, is regarded as an affirmation of faith, or the result of a reasoned argument concerning the nature of universals, does not in itself detract from its truth. Clearly it is valid for those who for different reasons would uphold the essentialist position and it is precisely this view that Vivekānanda seeks to convey with his concept of universal religion.

11 The One and the Many: Radhakrishnan's Concept of Religion

An analysis of the one and the many might take as its starting point the distinction between monotheism and polytheism and any kind of evaluation of polytheistic systems might well begin with the question whether the term polytheism should be necessarily be given a pejorative connotation. It does seem to be the case that monotheism is on the whole regarded as superior to polytheism and the view is advanced by some scholars that in the history of the spiritual development of mankind it is possible to discern a movement from the many to the one. In the Vedic religion, for example, it is claimed, that the movement from the many to the one has taken the form of a movement from polytheism, the worship of *many* gods often associated with natural phenomena such as the storm, the wind, the dawn, fire, and the more sophisticated worship of *puruṣa*, *hiranyagarbha*, and the golden embryo, through what has been referred to as henotheism (the worship of one god though not to the exclusion of other gods), to a form of monotheism to be found in the worship of that *One* which was in the beginning and which was generated by the power of heat.

But it can be argued that the evolutionary theory that perceives a commendable development in spirituality from the worship of the many to the worship of the one, and consequently a movement from a less desirable inferior position to a more desirable superior position, is in need of further examination and reappraisal. In support of this suggestion we might look at what Peter Winch has to say about the Zande practice of consulting oracles. He asks the question what grounds we have for saying that something is true or false, or that it does or does not make sense. It might appear to us that the Zande practice of consulting oracles does not make sense and is basically unintelligible, but it does not appear unintelligible to the Zande even when what we take to be contradictions are pointed out to him. The question is are we right and the Zande wrong? Is it the case that he is wallowing in a sea of mystical notions while we in our turn operate quite properly on the basis of intelligible and verifiable scientific notions? Is he mistaken and confused in his beliefs? Is it possible to maintain with Evans-Pritchard, for example, that we are confronted here with two fundamentally different concepts of reality and that our concept of reality is right and the Zande concept of reality false? Winch's argument is that it is difficult to understand what true and false can mean in this context. What we are confronted with are different forms of understanding and different standards of intelligibility. In order for us to understand another way of life it is necessary for us to extend our way of life into the orbit of the other way of life. The onus is with us to extend our understanding rather than insist on seeing everything in terms of our ready made distinctions between what is scientific and rational and non-scientific and irrational. What appears to the Zande to be perfectly rational and intelligible might appear to us to be irrational and unintelligible. But does this mean that we are right and the Zande wrong? Winch's argument is that when a society has its own language and traditions it also has its own concepts of rationality and intelligibility.[1] What Winch has to say about certain practices in primitive cultures can be applied to accounts of religious beliefs. Judgements concerning the truth and falsity, or superiority and inferiority, of religious beliefs such as monotheism and polytheism sometimes ignore the role played by different concepts of rationality and intelligibility in the different forms of life concerned.

As an illustration of this point it is possible to quote a brief discussion that took place between Gandhi and a Roman Catholic priest. The priest's assumption was that Hinduism was basically polytheistic. He suggested to Gandhi that if Hinduism were to become monotheistic, and move from the worship of the many to the worship of the one, Christianity and Hinduism would be able to serve India in cooperation with one another. Gandhi's reply was that Hindus were not polytheistic and that while they undoubtedly maintained that there were many gods they also declared that there was but one God, *Īśvara*.[2] This might be construed as a recognition of the presence of the one in the many rather than an acceptance of the need to move in evolutionary fashion from the many to the one. If it is insisted that the image worship characteristic of Hinduism is clear evidence of polytheism and even idolatry, Gandhi's reply is that it is simply indicative of man's need for symbols and that the one God is symbolised or personified in different forms. Only if a worshipper were to make a fetish of his stone or metal image could he be accused of image worship or idolatry.[3] Radhakrishnan makes a similar point when he distinguished between the Supreme as absolute spirit and as personal God. 'It is a difference between God as He is and God as He seems to us. Personality is a symbol, and if we ignore its symbolic character it shuts us out from the truth.'[4]

It is not my intention here to pursue the question of the need for a re-evaluation of polytheistic systems. What I am seeking to do is to extend our analysis of the many and the one to the concept of religion and religions with particular reference to Radhakrishnan. In place of polytheism and monotheism we might consider the relative merits of what might be called polyreligion and monoreligion, if such artificial terminology is permissible.

According to Ernst Troeltsch the 'earthly experience of the Divine Life is not One but Many'.[5] His mature position is that religions are culturally determined and his attitude epitomises the relativistic approach to religious pluralism representative of the more liberal theological stance. He was very much aware of the importance of historical change and of the significance of historical consciousness. He recognised that everything was subject to historical development including cultural phenomena and religio-ethical ideas. The principle of development is so fundamental, he maintains, that we have to acknowledge the same development in 'religious, ethical, and philosophical ideas' and in 'the character of individuals and peoples', as we find in 'forms of government and economic conditions'.[6] It follows that we have to recognise also the transitory nature of all things since historical consciousness seems to demand cultural relativity.

The emphasis placed by Troeltsch on cultural relativism and the linking of particular religions to specific cultures is further clarified by his insistence that all religions have a common goal in the 'beyond' or the 'unknown', and a common ground in the 'Divine Spirit'. Historical religions, however, although they move in the direction of ultimate unity and objective truth, manifest individual differences which are likely to remain. Hence according to Troeltsch, 'so far as the eye can penetrate into the future, it would seem probable that the great revelations to the various civilizations will remain distinct ... and that the question of their several relative values will never be capable of objective determination, since every proof thereof will presuppose the special characteristics of the civilization in which it arises.'[7] Mutual understanding occurs when each religion seeks to realise its own potential, yet at the same time is open to the influence of others in their quest for truth. For Troeltsch, whose views on this point are not far removed from those of Gandhi and Radhakrishnan, the 'earthly experience of the Divine Life is not one but many.' So his relativistic position would favour polyreligion rather than monoreligion, the many as opposed to the one.

The same could be said of Toynbee's position. The revelation of God to man given through the different world religions differs in degree rather than kind. The spiritual light that shines through the religions of the world derives from the God of love who reveals himself in accordance with man's ability to receive his revelation. The more the world continues to be unified the greater will be our acknowledgment of other cultures. Toynbee's recognition of the unification process at work in the world does not, however, lead him to maintain that a single syncretistic religion ought to be constructed out of the various elements of the different religions of the world. That would be an artificial construction and would not capture the imagination or the allegiance of men. Neither does he anticipate that historical religions will coalesce to form one religion, though he does express the hope that they would become more open-ended towards one another. Like Gandhi and Radhakrishnan, he believes that respect and reverence for other faiths would enable men to understand and practice their own religion better, and he advocates receptiveness to the truths and ideals of other faiths in order that arrogance and intolerance might be avoided.[8] His view is that it is possible to have 'conviction without fanaticism' and 'belief ... without arrogance or self-centredness or pride', given that the mystery of man's encounter with God is not confined to one religion. Like Troeltsch he favours the many as opposed to the one.[9]

It might be argued that the essentialist view of religion of which Radhakrishnan is a notable representative is the direct antithesis of the relativistic position we have looked at so far, since it supports the notion of religion as a self-subsisting essence or transcendental entity underlying all historical manifestations. In which case what we have from the essentialist standpoint is explicit support for the monoreligious rather than the polyreligious position, that is, the one, in the sense of a primordial essence, rather than the many. Yet as we shall see the essentialist does not necessarily favour the concept of the one to the exclusion of the many, or monoreligion to the exclusion of polyreligion. That is to say, he does not advocate the elevation of one particular, historical religion to a position of superiority over all other historical religions any more than Troeltsch does. This is particularly true of the essentialism of Radhakrishnan.

While Hegel may have been one of the first thinkers of recent times to regard religion as a self-subsisting essence, or a transcendental entity underlying all historical manifestations, it was Schleiermacher who proved to be the most notable Western representative of this position. He conceives of religion as pre-existing individual, historical manifestations of it, and maintains that as a transcendental entity it is the necessary prerequisite of the existence of all historical religions. Particular religions, in his view, may be regarded as concrete expressions of the primordial form of religion which is experienced by the immediate religious consciousness as 'the sense and taste of the infinite'.[10] Not that this experience makes particular religions superfluous in any way; in fact the existence of particular religions is necessary for the complete manifestation of the primordial form of religion because each religion embodies something of the essence of religion. That is, the existence of the many is necessary for the manifestation of the one. Historical religions can be considered true to the degree that they succeed in expressing the essence, or the primordial form of religion.[11] The multiplicity of historical or positive religions is for Schleiermacher the direct result of the work of the Spirit, and although they may contain much that is corrupt and degenerate, they also possess, to a greater or lesser degree, something of the true nature of religion.

Schleiermacher is often referred to as the theologian of

romanticism, the school that owed its origin to Goethe and protested against the tyranny of rationalism. His speeches on religion which were addressed to cultured despisers of religion are regarded as the religious programme of romanticism. They incorporate the sentiments of the romantic school particularly its views on nature and history, individuality and religion. What he endeavoured to do was to show his cultured, literary friends that religion is not just a theological system, or a set of theories, doctrines, principles or ideas, or even analyses of the nature of an incomprehensible being, but something that has to do with the soul of man. In this respect it is far removed from all that is systematic, for systems merely house the dead letter and not the spirit of religion. To discover what religion is, one must turn from what is usually called religion and look within at the pious soul. The kernel of religion is the exalted mind, the 'soul dissolved in the immediate feeling of the Infinite and the Eternal'. It is this which constitutes the essence or primordial form of religion.[12]

For Schleiermacher, therefore, the starting point of religion is man; it has a human ground. It originates in the soul's response and surrender to the Universe, the One, the Whole, the Godhead, the Infinite. True religion is 'the sense and taste for the Infinite'. Naturally this definition gave rise to accusations of psychological subjectivism against him especially in view of his rejection of rationalism. But it would be a mistake to assume that his stress on feeling, or sense and taste, implies simply an emotional response with no cognitive, intellectual content. While he would concede that conceptual thought cannot comprehend the fundamental unity, the One, the Infinite, the Absolute Spirit, grounding the ideal and the real, thought and being, or mind and nature, it is the case, nevertheless, that feeling, or intuitive awareness, or immediate self-consciousness, provides the basis for understanding the fundamental ground of knowledge. So feeling, for Schleiermacher, is not simply an emotion, or a sense of rapture; when he refers to the 'sense and taste for the Infinite' he is not engaging in subjectivism. Feeling is an *a priori* cognitive experience; it is the means whereby the ground of knowledge is understood. This is a point that Radhakrishnan may not have fully appreciated.

It is the injunction to recognise and understand that

religion has a human ground and that it originates in the pious soul's response and surrender to the Universe, that leads Schleiermacher to insist that it cannot be equated with its many outward finite forms nor confused with science or morality. What is known of the nature of things is not religion. 'Religion cannot and will not originate in the pure impulse to know'.[13] Religion is not to be equated with ethics either, though the excellence of ethical systems has to be acknowledged, and it also has to be recognised that one cannot be pious without being moral. Religion is, in fact, the natural counterpart to science and morality: an indispensable third as Schleiermacher calls it. It is the assurance that all things that influence us are One; that everything is part of the Whole.[14]

It is Schleiermacher's belief that the primordial essence of religion finds expression in the sorry form of earthly religions; that the one finds expression in the many. Each historical religion is a distinct, though impure, form of the essence of religion. The multiplicity of earthly religions, however, is necessary for the complete manifestation of the essence of religion.[15] While it is true to say that positive religions are full of much that cannot be regarded as religion and characterised by elements that they should make every effort to eliminate, such as empty customs, abstract ideas and claims to possess absolute truth, nevertheless they are forms of religion and embody much of the true nature of religion.[16]

Each historical religion is a distinct form of religion and a particular way of revealing it, for religion is the sum total of man's relation to God. There is no universal religion which is natural to everyone; individuals differ in their receptiveness to different religious feelings and experiences,[17] so antipathy to religious multiplicity should be avoided. Every man is entitled to develop his own religion, though most men will choose an existing form of religion if it corresponds to his own feelings, and it is none the less personal or individual on that account.[18] Christianity is just one of the positive, historical religions and of a high order. It expresses man's longing for the Infinite and brings to perfection the indwelling of the Divine Being in finite nature. The finite is brought closer to the Infinite through the work of mediation which participates in both the human and the divine spirit.[19] Not that this means, according to Schleiermacher, that we are entitled to regard Christianity as the only true religion. Nothing would be more irreligious than to deny multiplicity and demand uniformity. The many are necessary for the one to be truly revealed, and different types of religions are always possible given the different degrees of apprehension and receptivity that exist among men.[20] So this particular form of essentialism can be said to favour the concept of monoreligion in the sense of a primordial essence or transcendental entity, yet not to the exclusion of polyreligion since the many are essential for a true manifestation of the one.

A similar attitude to the one and the many finds expression in the work of Radhakrishnan and his predecessor Vivekānanda, two of the more systematic philosophers of India in the modern period. A significant tenet in Vivekānanda's teaching is his belief in the basic oneness of existence and the essential unity of all religions. According to his philosophy there is but one life, one world, one existence, and God permeates everything that exists from stones and plants to human beings. Differences between one form of life and another is a difference of degree rather than kind. It would be contrary to Vedāntic teaching for instance to claim that animals were created simply in order to provide food for man.[21] Similarly he upholds the concept of universal religion, but not in the sense of a single ritual, or mythology, or philosophy, for the whole of mankind, rather in the sense that every particular, historical religion proclaims an aspect of the universal truth according to its own insights. No one form of religion will do for everyone so each religion has to be regarded as a single pearl on a string of pearls.[22] Like Schleiermacher, Radhakrishnan maintains that religion is one in essence but diverse in manifestation, and the advantage of supporting a tolerant attitude is that it teaches us not to look for defects in religions other than our own.[23] For Vivekānanda, the Advaitist and the Visistadvaitist would not claim that the Dvaitist is wrong in his perception of religion but that he holds a lower and possibly partial view which is on the way to truth.[24] It would appear from this assessment that the finest pearl on the string for Vivekānanda, despite his insistence on an attitude of toleration, is Advaita Vedānta! Yet he is at pains to point out that everyone should develop his own vision of the universe and act in accordance with his own ideals. The existence of so many different religions in the world is after all a 'glorious dispensation of the Lord' and since all religions are good and in essence the same, they should continue to increase in number 'until every man had a religion unto himself'.[25] Clearly Vivekānanda's attitude to the one, or monoreligion, in the sense of a transcendental essence, had no adverse effect in his attitude to the many, or polyreligion. On the contrary, since all religions are in essence one it is eminently desirable that diverse manifestation of the essence of religion should continue to increase.

Radhakrishnan shares Vivekānanda's belief in the unchanging essence of religion, the essential unity of religions and the oneness of existence. He seeks above all to convey his insight into the meaning and purpose of earthly life in order to promote his concept of the religion of the spirit. Earthly life, he claims, is the gradual revelation of the divine or the eternal in man. The inner self of man is akin to the Supreme one; it mirrors the divine. In the depths of man's spiritual experience the barriers between the self and ultimate reality fall away and the isomorphism of God's spirit and man's spirit is revealed. His essentially spiritual interpretation of the universe enables him to see the cosmic process as a movement with a specific goal and an inherent teleology. He is at one with Vivekānanda in maintaining that there is no discontinuity between animal life and human life, or between human life and spiritual life, since all forms of life are expressions of the Divine Spirit. Indeed spiritual life might be regarded as the fulfilment of human life and the ultimate goal of the cosmic process could be seen as the establishment of a spiritual kingdom of free spirits. What this means is that it is quite impossible for Radhakrishnan to view the world as illusory in any way because for him it is the manifestation of the Divine Spirit. But he is careful to point out that its reality is dependent rather than absolute; it is not ultimately real, which is precisely what the doctrine of *māyā* seeks to convey. The world depends on the immanent activity of God without which it would cease to be. It is a manifestation of divine, creative activity, but its inherent mutability and eventual dissolution does not affect in any way the absolute reality of God. The world may be dependent on God, but God is not dependent on the world.[26]

The social implications of this spiritual interpretation of the universe are evident. Belief in the oneness of existence means that all men are bound together in one spirit, hence Radhakrishnan's claim that the common aim of religion in all its forms is to preserve those spiritual values that unite mankind. It follows that a life of service and sacrifice is the prerequisite of those who would promote the religion of the spirit. It is man's bounden duty to create and defend those institutions which preserve the ideals of freedom, justice and truth and promote the development of a truly human life. Equally it is man's responsibility to condemn those institutions that would degrade and humiliate the more unfortunate and socially deprived sections of society. Clearly the caste system and the attitude to women prevalent at the time in Hindu society would merit condemnation on that account. It is significant, however, to note that while Radhakrishnan explicitly acknowledges that the caste system had resulted in much evil and suffering, and had degenerated into an instrument of oppression and intolerance perpetuating inequality, he also maintains that it was based on sound principles. When he says this he has in mind the system of trade guilds whereby one's sphere of work is clearly delineated and in this respect he shares the views originally held by Gandhi concerning *varṇāśramadharma*, namely, that there are certain functions and duties that are related to one's order and status in society. No notion of inferiority or superiority is involved in any way by divisions of this kind which are regarded as natural and a matter of custom. It could be argued that functional distinctions based on the differing abilities of different members of society contributed significantly towards the stability of social life. However, it is only a short step from functional distinctions which might be approved of to the caste divisions which would meet with disapproval, especially since the latter led eventually to the development of the concept of untouchability. This is explicitly acknowledged by Gandhi and is implicit in what Radhakrishnan has to say about stereotyping people without regard to their aptitude and endowment, a practice which leads to a life of enslavement.

Radhakrishnan's spiritual view of the universe and his recognition of the common ground of all religions has implications also for his attitude to religions other than his own. Like Schleiermacher and Vivekānanda he acknowledges that each religion takes its own path to the realisation of the goal of union with the Divine, but he insists that they are at one in essence. It follows that no single individual religion can lay claim to exclusiveness or superiority. That being the case proselytising or missionary activity based on the concepts of exclusiveness and superiority has to be abandoned. All religious traditions are but imperfect expressions, or sorry forms as Schleiermacher calls them, of the immutable essence of religion which is ultimate truth. The aim of religious education should be to learn about the basic principles of the great religions of the world and to promote international understanding and the creation of a world community and a world culture. Interreligious rivalry militates against such an aim and should be abandoned.[28]

Radhakrishnan then is at one with Schleiermacher and Vivekānanda in maintaining that religion is one in essence. Knowledge of the primordial form of religion for him is acquired as a result of an intuitive apprehension of the nature of ultimate reality which in turn is apprehended by means of *jñāna*, gnosis, or integral insight. It is a state of ecstasy; it is what is meant by union with God and is a mystical experience common to all religions. Hence the importance of learning about the basic principles of all world religions.[29] In Radhakrishnan's view we need to:

> bring together in love those who sincerely believe in God [for] if we persist in killing one another theologically, we shall only weaken men's faith in God. If the great religions continue to waste their energies in a fratricidal war instead of looking upon themselves as friendly partners in the supreme task of nourishing the spiritual life of mankind, the swift advance of secular humanism and moral materialism is assured'.[30]

The main purpose of religion, according to Radhakrishnan, is to deliver man from meaninglessness and to give him eternal status. The ultimate dream of all the great religions of the world is to divinise the life of man. This is the '*mokṣa* of the Hindus, the *nirvāṇa* of the Buddhists, the kingdom of heaven of the Christians'. The world process reaches its consummation when every man knows himself to be the son of God and immortal spirit.[31]

It is obvious that Radhakrishnan, like Schleiermacher, favours

monoreligion, or the one, in the sense of a primordial transcendental essence of religion, yet not to the exclusion of the
many historical forms of religion or polyreligion. Different
religions are separate paths to the realisation of the goal of
union with the Divine but they are all one in essence. Hinduism, for example, takes its stand on the life of the spirit and
maintains that theological expressions of religious experience
are bound to be varied. But since it is a movement rather than
a position, or a growing tradition rather than a fixed revelation, it is able to accept all forms of belief as equally valid.[32]
The Hindu faith, for Radhakrishnan, is not to be equated with
dogmatism; its distinctive characteristic is insistence on the
inward life of the spirit because at the centre of man's being,
in his inner self, is that which is akin to the divine and the
essence of reality, and this is precisely what the Upanisadic
aphorism *tat tvam asi* affirms.[33]

From his idealist philosophical standpoint Radhakrishnan
propounds what is basically an essentialist view of the nature
of religion. Schleiermacher proposes a similar view, as we have
seen, and maintains that the transcendental unity of religion
is the necessary prerequisite of the existence of historical religions. They are concrete expressions of the primordial form
of religion which in turn is experienced as the 'sense and taste
for the infinite' or 'the feeling of absolute dependence'. This
view is not far removed from Otto's concept of the numinous,
or Hocking's reconception theory which seeks a better understanding of the essence that underlies all forms of religious
life. The feeling of absolute dependence, or the sense and
taste for the infinite, is presupposed in every type of religious
consciousness according to Schleiermacher, and is an indication of man's finitude. And since God can be contemplated
and worshipped in a variety of different ways it would be irreligious of us to insist on religious uniformity. Radhakrishnan
makes the same point when he maintains that immediate self-
consciousness, or intuitive awareness, is the common ground
of all religions and that particular religious traditions are simply imperfect expressions of the immutable essence of religion
which is ultimate truth. He regards intuitive awareness as self-
validating. It is *aparoksa*, non-sensuous and immediate knowledge, rather than *pratyaksa*, knowledge presented to the senses.
It is knowledge that springs from the fusion of mind and reality

and as such needs no external verification of its validity.[34] While profound intuitions are rare it is possible to have experiences of a less profound nature through art, poetry and loving relationships.[35] Hindu thinkers refer to the ineffability of intuitive experience but they acknowledge that there can be different interpretations depending on the religious tradition in which a person is nurtured. Whenever a particular interpretation of intuitive awareness is regarded as ultimately true, however, and applicable to all men in all circumstances, then intolerance and fanaticism ensues. And as Radhakrishnan points out:

> Mankind at each period of its history cherishes the illusion of the finality of its existing modes of knowledge ... [and consequently] the world has bled and suffered from the disease of dogmatism, of conformity.[36]

The question that arises with regard to the essentialist position is whether the concept of a transcendental unity underlying all positive, historical religions is, as Hans Küng maintains, simply an affirmation of faith? If it is possible to maintain the existence of a primordial form of religion, as the essence, or transcendental unity, or *a priori* condition, of all particular historical religions, then we have to ask what it means to say that it is experienced as the numinous, or the sense and taste for the infinite, or as the feeling of absolute dependence? Furthermore, how do we go about isolating it as an essence or transcendental unity, and how do we determine the truth of particular religions by means of this primordial form of religion? Is Cantwell Smith right to maintain that the quest for the essence of religion simply leads us further away from a true understanding of particular religious traditions? Is Troeltsch right to claim that historical investigation can point to no universal principle underlying the appearance of particular historical realities, and that those theological works which refer to the essence of religion as underlying individual religions must be viewed with misgiving? Is he right also to maintain that such theological works elevate the concept of essence or principle to a normative position while at the same time affording the discipline of historical investigation an inferior status?

This essay seeks to show that Radhakrishnan's concept of the religion of the spirit bears a resemblance to the views of

Troeltsch and Toynbee in the sense that he acknowledges the need to accept that earthly experiences of the Divine Life are not one but many, to use Troeltsch's phrase, and that reverence for other faiths, as Toynbee maintains, leads to a better understanding of one's own faith. But it also makes clear that Radhakrishnan's stress on the importance of the many is not to the exclusion of the one. On the contrary, for him the one in the sense of an immutable essence is necessary for the existence of the many, and in this respect he echoes the essentialist teaching of Schleiermacher, Otto and Hocking, and other like-minded idealists.

It may not be possible to establish to everyone's satisfaction the view that historical religious traditions are relative expressions of a primordial form of religion which is mystically experienced and intuitively apprehended or that they are finite forms of a transcendental essence of religion. But the fact that it may be an affirmation of faith, as Küng maintains, does not necessarily detract from its truth. That would certainly apply to those who would uphold the validity of the essentialist position and it is the truth of that position that Radhakrishnan seeks to convey with his concept of the religion of the spirit.

12 *Śūnyatā*: Objective Referent or *Via Negativa*?

This essay examines the concept of *śūnyatā* as it is formulated in the Hṛdaya sūtras of the Buddhist *prajñā-pāramitā* literature and in the *Mūlamadhamaka-kārikās* of Nāgārjuna.[1] An attempt will be made to point out some of the difficulties involved in seeking an objective referent for the term and in preserving the tension implicit in the affirmation of the middle way. I hope to show that the *via negativa* approach has positive implications for understanding *śūnyatā* and that in the final analysis we may have to look for its meaning in the way it is used in the Buddhist way of life.

The Hṛdaya sūtras epitomise the teaching of the *prajñā-pāramitā* or perfection of wisdom literature and they express concisely one stage at least of the dialectics of *śūnyatā* in the puzzling phrase:

Form is emptiness and the very emptiness is form.[2]

There may be, as is often suggested by scholars, different ways of looking at the concept of *śūnyatā* but they would all include the view that what we consider to be real, such as the world around us, is, from the standpoint of *prajñā* or transcendental wisdom, devoid of reality or *svabhāva*, own being. That is to say, when phenomena are considered or looked at as they are in themselves they are found to be empty.

The term 'form' in the context of the phrase 'form is emptiness' is one of the five *skandhas* or constituents which Buddhist believe make up the individual self. The other four *skandhas* are feeling, perception, impulse and consciousness. What is said of 'form' in the Hṛdaya sūtras applies equally to the other four *skandhas*, hence 'form' can be taken to represent the other four constituents of the self. But 'form' also represents conditioned events because, as Conze points out,[3] the five *skandhas* are coextensive with the conditioned world and synonymous with conditioned events or *dharmas*. To say that 'form is emptiness' is equivalent to saying that the conditioned world, including the self, is devoid of independent being or *svabhāva*.

If the phrase 'form is emptiness' were to be expressed symbolically it would take the form A = –A. This is clearly a violation of the law of identity, namely that A = A and also a violation of the law of contradiction, namely that A cannot be both A and –A. Buddhist philosophy maintains that there is a distinction between what it calls conventional and absolute levels of truth. Hence it is possible by shifting levels as it were to state that A is both A and –A. But absolute truth, as Nāgārjuna shows, is not taught without dependence on conventional truth. That is to say, mundane truth and absolute truth are not mutually exclusive; they do not refer to different realms of knowledge. This accounts for such paradoxes as the Bodhisattva leading innumerable beings to *nirvāṇa* and yet no beings at all being led to *nirvāṇa*, for if a Bodhisattva should perceive a being he could not be called a Bodhisattva, an enlightenment being. It is true that the Bodhisattva in his compassion resolves to save all beings yet it is equally true that in his wisdom he knows that in actual fact there are no beings to be saved. What we have here is an indication of the different way in which things are perceived.

The denial of the reality of the conditioned world expressed in the phrase 'form is emptiness' is an explicit rejection of the Abhidharma doctrine of the Theravāda schools of Buddhism concerning the reality of conditioned *dharmas*. Abhidharma philosophy propounds what has been called an 'analytic theory of emptiness'.[4] It removes the notion of the substantiality of phenomena by a process of analysis that reduces phenomena to momentary *dharmas* or bursts of existences. The doctrine of *pratītya-samutpāda* or dependent origination supports the rejection of belief in the inherent substantiality of phenomena by claiming that one thing arises only in dependence on something else. Thus the Theravāda teaching is that no one thing has self-substantiality or its own substantial nature whereby it can claim independent existence. But Abhidharma philosophy retains the concept of the reality of momentary *dharmas*, or analyzed elements, and so fails to propound a complete or full blown theory of emptiness. It was left to the *prajñā-pāramitā* literature to propound such a theory, but it has to be acknowledged that it was the seed sown by Abhidharma philosophy in its analytic theory of emptiness which later bore fruit in the *śūnyatā* doctrine of the Mahāyāna tradition. What was initially expressed in the *prajñā-pāramitā* literature finds its logical expression later in the philosophy of Nāgārjuna who rejects not only the view of the reality or substantiality of 'unanalyzed elements' but also the notion of the reality of 'analyzed elements' or momentary *dharmas*. The phrase 'form is emptiness' epitomises such a rejection.

The question arises whether the denial of the reality or substantiality of the conditioned world leads automatically to the affirmation of *śūnyatā* as a kind of transcendental entity. If it does then it would be natural to expect a statement to that effect in the sūtras. But what we have is not an affirmation of *śūnyatā* as the absolute, or unconditioned, or ultimate, or transcendental, but the statement that 'emptiness is form'. That is, 'emptiness' far from being a transcendental entity is itself empty. If this is not to be taken as an example of tautology then it is necessary to ask what it means to say that emptiness is form, and whether it means something different from saying form is emptiness. The answer might be that to say emptiness is form is not to say that it is form in the Abhidharma sense, namely, synonymous with momentary *dharmas* or what might be called analyzed elements of phenomena. Neither does it mean that emptiness is immanent in form like an unconditioned being or absolute permeating conditioned existence. Nor does it mean that emptiness underlies form as a state of non-being. It would be a mistake to assume that the denial of the reality of form leads either to an affirmation of an immanent absolute or to the acceptance of complete nihilism. In point of fact *śūnyatā* cannot be classified as either being or non-being, absolutism or nihilism.[5] When Conze equates emptiness with the absolute or transcendental reality he tends to give it a substantial essence. Yet when he goes on to describe *śūnyatā* as infinitely near and as being the same as the world, he seems to be contradicting his original statement concerning the transcendental nature of emptiness.[6] If he were to maintain that by his use of the terms transcendental and absolute he is simply pointing to the immanence of the absolute in conditioned existence, then he is classifying *śūnyatā* as being itself. Hiryanna, on the other hand, finds it difficult not to conclude on the

basis of the evidence available in Hindu philosophical literature that the Mādhyamika position is nihilistic, and he claims
to share the view of both the Hindus and Jains that the doctrine of *śūnyatā* is nihilistic.[7]

But if we maintain that *śūnyatā* is neither absolutism nor
nihilism what does it mean to say the emptiness is form? If it
is not immanent in form as the absolute nor the nihilistic
ground of form, how is it to be defined? Is it form in the sense
that it is no different from form, or the conditioned, and has
no existence as a separate entity whether as the ground of
being or as an original state of non-being? Is emptiness form
looked at from the standpoint of absolute truth? Is the statement 'emptiness is form' another way of saying that *nirvāṇa* is
saṁsāra? Nāgārjuna maintains that no state of *nirvāṇa* exists
which is distinct from *saṁsāra*?[8] The distinction only applies
when the two are looked at from the standpoint of relative or
conventional truth. In reality nothing differentiates *nirvāṇa*
from *saṁsāra*. In the same way nothing differentiates emptiness and form. Form is emptiness and the very nature of
emptiness is form, but emptiness has no separate existence or
essence, rather it is form looked at from the vantage point of
wisdom or *prajñā-pāramitā*.

From what has been said it is evident that *prajñā* could be
regarded as the means whereby *śūnyatā* is realised. It has in
fact been referred to as the ontic means to the realisation of
an ontological end. But such a description is misleading.[9] Not
only is there no ontological end as such but even the concept
of *śūnyatā* is empty; hence the insistence on *śūnyatā śūnyatā*,
i.e., emptiness of the very concept of emptiness. The concept
is simply a designation, a means of communication; it has no
substantial essence. Although *prajñā* is sometimes described as
the wings of bird that facilitate the flight to enlightenment, in
fact it is itself *śūnyatā*. Conventionally it can be said that *prajñā*
enables one to apprehend the meaning of *śūnyatā*, that is,
emptiness is the goal of wisdom. But in reality *prajñā* is *śūnyatā*;
there is no distinction between higher wisdom and emptiness.
The isomorphism of *prajñā* and *śūnyatā* is such that to know
emptiness is the same as realising emptiness.[10]

As I have indicated the doctrine of emptiness found in the
prajñā-pāramitā literature is given logical expression in the
philosophy of Nāgārjuna. Mādhyamika philosophy can in fact

be regarded as a systematised form of the doctrine of *śūnyatā*.
It has been described as the heart of Buddhism and a critique
of Abhidharma realism in the same way as Advaita is regarded
as the heart of the Upaniṣads and a critique of Sāṁkhya realism.[11] As the term Mādhyamika implies it is the middle way. It
is the *via media* between eternalism and nihilism, being and
non-being. The four-fold method of expression, *catuṣkoti*, used
by the Buddha to show the inapplicability of undetermined
questions,[12] became an integral part of the Mādhyamika dialectic and a justification of the claim that all views about ultimate reality are inherently contradictory. The tetralemma as it
is called is 'a spiritual answer to the problem of grasping after
self-existent entities'.[13] Nāgārjuna takes the middle way between
affirmation and negation and calls it *śūnyatā*.

Nāgārjuna then does not equate *śūnyatā* with non-being in
the Nietzschean sense of *non-être* or *Nichtsein*, nor with being in
the Tillichian sense of ground of being. *Śūnyatā* is beyond
both being and non-being yet it cannot be regarded as a separate distinct entity; it is not beyond in the transcendental sense
of the term. In fact it is claimed that 'Whenever existing things
exist by nature of their inter-dependence this is called emptiness'.[14] *Śūnyatā* can be said to be the logical expression of the
silence of the Buddha who when asked whether the self exists
made no reply. Later when his disciples requested an explanation he replied that an affirmative answer would have resulted
in the accusation of eternalism while a negative answer would
have produced the accusation of nihilism neither of which was
correct. It might be asked why the Buddha should have taught
the doctrine of the *skandhas* as constituents of the self and
momentary *dharmas* as constituting reality if silence would have
been a more accurate reflection of his position. Nāgārjuna's
explanation is that the Buddha's teaching was determined by
the ability of his hearers to understand and by their general
powers of comprehension: it was a step in the direction of
śūnyatā. But why propound even the concept of *śūnyatā* if
silence is a more accurate course to adopt when dealing with
the nature of reality? Nāgārjuna's affirmation of the emptiness
of the concept of emptiness, *śūnyatā śūnyatā*, goes some way
towards meeting this objection. Clearly he is of the view that
if silence is inadequate and some form of designation is called
for then *śūnyatā*, which is itself *śūnyatā*, is the best form of

designation. It is a means of communicating knowledge and in Nāgārjuna's view preferable to the Abhidharma philosophy which, while correct in its denial of the notion of substantiality, was wrong in its acceptance of the reality of momentary *dharmas* or discreet entities. Such an analytic theory of emptiness, in Nāgārjuna's view, did not go far enough.

The silence of the Buddha and the problem of communication that it represents anticipates, and in a sense is the basis of, the Mādhyamika rejection of all *dṛṣṭi* or viewpoints.[15] The Mādhyamika dialectic in fact shows the inherent contradiction of all *dṛṣṭi* and the inability of reason to arrive at a universal paradigm of rationality. The dialectic method of Nāgārjuna is one of logical analysis whereby the logic of the *dṛṣṭi* in question is applied. There is no Mādhyamika logic as such; no single philosophical method is applied. Problems are resolved like the treatment of an illness.[16] By using the logic of the viewpoint in question and *reductio ad absurdum* arguments (from which the Prasangika school of Mādhyamika philosophy derived its name) Nāgārjuna succeeds in pointing out the inherent contradictions and limitations of all viewpoints. The main purpose of the dialectic is to show that there can be no all-embracing paradigm of rationality and no single answer to the question of the nature of reality.

Wittgensteinian philosophers of the present day might well be interested in the conclusions of this philosophical school of Buddhism and attempts have been made by some scholars to draw comparisons between Wittgenstein and Buddhism. What Nāgārjuna does, however, is to point to the futility of accepting a particular *dṛṣṭi*, or what might be called in some philosophical circles a concept of rationality, as the norm or criterion for evaluating other viewpoints.[17] It might be asked whether the Mādhyamika dialectic itself does not involve the acceptance of a particular viewpoint since it is difficult if not impossible to criticise from a non-position. This is the crux of the arguments of Nāgārjuna's opponents. Is not *śūnyatā* another theory or *dṛṣṭi*? Does not negation imply that the negative viewpoint is valid? Nāgārjuna's reply is that *śūnyatā* should not be regarded as another viewpoint simply because it points to the limitations of all viewpoints. The self-existence of *śūnyatā* does not have to be accepted in order to refute other viewpoints. To be aware of the limitations of all *dṛṣṭi* is not necessarily in itself a *dṛṣṭi*.

If it were to be so regarded it could be shown by its own logic to be empty. *Śūnyatā* is in fact *śūnyatā*, so it could be argued that there is no viewpoint here which is normative or paradigmatic for all viewpoints.[18]

What may be asked here is how it is possible for *śūnyatā* itself to be apprehended if reality transcends all thought or reason? The reply to this question is, as we have seen, that it is apprehended by means of *prajñā* the higher wisdom that is in some way transcendental. If we press the issue and ask how such wisdom is arrived at we reach an impasse, for *prajñā* transcends the subject–object dichotomy yet must not be confused with instinctive apprehension or intuition in any sensory sense. It is ultimate truth; it is *satori*; it is *śūnyatā*. An examination of the epistemological problems raised by the concept of *prajñā* takes us beyond the scope of this essay so we have to be content with simply raising the issue here.

To return to the claim that it is not possible to equate *śūnyatā* with either being or non-being; it can be inferred from this that Mādhyamika philosophy is not propounding any particular kind of ontology. The understanding of the concept of *śūnyatā* in fact involves nothing being attained and nothing being relied on, that is, no substantive view or position. To equate *śūnyatā* with the Vedāntic concept of the *Brahman-Ātman* identity as some scholars have attempted to do is to misunderstand *śūnyatā*.[19] Nāgārjuna's eight-fold negation illustrates this point. He claims that emptiness implies no production and no extinction, no permanence and no annihilation, no unity and no plurality, no coming in and no going forth. There is neither being nor non-being and antithetical statements about ultimate reality are denied. If it is maintained that *śūnyatā* functions as a sort of absolute the presupposition is that it has an objective referent.[20] Streng's thesis, forcibly argued, is that 'Nāgārjuna presumes no "absolute" in relation to a "particular" but empty structures of particulars'.[21] If by this he means that there is nothing but particulars which are empty of self-existence, he is reiterating the position of the *prajñā-pāramitā* literature that emptiness or *śūnyatā* has no substantial essence, is not a transcendental entity, and is in fact no different from form and empty of self-existence. But insistence on the emptiness of particulars, or conditioned existence, means that Nāgārjuna is not compelled to make a commitment to empirical reality, contrary to the philosophers of the Abhidharma tradition and of course to the empiricists and philosophical positivists of the Western tradition.[22]

Nāgārjuna's insistence on the emptiness of conditioned existence involves him in a reinterpretation of the concepts of *dharma* and *pratītya samutpāda*. While he approves of the denial of the substantiality of phenomena implicit in those concepts he rejects the explicit acceptance of the *svabhāva* or self-existence of momentary *dharmas* and *pratītya samutpāda*. He substitutes as we have seen a more complete theory of emptiness for the more analytic theory of emptiness of the Abhidharma tradition and endeavours to show that neither *dharmas* nor *pratītya samutpāda* have *svabhāva* or self-existence. His rejection of the self-existence of dependent origination is a clear expression of his insight into the nature of emptiness and takes the form of an analysis of conditioning causes and makes use of the logical method of necessary consequence.[23] He points out, for example, that no existing thing can originate from itself, or from something else, or from both itself and something else, or from no possible cause. If something originated from itself it would imply that it created its own substance. If it originated from something else it would mean that its substance would be essentially the same as the conditioning cause. If it were claimed that it originated from no cause then we would have the fallacy of a non-cause producing an entity. His argument against conditioning causes is fourfold:

1. Non self-existing conditioning causes cannot produce other existences. That is, where a conditioning cause has no *svabhāva*, self-existence, there can be no *parabhāva*, other existence, otherwise we would have the fallacy of a non self-existing conditioning cause producing an existence or entity.

2. If a *dharma* or momentary burst of existence were considered to be other than its objective counterpart, as for example a mental phenomenon, and had no objective counterpart in the first place, it would not be possible for it to acquire an objective counterpart as a conditioning cause.

3. If a momentary *dharma* has no *svabhāva* then its foregoing

moment has no self-existence either in which case it is not possible to speak of a conditioning cause.

4. Where there is no self-existence there can be no relational existence and this being the case the decisive factor in dependent origination, namely, this exists that appears, has no meaning.

What Nāgārjuna is seeking to show is that conditioning causes do not account for existence because we cannot extract from them what does not exist in them in the first place. Entities cannot result from non-self-existing conditioning causes.

This analysis involves the denial of the self-existence of *dharmas* and of dependent origination, *pratītya samutpāda*. For Nāgārjuna dependent origination is in fact emptiness, but not in the sense that it has its own ontological status.[24] It neither is nor is not; it is simply a designation, a means of conveying knowledge, and he who is wise has recourse to neither being nor non-being.[25]

It might be argued that if everything is empty then there is no origination or extinction and consequently no four noble truths, no three jewels, and no enlightenment. Nāgārjuna's reply is that such an objection simply shows an inability to comprehend *śūnyatā*. The point is that the concept of emptiness is not taught in isolation from practical behaviour. Its meaning is to be found in its use. When emptiness 'works' then everything 'works'. What we call emptiness is dependent origination and since no *dharma* originates independently there can be no *dharma* that is not empty. So contrary to the objection raised we can say that if existence is *not* empty then there is no origination and therefore no four noble truths.[26] Nāgārjuna sums in up in these words:

You deny all mundane and customary activity when you deny emptiness (in the sense of) dependent origination (*pratītya samutpāda*).[27]

So he who perceives dependent origination understands sorrow, origination, destruction and the path of release.

Nāgārjuna also insists on the emptiness of unconditioned existence which involves him in a reinterpretation of the concept of *nirvāṇa* as a non-existing entity. If it were to be regarded as an existing entity, according to Nāgārjuna it would have to be classified as a constructed product or *saṁskṛta* dependent on something else. On the other hand *nirvāṇa* is not a non-existent thing; it is neither existent nor non-existent, nor is it both existent and non-existent for that would make it a composite product and *nirvāṇa* is non-composite or *asaṁskṛta*. But who is able to understand that *nirvāṇa* is neither existent nor non-existent? As we have seen the post-mortem existence of the Buddha, or his non-existence, or both, is considered to be inexpressible.[28] We are confronted again here with silence in the face of undetermined questions because for similar reasons emptiness is considered to be inexpressible. We may not say that emptiness is or that it is not. The purpose served by the term emptiness is simply the communication of knowledge. It is a designation. In the same way, by stating that *nirvāṇa* is neither existent nor non-existent what we are really saying is that nothing differentiates *nirvāṇa* from *saṁsāra* or *saṁsāra* from *nirvāṇa*. As Nāgārjuna states:

> The extreme limit (*koṭi*) of *nirvāṇa* is also the extreme limit of existence-in-flux; there is not the slightest bit of difference between the two.

And again:

> Existence-in-flux has no beginning, no ending, is without bounds.[29]

Nirvāṇa as reinterpreted by Nāgārjuna then is synonymous with emptiness. It is not to be differentiated from *saṁsāra* either, any more than emptiness is to be differentiated from dependent origination.

I have suggested that it would be a mistake to subsume the Mādhyamika philosophy of Nāgārjuna in Advaita Vedānta and thereby change a dialectic philosophy into an ontological philosophy. Equally it would be a mistake to translate *śūnyatā* into a transcendental absolute such as a *Tathāgata*. To do this constitutes a denial of *pratītya samutpāda* and the notion that there is no self-existing entity. Nāgārjuna refers to the *Tathāgata* as the 'fully completed' one, but he insists that no kind of 'fully completed' being exists who is not dependent on the *skandhas* and wherever there is dependence there is no self-existence. Those who conceive of the *Tathāgata* or the Buddha as existing or not existing in *nirvāṇa* have only a crude idea of *nirvāṇa.* Furthermore, according to Nāgārjuna, those who describe the Buddha in detail do not really perceive the *Tathāgata* for the 'fully completed' one has no self-existence.[30]

I have attempted to show in this essay what the concept of *śūnyatā* means in the *prajñā-pāramitā* literature as epitomised in the Heart Sūtras and how it has been logically developed in the philosophy of Nāgārjuna. It remains to enquire what conclusions can be drawn from this. It is exceedingly tempting to conclude that what we have here is a form of nihilism. It is true that the classification of *śūnyatā* as nihilism is explicitly rejected in the *Kārikās*, but since all viewpoints are shown to be inherently contradictory, even the acceptance of *śūnyatā* as a viewpoint, it would appear that we are ultimately left with nothing. K.V. Ramanan may be right to point out that the *Kārikās*, while considered the best-known work of Nāgārjuna, is primarily abstract and negative in its emphasis. He maintains that a clearer picture of Mādhyamika philosophy is to be found in the *Mahā-prajñā-pāramitā Śāstra* despite the doubts expressed concerning Nāgārjuna's authorship of it. In his view the *Śāstra* provides the negative arguments of the *Kārikās* with a more concrete setting.[31] But his insistence that *śūnyatā* implies (a) no *svabhāva* in relation to conditioned existence; (b) the indeterminate nature of ultimate reality and (c) non-clinging to the determinate as ultimate, makes it difficult to see what concrete setting can be provided which is consistent with the emphasis of the *Kārikās.*[32] If as Ramanan suggests, no *dṛṣti* is ultimate, not even *śūnyatā*, and ultimate truth is not confined to any particular viewpoint,[33] then how is it possible for him to hold the view that the ultimate nature of conditioned existence is unconditioned reality or that indeterminate reality is the ground of determinate entities.[34] He is on surer ground when he claims that in the *Kārikās* there is no account of the real as the ground or immanent nature of the determinate and that this is precisely what is to be found in the *Śāstra.*[35]

What can be concluded concerning the concept of *śūnyatā* is that it indicates the impossibility of equating reality with an essence apart from particulars in Platonic fashion, or of grasping the essence of reality in particulars, an insight which Socrates had when he rejected the usual answers given about the nature of justice, and a fact that Kierkegaard referred to as a foreshortening of eternity. The *via negativa* of Nāgārjuna, however, does not prevent him from recognising that the particular instance, while it cannot be regarded as the essence of reality, is nevertheless necessary to convey the meaning of *śūnyatā*. The realisation of the non-substantiality of momentary *dharmas* and the non-ultimacy of *dṛṣṭi* may also be regarded as a prerequisite for the understanding of *śūnyatā*, although it cannot be interpreted as pointing to an affirmation of nihilism. Can it be that the meaning of *śūnyatā* ultimately has to be sought in the way it is used in a form of life rather than in any attempt to locate an objective referent?

13 Conceptions of the Self in Wittgenstein, Hume and Buddhism: An Analysis and Comparison

The purpose of this paper is to show that Wittgenstein's arguments against the Cartesian model of the self find some parallels in the Pudgalavādin (Personalist) controversy within Buddhism, and that Hume's rejection of the notion of the self as an abiding entity, together with his claim that the self is simply a bundle or collection of distinct impressions and ideas, bears a certain resemblance to the Buddhist doctrine of *anatta* (no-self). The motive for propounding these notions of the self clearly differs in each case, but this does not detract from or affect the way in which I have attempted to draw comparisons. For the sake of clarity the paper is divided into three sections, but the interrelation between the sections and the unity of the whole is hopefully preserved by the comparisons I have attempted to draw.

Descartes' application of radical doubt to all inherited beliefs and opinions and all that hitherto had been termed knowledge resulted in the affirmation of his own existence. Since he could not doubt his thinking it followed that he could not doubt that he existed. The *cogito* assured him of his existence because in order to think at all it was necessary for him to exist. Whether it could have enabled him to know himself is another question. His equation of the ego with consciousness distinct from the body yet inhabiting the body makes it possible for his critics to contend that he really could not have been able to know who he was. Such a contention, of course, involves rejecting the notion of the self-identifying nature of consciousness, or put in another way, it involves rejecting the claim that I am able to know who I am by examining my consciousness.[1]

The equation of the 'I' with consciousness has been variously described as an 'illusion', a 'fantasy' and as 'a misleading Cartesian model'. Wittgenstein claims that the use of the 'I' as subject creates the illusion of something bodiless inhabiting the body.[2] The nature of the 'misleading Cartesian model'[3] is that the mind consists of internal thoughts, feelings, sense impressions, etc., behind which lies the 'I'. This ego of ours is far removed from objects in the outside world seated as it is behind our thoughts and feelings. It is even further removed from the 'I' of other people since the other person's 'I' is itself behind his own thoughts and feelings.

Linked with this notion of an enduring entity or ego and comparable with it is the theory of language which maintains that when we speak we express thoughts. The words we use are in themselves mere lifeless sounds and are translated into thoughts by those who hear them. Words are a bridge or a means of communication between thoughts and they acquire meaning from their relationship with thoughts. Words and language presuppose thoughts: the former are on the outside and the latter on the inside. Behind thoughts, and even further inside, is the 'I', the initiator of thought. Wittgenstein sought to reveal the illusory nature of the whole Cartesian interpretation of inner and outer by examining the use of language. His claim is that we need to 'make a radical break with the idea that language always functions in one way, always serves the same purpose: to convey thoughts.'[4] He maintains, for example, that to say the use of the word red necessarily involves the mental image or representation of the colour red can be shown to be fallacious. It is a mistake to believe that words only have meaning when they refer to aspects of experience in this way. Words acquire meaning from the way they are used in ordinary language. When we use language we are sharing in an activity or a form of life.[5] Words are like tools and serve the same diverse function as tools.[6] They have different meanings in different contexts. There is no prior criterion of meaning for the use of words in language, nor do they have the same meaning in all usages; they have different meanings which can be discerned only from they way they are used. This appeal to the use of language can be referred to as an appeal to a form of human linguistic activity or to a form of life.[7] This conception of language as a shared activity enables Wittgenstein to reject the notion of a private language whereby words are related to thoughts and acquire meaning only by reference to private inner egos.

The Cartesian model that the 'I' hides behind a veil of flesh has implications also, as we have suggested, for knowing the self and knowing others. On the basis of this model we can only know the self, the subject of experiences, the 'I', by way of introspection. Only by looking within, behind the veil of flesh, are we able to examine our own egos. Introspection, however, will not give us knowledge of the egos of others. We are not able to examine the egos of others by looking within them. Introspection is an intensely personal activity. It follows that we can only know the inner selves of others indirectly by way of inference and analogical reasoning. The resemblances and similarities between the experiences and attitudes of others and our own experiences and attitudes enable us to infer that there are other egos similar to our own.

But what does it mean to say that we only have indirect knowledge of another's ego and direct knowledge of our own egos? What does introspection mean? What is involved in the process of looking within and examining our inner selves? Is such internal awareness of the ego possible? If so what would it be like to know it? Referring to William James' comments on introspection Wittgenstein maintains that what James showed was: 'not the meaning of the word "self" . . . but the state of the philosopher's attention when he says the word "self" to himself and tries to analyse its meaning.'[8]

And what does it mean to say that we have knowledge of the inner selves of others indirectly through inference and analogical reasoning? Is it not the case, on the Cartesian model, that the analogical argument presupposes an initial solipsism? Does it not presuppose an 'I' fully aware of having experiences? I do not know prior to the analogical argument that others beside myself are capable of having experiences. If I did know that, the analogical argument would be rendered superfluous, for I cannot presuppose with regard to the experiences of others the very conclusion that the analogical argument is designed to reach, namely, that there are other experiencing subjects. I cannot draw the conclusion by means of analogical reasoning that there are other experiencing subjects until I know myself as an experiencing subject. This is the solipsistic basis of the analogical argument.[9]

We contended earlier that it is possible to reject the notion of the self-identifying nature of consciousness on the grounds that the solipsistic self is not able to know who he is. Strawson argues this point most forcefully. He shows that if a gap is allowed to develop in the concept of a person between the 'body' and 'consciousness', and the 'I' is equated with 'consciousness' and regarded as merely inhabiting the 'body', it results in the 'I' no longer being able to know itself. To be able to identify myself I must be able to pick myself out from others similar to myself; but it is not possible to pick out a consciousness and say of it – 'this is who I am', because I am not able to distinguish it from other consciousnesses. I have no notion of 'different, identifiable subjects of experience – different consciousnesses.'[10] Wittgenstein argues along similar lines when he says that he is puzzled that the feeling of an 'unbridgeable gulf' and 'difference in kind' should arise between consciousness and the brain process and yet not enter into the considerations of ordinary life, which leads him to ask what 'turning my attention on to my own consciousness' could possibly mean.[11] He refers to it as the 'queerest thing' and concludes that the whole notion of an ego inhabiting the body needed to be abolished.[12]

But if the Cartesian model needs to be rejected, and if we do not know the self by way of introspection and the selves of others by way of analogical reasoning, how then do we know the self? What Wittgenstein sees 'at the source of the visual field' as he calls it, 'is a small man in grey flannel trousers, in fact L.W.' He does not establish a relationship between himself as a person and what he sees around him. All he does he says is: 'alternately I point in front of me and to myself'.[13] This act of pointing places the 'I' on the same grammatical level as 'he', or to put it another way, on the same level as other people. He knows himself and others as a physical presence among other physical presences. If I were a single pure consciousness, he says, would it be possible for me to ascribe predicates to myself and would I know to whom I would be ascribing them?[14] J.R. Jones puts this point clearly when he submits that:

(1) 'people' are a special class of space occupants: perceptible, mobile 'presences' of characteristic appearance and behaviour; (2) that I am one such occupant of space; and (3) that it is *as* one such occupant of space, and in no other way, that I know *who* I am.[15]

But am I not something more than just a physical presence? Suppose, says Wittgenstein, I change my face: how is the waiter who brings me soup to know which is me? The waiter would not know who ordered the soup but I would.[16] If it is conceded that I am not able to know myself except as a physical presence what do I ascribe to myself in addition to physical characteristics? Clearly I must ascribe to myself experiences and intentions. But the point is that I ascribe them to an occupant of public space and not to something bodiless inhabiting the body. And when I ascribe such experiences and intentions to myself I ascribe them to the same person as you ascribe them to, which is what is meant by saying that 'I' is on the same grammatical level as 'he'. For me to be able to ascribe experiences to myself presupposes the existence of other subjects to whom it is possible to ascribe similar experiences and intentions.

Another argument for claiming that we know ourselves and others as occupants of space is the use of language. The presupposition of language is that statements are means of communication binding us together, which makes the notion of an ego inhabiting the body yet in some way distinct from it untenable. The same applies to other means of communication. For example, I know you are in pain by your groaning and behaviour, for these activities are not simply signs which only indirectly reveal your pain; I see your pain in your facial expressions. As Wittgenstein points out:

> Do you look into *yourself* in order to recognize the fury in *his* face . . . I see the look that you cast at someone else. And if someone wanted to correct me and say that I don't really *see* it, I should take that for pure stupidity . . . 'We see emotion' . . . We do not see facial contortions and make inferences from them . . .[17]

The point that is being made here is that the basis of our knowledge of another person is that he is a presence in space with whom we communicate in language. We know ourselves and others as members of a human community which is bound together by language, and the nature of that community and language, its institutions and literature, will directly influence the identity of the self.

Wittgenstein argues against the Cartesian model of the self. His position is that there is no private experience without the prior existence of a public shared world. The empiricist, on the other hand seeks to construct a public world from the starting point of immediate experience. Hume's attempt to understand the concept of the self is influenced by those philosophers who claim to have an awareness of the self. He looks for an impression to account for the idea of the self and fails to find it. This is hardly surprising since he is searching for an impression of the self that supposedly unites all our different impressions. Confronted with the notion of the self as some kind of unitary principle behind sensations or successive perceptions binding them together, he has to conclude that there is no such thing as the self as an abiding entity and that there is simply a bundle of sensations. The two prominent factors in human nature, in his view, are change and complexity neither of which are conducive to belief in the self as an abiding entity or as an immutable, simple substance. Since it would be a mistake to ascribe absolute identity to changing, complex things he concludes that the 'identity, which we ascribe to the mind of man, is only a fictitious one, and of like kind with that which we ascribe to vegetables and animal bodies' which over the years 'endure a *total* change, yet we still attribute identity to them' even though 'their form, size, and substance are entirely altered.'[18] Kemp Smith suggests that what Hume means by 'fictitious identity' is that the absolute constancy necessary for identity is not part of man's essential nature and is not to be found in his mental or physical makeup.

Referring to the obvious complexity of human nature Hume notes that a man's thinking is affected by changes of environment or disposition.[19] So given that change and complexity are characteristic of human nature and that change involves simple substances becoming totally different from what they are, i.e. that change affects their absolute identity, the question arises what kind of identity can we attribute to the changing, complex self? Hume contends that a measure of identity is preserved throughout the process of change by means of uniform relations. But what does this mean? Clearly Hume does not mean that uniform relations refers to some kind of mysterious entity holding the complex self together.[20] In fact he refers to it as the relation of causation and he speaks of the self as 'nothing but a bundle or collection' of distinct impressions and ideas. He compares the unity of the self to a republic or commonwealth, the members of which 'are united by the reciprocal ties of government and subordination'. As a republic changes its laws, constitution and members, so also a

> person may vary his character and disposition, as well as his impressions and ideas, without losing his identity. Whatever changes he endures, his several parts are still connected by the relation of causation.[21]

It is Kemp Smith's contention that, in describing the self as a bundle of perceptions, Hume is overstating his case in order to counterbalance the equally one-sided view that the self is simple and self-sufficient, and that he is not in fact denying the existence of a continuing self.[22] If that is so, we are entitled to ask what the nature of the continuing self is that, according to Smith, Hume is not denying? Is it human nature as Smith suggests?[23] But if human nature is merely another name for the self, and is to be regarded as the centre of all knowledge determining our perceptions, propensities, instincts, feelings and emotions, we may well ask if the problem confronting Hume at the outset has been satisfactorily resolved. Clearly not to his own satisfaction for he admits that his account is very defective.[24]

The problem seems to be that for Hume identity implies simplicity and constancy or unchangeableness. An identity compatible with complexity and change, therefore, is purely imaginary. His disagreement is with those who define the complex, changing self in terms of identity. Hence for him the self has to be understood in terms of causal relation because the identity we attribute to the human mind 'is not able to run the several different perceptions into one, and make them lose their characters of distinction and difference, which are essential to them'[25] So personal identity can be understood only through causation which is a matter of belief and not the result of immediate experience.[26] It is apprehended by the memory 'showing us the relation of cause and effect among our different perceptions'[27] but the sense of unity is provided for finally by causal dependence.

It is suggested that Hume's misunderstanding arises from his assumption that the term self is the name of something, an entity or an impression. He looks for an entity which relates to the notion of consciousness or ego and when he fails to find it he is puzzled. He starts with perceptions and embarks on the task of constructing the notion of the self from these perceptions. But to search for the self in this way is to ignore the role played by the term in the use of language; it takes no account of the different contexts in which the term self is used.

Hume's reference to a bundle of sensations and a collection of perceptions or impressions, together with his emphasis on causal relation, bears more than a slight resemblance to the Buddhist doctrine of *anatta* (no-self). This doctrine has a religious connotation, as will become clear in the course of this analysis, but it is not without philosophical implications. Hume's attempt to understand the concept of the self is influenced by those philosophers who claim to have an awareness of the self as an abiding entity; the Buddhists propound the *anatta* doctrine in the context of a general belief in the *Ātman* (Self) as the absolute or ultimate reality. Hume sees no grounds for postulating the idea of the self as an unchanging, simple substance because of the complexity and mutability of human nature; the Buddhist refers to the impossibility of postulating the idea of an unchanging self in the realm of momentary *dharmas* (bursts of existence) where everything is subject to *anicca* (impermanence). According to Buddhist teaching the untutored or misinformed might regard the self as consisting of one of the five *skandhas* (constituents), regarded as the component parts of a human being and classified as form, feelings, perceptions, impulses and consciousness. But to associate the self with one of the *skandhas* in this way, or with the aggregate of *skandhas*, is either to show a lack of acquaintance with the *dharma* (teaching) or to be misinformed about it. As the Buddha states:

> Now, what do you think, brethren, is form, or any other constituent of the 'personality', permanent or impermanent?

Impermanent, O Lord!
Does then impermanence conduce to suffering or to ease?
To suffering, O Lord!
But is it fitting to consider that which is impermanent, linked
to suffering, and doomed to reversal, as 'this is mine, I am
this, this is myself'?
No, indeed not, O Lord!
Therefore, brethren, whatever form, or other skandha, there
may be – past, future, or present, inward or outward, gross
or subtle, low or exalted, near or far away – all that should
be seen by right wisdom as it really is, i.e. that 'All this is not
mine, I am not this, this is not myself'.[28]

The *anatta* doctrine is further illustrated by the encounter
of King Milinda with the venerable Nagasena. At the close of
a discussion on the nature of the self the King is made to see
that as a chariot is so designated in dependence on the pole,
axle, wheel, and other constituent parts, in the same way
'Nagasena' is so designated in dependence on the five *skandhas*.
The discussion is summed up thus:

Where all constituents parts are present,
The word a 'chariot' is applied.
So likewise where the skandhas are,
The term a 'being' commonly is used.[29]

The problem of personal identity raised by such an analysis
takes different forms. Within the Buddhist context the
Pudgalavādins (Personalists) meet the problem by rejecting
the doctrine of *anatta* and positing a particular doctrine of the
self. They speak of a personal entity which is neither identical
with the *skandhas* nor different from them, but rather independent of them. This personal entity, or person as it is called
in preference to the term self, is not simply a designation, nor
is it a totally independent entity but 'a kind of structural unity
which is found in correlation with the Skandhas of one individual.'[30] The phrase 'structural unity' appears at first sight to
be similar to Hume's 'system of different perceptions'. Kemp
Smith places the word 'system' in italics, possibly to indicate
that the bundle or collection of distinct ideas is not just a
bundle or collection but is bound together in some way by the
unifying principle of causal relation. The 'system of different
perceptions' is constitutive of the self for Hume; 'structural

unity' is indicative of the self for the Pudgalavādins. But the resemblance between the two concepts is more apparent than real as we shall see.

The Pudgalavādins argue that if the term persons simply means the *skandhas*, and if, according to the Buddha's teaching, the *skandhas* are part of the range of grasping or the burden then, since there is no distinction between the person and the *skandhas*, the phrase 'the bearer of the burden' can only mean that the burden bears itself. In reply to this Vasubandhu, who upholds the *anatta* doctrine, maintains that the Buddha used the term person to conform to ordinary usage but that in fact the term relates to a series of consecutive momentary *dharmas* (existences). The Pudgalavādins do not reply to Vasubhandu on this point but continue to insist on the reality of the person independent of the *skandhas* and that a person is a conscious subject, for 'if the person does not exist, who is it then that wanders about in Samsara? . . . To say that the self does not exist, in truth and in reality, is a wrong view.'[31] For the Personalists only the person abides in what is otherwise the realm of becoming:

> You say that all thoughts and mental activities change incessantly, and that each mental act lasts only for one moment. How then can it know all the dharmas? Only an abiding Person can be omniscient.[32]

The explicit reference of the Pudgalavādins is to the person 'arising' and 'being born' or 'reborn' and 'acquiring certain constituents' which make him into 'this man'. That is to say, the person exists apart from or independent of, although correlated with, the constituents of form, feelings, perceptions, impulses, and consciousness. How such knowledge is arrived at is not explicitly stated, but what is implied is that the person is intuitively aware of himself as a 'structural unity'. We noted earlier the apparent similarity between this 'structural unity' and Hume's 'system of different perceptions', but the differences between the two concepts are clear. The Personalists conceive of the person as existing independent of the *skandhas* although correlated with them; Hume's 'system of different perceptions' has no existence apart from the bundle or collection of distinct ideas. In this respect Hume is closer to the *anatta* doctrine which states that:

apart from the causally linked sequence of impersonal dharmas there is no one who acts, there is no one who gives up one set of Skandhas, and takes up others instead.[33]

The Pudgalavādins on the other hand, as our analysis shows, are much closer to the Cartesian model. In fact there is a most marked resemblance between the Pudgalavādin concept of person as an abiding entity independent of the *skandhas*, and the Cartesian ego, which is distinct from yet inhabiting the body, and equated with consciousness.

The problem of personal identity raised by the doctrine of *anatta* is further met by an interpretation that regards the doctrine as a denial of an unchanging principle or entity in the *skandhas* but not a denial of the true self. This Vedāntic reinterpretation, much beloved of some Western commentators on Buddhism, retains the structure of the *anatta* doctrine while simultaneously upholding the content of the *ātman* doctrine. The true self (*ātman*), it is maintained, is distinct from the empirical self, which is no-self (*anatta*) and simply an aggregate of *skandhas* lacking true personal identity and epitomising the transience of human existence.[34] Such an interpretation, it has to be said, which maintains 'a soul affirming primitive Buddhism followed by a soul-denying scholastic Buddhism',[35] finds no corroboration in the relevant texts. It reflects more a desire to hold on to the concept of an ego underlying the *skandhas* than an attempt to understand the true import of the doctrine of *anatta*. And presumably on this interpretation it is the transcendental self which is aware of itself as the true self and the *skandhas* as constituting the nature of the empirical self. The problems of solipsism inherent in this interpretation are evident from what has already been noted. To maintain an Upanishadic interpretation of the *anatta* doctrine is to attribute to Buddhism the very notion of the self it seeks to deny and in the context of which it was first propounded. It subsumes Buddhism in Advaita Vedānta where the true self within man is considered to be at one with the Paramātman of the universe, a concept epitomised in the *tat tvam asi* text as interpreted by Śankara.

As we have seen, the self, according to the Buddhist, is a designation, an appellation, a conceptual term for what is in reality a psycho-physical organism consisting of five *skandhas*.

The term person is used in connection with the *skandhas* to
conform to ordinary usage, but in reality there is no abiding
self, only an aggregate of *skandhas* which in turn are a simply
a succession of momentary *dharmas*. In this respect the *anatta*
doctrine corresponds to Hume's negative insight into what the
self is not, namely, an abiding entity. A wandering monk puts
the question to the Buddha: 'Is there an Ātman?' and the
Buddha makes no reply. 'Is there no Ātman?' inquires the
monk. Again the Buddha is silent. The monk departs and
the disciple Ananda questions the Buddha on his silence. The
Buddha replies:

> Had I replied 'there is a self' I would have been called an
> eternalist. Had I replied 'there is no self' I would have been
> called an annihilationist. It is as wrong to maintain that I
> have a self as it is to claim that I have no self; both are
> inaccurate, and both derive from a false notion of 'I'.[36]

The notion of the self that the Buddha is neither affirming
nor denying in this context is the notion of an abiding entity.
But his failure to deny the notion, as the Buddha's explanation suggests, can be taken as an indication of his concern for
the puzzlement and confusion such a reply would have caused
the questioner who by his questions showed that he was not
yet able to understand the implications of the *anatta* doctrine.

The question that arises is what is the role of the 'I' in
Buddhist thought and how does it compare with the ordinary
use of the term?

According to Buddhist teaching the self has to be seen as a
causally linked combination of interdependent mental and
physical *skandhas* working together in a stream of becoming or
in the flux of momentary *dharmas*. There is no self other than
this.[37] The Buddhist is not as concerned to find the principle
of connection between the *skandhas* as Hume is to discover the
principle binding the successive perceptions together. The
Buddhist is not affected by the Humean notion that identity
necessarily implies simplicity, constancy and unchangeableness.
He considers the notion of the self to be entirely compatible
with complexity, momentariness and flux. Unlike Hume he
does not embark on the task of constructing the idea of the
self from a bundle of perceptions or an aggregate of *skandhas*;
he simply gives the name self to the aggregate of *skandhas* and

leaves it at that. He is not denying that there is a self in the sense that it is the name given to an aggregate of constituent parts; there is a psycho-physical organism and that is what is designated the self. It is the name for a physical presence among other physical presences, and for an experiencing 'subject' among other experiencing 'subjects'. The Buddhist could not conceive of a self apart from the psycho-physical organism and in this respect his view is not dissimilar to that of Wittgenstein.

The Buddha recognises, however, that for some the self or ego is mind or consciousness, but in his view it is better for a man, if he has the choice, to regard his physical body as the self rather than his mind or consciousness. Yet in reality neither the body nor consciousness can be regarded as the self so the Buddhist does not engage in what Ryle calls the redundancy of soliloquy; the self as a designation for an aggregate of *skandhas* cannot be regarded as communicating information to itself. The role of 'I' in Buddhist thought is not to denote an abiding entity inhabiting the body yet distinct from it; rather it denotes a psycho-physical organism consisting of form, feelings, perceptions, impulses and consciousness. It is unfortunate that it tends to create a false notion of the self as in the case of Bikkhu Khemaka who said, 'I have a feeling "I AM" but I do not clearly see "This is I AM"'.[38] But in fact, the Buddhist view is that the role of 'I' is related to the aggregate of *skandhas*; it is simply an appellation for the psycho-physical organism apart from which it has no meaning or significance.

I have compared the *anatta* doctrine to the negative insight of Hume as to what the self is not, namely, an abiding entity but something more needs to be said. There is a religious motivation for the Buddhist denial of the self as an abiding entity. The purpose of the *anatta* doctrine is to cut at the very roots of *tanha* (craving or grasping) which binds man to *samsara* (cyclical existence) and the world of *dukkha* (suffering). The *anatta* doctrine is a corollary of the noble truth that the way to remove *dukkha* is to eliminate *tanha* which is the cause of *dukkha*, which in turn is the essence of *samsara*, the world of birth, death and rebirth. To understand the *anatta* doctrine in Buddhism is to be liberated from the samsaric world; to have a Humean insight into what the self is not produces no such liberating results. To know the self in the Wittgensteinian sense,

while it means rejecting the Cartesian notion of an ego separate from yet inhabiting the body, still allows for the possibility
of craving and selfishness, for such a philosophical analysis of
the self leaves everything as it is.

In the context of this paper, which began with a reference
to the Cartesian model of the self, a question that could be
put to the Buddhist propounders of the doctrine of *anatta* is
this: how is the non-self aware of its non-selfhood? Or to put
it another way: how does the non-self know itself as non-self
and as simply an aggregate of *skandhas*? It could be said that
the question presupposes there has to be ego to formulate the
question in the first place. But the import of the *anatta* doctrine is that the *skandhas* are all there is. To assert that a self
binds the *skandhas* together is to believe in an abiding ego
with all the adverse consequences of such a belief for the
spiritual life. The implication of the doctrine of *anatta* is that
the aggregate of *skandhas* which make up the psycho-physical
organism, and which is given the appellation self, knows itself
as such, namely, a physical form with feelings, perceptions,
impulses and consciousness existing among other psycho-physical
presences. What is explicit in the doctrine is that the self is not
an abiding entity inhabiting the body yet distinct from it. In
no way can it be confused with the 'misleading Cartesian
model'.

14 Symbols and Religious Language

If we were to attempt to define a symbol we might say that 'whatever has meaning is a symbol and the meaning is whatever is expressed by the symbol'.[1] Given such a comprehensive definition it could be argued that all words and figures are symbols and similarly that all acts are symbols since words, figures and acts have meaning. A more precise definition might be that 'the essence of a symbol is ... that its importance, value and meaning is not inherent in the intrinsic properties of the symbol itself, but in the thing symbolized' and that the relationship between the symbol and the thing symbolised is conventional and arbitrary rather than intrinsically caused.[2] The implication of this definition is that symbols are conceived as developing within social structures and cultural environments, or within what might be called forms of life, and that we look in vain for what is called 'a cross-cultural, pan-human pattern of symbols'.[3] That is, the choice and development of a symbol is the result of its acceptability and of decisions taken within particular social, religious or cultural contexts. Furthermore, the relevance of a symbol, or its value, meaning and importance, is to be found within these contexts and is related to that which is symbolised.

Whatever definition is adopted we can still consider views that have been expressed about the characteristics of symbols. They include those of acceptability, innate power and necessary character. It is maintained, for example, that symbols have an acceptable character because they are socially determined. It may be possible for an individual to conceive of a particular symbol but its acceptance is a social act. It is the reaction of a group that determines the acceptance and continuance of a symbol. This is what is meant by saying that the relation between a symbol and the thing symbolised is conventional and arbitrary; its meaning is what the people who accept it determine.

It is maintained further that a symbol has its own innate power.[4] But if by innate power is meant that in some way or other a symbol possesses an inherent power in the magical sense, or that its meaning lies within itself, then that is at odds with the view that the acceptability of a symbol, its value, importance and meaning, is related to the thing symbolised. It is not possible for a symbol to possess innate power in the magical sense and at the same time to be socially determined. If we take as an example the maple leaf flag as a symbol for Canada, we may question whether the innate power of this symbol means that no other flag could possibly serve the same symbolic purpose. Clearly this is not the case since at one time a different flag served as a symbol for Canada. A symbol then like a sign can be exchanged, and in the case of Canada the creation of a new symbol, the maple leaf flag, was a social act acceptable to the community which continues to recognise itself in that symbol.

Another characteristic of a symbol it is claimed is its necessary character. This description escapes the magical connotation of innate power on the one hand and the conventional and arbitrary connotation of social determination on the other. It implies that within a particular culture a certain kind of symbol is the natural one to choose. For example, a willow tree might be accepted as the ideal symbol for an unhappy form of life. Its naturalness is indicated by its drooping branches and its necessary character becomes evident if we tried to substitute a holly bush for it. The unacceptability of the holly bush would be related to the natural associations of the willow tree within a culture and would point to the necessary character of the willow tree as a symbol for an unhappy life. The same point could be made about the maple leaf as the natural symbol for the Canadian flag. The predominance of the maple tree in Canada makes its leaf the natural symbol for the country's flag, and its necessary character would become evident if we tried to substitute an oak leaf for it.

Another claim made on behalf of symbols is that they are representational and participate in the reality to which they point. But what does this mean? Is it the case that participation follows necessarily from representation? If the essence of a symbol together with its value and meaning lies not within itself but in that which it symbolises, does this mean that its efficacy is determined by the extent to which it participates in the reality it symbolises? The ambiguity implicit in the idea of participation may be clarified somewhat by the explanation that one who is chosen to represent an institution or a high-ranking person, for example, is said to participate in the honour of what or whom he represents. If so, representation would seem to be the primary factor in this situation, and that it is only in the sense of representing something other than itself that a symbol can be said to participate in the reality of what it symbolises and 'radiates the power of being and meaning of that for which it stands'.[5]

The question that might be raised at this point is whether the value, meaning and importance of symbols depend solely on their relation to the thing symbolised, that is, their participation in the reality to which they point, or whether because of their shared application within a culture they simply manifest the life they have. If in the light of this we ask what life is manifested or what it is that symbols show, we might get the reply that they show themselves in such a way that those who accept them and live by them understand what it means to talk of such things as the holy, for example, or the ultimate. The basic question here is whether or not we understand what it means to speak of the ultimate from the use of concrete particulars, or from the shared application of symbols in a particular culture or form of life. The relation of a symbol to what it shows may not necessarily be like the relation of a diagram or plan to a house. The symbol may itself be the object of thought and manifest itself in such a way that from the life it has, and from its shared application within a culture, we know what it means to speak of the ultimate or the holy. That is, it is itself a picture of the holy and the whole weight of evidence for the holy is in the picture. I shall return to this point in our discussion of religious language.

It may also be asked whether anything more is involved in saying that symbols are representative beyond the fact that they stand for what is symbolised. One suggestion is that a basic characteristic of representative symbols is that they point beyond themselves to something which cannot be grasped immediately and has to be mediated.[6] That something could be what Bernard Lonergan calls 'the world of the adult mediated by meaning and motivated by values' as distinct from 'the world of mediacy of the infant'.[7] The transition from the one world to the other involves a process of learning, according to

Lonergan, which includes asking questions, reflecting, deliberating and formulating views about the nature of reality. But it is not always easy to formulate views clearly and precisely because of the obscure nature of the world. Symbols, therefore, intimate to us 'the kind of world in which we become our true selves'.[8] Again, that something which cannot be grasped immediately could be what is called 'a particular kind of reality, different from that of daily life subject to ordinary speech' which requires the use of symbols in order to speak about it at all.[9] It is for this reason that Ricoeur can refer to symbols as the meeting point of different realities.[10] Such dimensions of reality that need to be expressed in symbols are not normally encountered in ordinary day-to-day experience.

If it is accepted that symbols perform a mediatory function, then their integrating power should also be accepted.[11] The cohesive and integrating effect of symbols in social groups might be illustrated in the political sphere by documents or events, and in the religious realm by holy books. But symbols could have the opposite effect depending on the nature of what is mediated. They could have disintegrating powers also, as illustrated, for example, by the political symbol of the swastika or the religious symbol of the golden calf in the history of Israel.

The same questions which were raised in connection with the notion of participation and acceptability may be asked again here in relation to what is described as the mediatory function of symbols. As we have seen Lonergan suggests that symbols intimate to us the kind of world in which self-realisation is a possibility, or the kind of reality which requires the use of symbols to speak about it. But it could be argued that we understand what it means to talk of a reality not normally encountered in everyday life, not because symbols serve a mediatory function, rather because they constitute a form of language which in itself enables us to picture and understand the kind of reality to which Lonergan and Ricoeur refer. What needs to be recognised is the danger of assuming that symbols are *necessarily* means of communicating or mediating something. Do we say, for example, that we smash a picture of a loved one in order to express, communicate, or mediate our anger – or is this the form our anger takes? Similarly, we might say that our understanding of the kind of reality not normally encountered in everyday life takes the form of symbolic language and to understand the nature of that reality we need to explore the grammar of our response. That is, we need to see symbols as a form of language and seek to elucidate the life they have.

When we turn to examine religious symbols as they find expression in religious language and seek to elucidate the life they have there, we may note at the outset that religious language assumes a threefold form and has been referred to as (a) analogical, (b) as serving a moral purpose, and (c) as symbolic.

(a) Those who refer to religious language as the language of analogy would argue, for example, that descriptions applied to God in religious discourse cannot be taken literally. There is a difference between what is called the ordinary use of language and the way language is used in religious discourse. The statement 'God is good' does not have the same meaning as 'John is good', because goodness as applied to God does not have the same meaning as goodness as applied to John. The term goodness is not being used univocally in these statements, yet neither is it being used equivocally or in a completely different sense. The fact is that the relation between goodness as applied to God and goodness as applied to John is analogical.

The doctrine of analogical predication, which is the way Aquinas attempts to resolve the problem of religious language, seeks to show that human goodness only approximates to divine goodness which is the ideal norm, and that we have an indication of what it might mean to talk about the goodness of God by analogy with what we know about human goodness; the one corresponds to the other. Human goodness indicates what goodness might mean when applied to God.[12]

The distinction here is between the literal and analogical use of language. In religious discourse language is used analogically rather than literally though the existence of God to whom descriptive terms are applied is nevertheless presupposed. What the doctrine of analogy does is indicate how statements can be made about God without detracting from the mystery of divinity.[13]

It will be seen that the ordinary use of language is regarded in this context as the paradigm of rationality or, as Hick describes it, the secular meaning of a word is considered primary since it determines the definition of that word.[14] Religious language then is an adaptation of ordinary language and in order that ordinary language should not be stretched to breaking point, or eroded by a thousand qualifications, it is necessary in religious discourse to resort to analogical predication. It could be argued that the fundamental mistake here is to assume in the first place that there is a single paradigm of rationality to which all modes of discourse must conform, or that the secular meaning of a word is primary and religious discourse an adaptation of ordinary language. I shall return to the possible conceptual confusion involved in imposing the grammar of one mode of discourse on another. At this point we might look at the attempt that has been made to describe religious language as something that serves a moral purpose, or as a psychological aid to moral endeavour.

(b) The view of religious language as serving a moral purpose is to be found in R.B. Braithwaite's lecture on the nature of religious belief. He notes in this lecture that from the standpoint of the positivists meaningful statements are either logical or mathematical propositions or empirical statements. Religious statements, he claims, do not belong to either of these two categories since they are neither logical or mathematical propositions nor empirical propositions. If they were placed in the former category they would forfeit the claim to be related to existence, and if they were placed in the latter category they would have to be falsifiable in principle. If this is the case in what sense we may ask can they be regarded as meaningful assertions?

Braithwaite argues that they serve a moral function: they express the intention of the person who makes the assertion to act in a certain way. For example, when a Christian asserts that God is love, he is indicating his

intention 'to follow an agapeistic way of life'.[15] The stories associated with religions, such as those concerning
the beginning of the world or the last judgement, should
not be regarded as historical facts; they are simply psychological aids to moral effort. They are not true in the
sense that 'the empirical propositions presented by the
stories correspond to empirical fact',[16] rather the relation between the religious stories and the moral way of
life is a psychological and causal one. So according to
Braithwaite, these stories help a man to pursue a moral
course of action, and the fact that they need not be
considered to be empirically true makes no difference
to their moral significance.[17] It is not quite clear whether
Braithwaite considers the stories about creation and
judgement, for example, to be empirical statements
which need to be shown to be false, or whether he
thinks they are accepted as empirically true by religious
believers when in fact they ought not to be considered
as empirically true in the first place. In either case he
maintains that these stories should not be accepted as
empirical statements in themselves or by religious believers, but rather as psychological aids to moral action.[18]

A similar criticism can be levelled against the empiricist view of religious language as was made against the
theory of analogical predication. Braithwaite presupposes
that for a religious assertion to be meaningful it must
be either an empirical proposition or serve a moral function. For a religious story to be accepted as empirically
true it must be capable of being tested empirically.[19]
Since stories about creation and judgement cannot be
tested empirically they cannot be considered meaningful in that sense, so they must be regarded as serving a
moral function. But the fundamental mistake here is to
assume that there is a single paradigm of rationality to
which all modes of discourse must conform. What
Braithwaite fails to realise is that in the case of religious
discourse 'the grammar of "belief" and "truth" is not
the same as in the case of empirical propositions'.[20]
Furthermore, it could be argued that far from serving
simply a moral function or acting as psychological aids
to moral endeavour, religious stories are in fact *expressions*

of a moral outlook which is directly related to religious beliefs. Religious language is not contingently related to moral conduct as a kind of psychological aid; 'it is internally related to it in that it is in terms of this language that the believer's conduct is to be understood.'[21]

Some critics of Braithwaite insist on retaining the referential nature of religious language and they accuse him of being a reductionist when he fails to preserve it. Hick, for example, insists on the factual and not merely symbolic nature of belief in the love and power of God when he claims that 'religious beliefs must be regarded as assertions of fact, not merely as imaginative fictions'.[22] The symbolic, for Hick, implies it would seem something less than real, or at least something that is not on the same level as the factual, and this view is quite different from that of Tillich who claims that religious language is symbolic language.

(c) A very full and comprehensive examination of religious symbols is to be found in Tillich's works. For him the language of faith is the language of symbols.[23] His acceptance of Otto's analysis of the holy means that he acknowledges the mysterious and fascinating nature of the holy and the ambiguity characterising man's experience of it. Awareness of the holy is awareness of the divine presence and, in Tillich's terminology, awareness of the nature of ultimate concern. Its ambiguous character, with its creative and destructive potential for man, is manifested for example in the auspicious and threatening form of Śiva, the destroyer god of the Hindu triad, and in Tillich's view it is necessary for such characteristics to be expressed in symbolic terms. Hence his claim that religious faith can only be adequately expressed in symbolic language.

If we ask why ultimate concern cannot be expressed directly rather than through the mediatory function of symbols, Tillich replies that immediate or direct expressions do not succeed in communicating the power of the holy. The nature and character of ultimate concern is such that it demands symbols in order to be adequately expressed since symbols point to the ultimate, unlock dimensions of the soul we would otherwise be unaware of, and open up levels of reality which would otherwise remain closed to us.[24] Tillich uses Picasso's painting 'Guernica' as an example of the dual function of symbols: the painting expresses starkly man's predicament. In the destruction of the small town of Guernica by Fascist planes we can see man's guilt, anxiety and despair manifested clearly. The expressive style of the painting has religious implications: it points to man's finitude, his bondage to demonic forces, and his estrangement from the 'ground of being'. In short it is a symbol of the Cross; an expression of the human predicament; and it raises existential questions about the meaning of existence. The painting offers no answers, but since the human predicament is courageously expressed, answers are anticipated, because depth dimensions are unlocked and other levels of reality opened up.[25]

Religions for Tillich are concrete expressions of ultimate concern and take the form of words and events. One such word is 'God' which is the most fundamental symbol of the holy. If we object that 'God' cannot be referred to as a symbol only,[26] Tillich replies that the very objection shows a certain confusion about the true nature of symbols. The assumption behind the statement is that the symbolic is somehow less real than the literal or the empirical and therefore less true. But in fact the truth and reality of a religious symbol has nothing to do with empirical reality; it has to do with the ultimate and with dimensions of reality not open to the more literal approach. A religious symbol is true when it is an adequate expression of ultimate concern. When it ceases to exercise that function it dies. But if as Tillich maintains 'God' is a symbol we may ask what is symbolised by it, and the reply we receive is that it symbolises being itself or the ground of being, the only non-symbolic term for the ultimate.[27] Since this concept preserves the character of ultimacy for Tillich, it is less susceptible to the charge of idolatry the essence of which is that finite and concrete concerns are elevated to the status of ultimate concern.

It is evident that Tillich shares the belief that the

language of religious discourse cannot be taken literally. Yet his concept of the ground of being as that to which the symbol 'God' points indicates a desire on his part to preserve the notion of an objective referent. He is not content to believe that the symbol 'God' simply expresses the subjective outlook of the religious believer,[28] for the subjective aspect of religious symbols, he maintains, is not 'unrelated to the objective referent of the symbols, but rather has an essential relation to it'.[29] Clearly he resists the view of those who would insist on the factual rather than symbolic nature of belief in the love of God,[30] and he rejects also their view that the qualities of love, power and justice should be regarded as attributes of a divine being rather than symbols taken from finite experience to refer to the ground of being.[31] Nevertheless he returns to a similar referential use of religious language when he refers to the subjective factor of a religious symbol as bearing an essential relation to its objective referent. His basic assumption seems to be that religious language has to be referential in one sense or another, and although he dispenses with the literal, factual interpretation of religious discourse he retains the notion of the transparency of a symbol to the referent for which it stands. That is, he hypostatises the ultimate. This view differs from that put forward by Wittgenstein who maintains that religious stories present us with a picture of divinity which is in itself the reality of God. That is, the whole weight of evidence is in the picture itself which is non-referential and does not necessarily refer us to external facts. So it could be argued from this point of view that to use the concept 'ground of being' in an objective, referential sense does not necessarily make religious discourse more meaningful.

This alternative view of religious language which Wittgenstein presents emphasises the fact that religious beliefs play the kind of role in a man's life that a picture plays. Stories, pictures and catechisms make up the language of religious belief and we understand the nature of belief when we explore the grammar of this language. The exploration we engage in is not aimed at seeking an explanation for religious belief; it merely seeks to elucidate the role it plays within a culture. Wittgenstein for example says:

> Suppose we said that a certain picture might play the role of constantly admonishing me, or I always think of it. Here an enormous difference would be between those people for whom the picture is constantly in the foreground, and the others who just didn't use it at all.[32]

On this view it is suggested that religious stories, pictures and catechisms, introduce us to the reality of God. They present us with a picture of divinity which is itself the reality of God. We understand what 'God' means through these stories and pictures.[33] The fact that we do not see what the picture represents does not detract from the reality of God because it is not the purpose of the picture to refer us to external facts. Rather the picture itself determines our attitude to the facts. What this means is that the criterion for the meaningfulness of religious discourse is to be found within religion itself and not in accordance with its verifiability or falsifiability by empirical norms. To insist that what is considered intelligible in one context must be intelligible in the same way in all contexts, or that the same criteria of intelligibility must apply in all modes of discourse, may be regarded as philosophical prejudice. To attempt to establish general criteria of intelligibility or meaning that can be applied to all significant utterances is similar to presupposing that there is a single paradigm of rationality to which all modes of discourse must conform. As we have seen the ordinary use of language is regarded by some as the paradigm of rationality and they claim that the secular use of a word is primary. But as Winch points out we may be guilty of arbitrary linguistic legislation when we insist that a word must have a specific meaning:

> The 'must' is not a logical 'must' but simply the 'must' of their own preferences, or the 'must' of one context which they have elevated consciously or unconsciously to be a standard for all others.[34]

When we sum up what has been said hitherto we can say that the theory of analogical predication, and the empiricist view of religion as a psychological aid to moral endeavour, share the common belief that the language of religious discourse cannot be taken literally. They differ from one another in that upholders of the doctrine of analogy presuppose the existence of God to whom descriptive terms are applied, while upholders of the empiricist view do not make the same assumption. For the latter the assertion 'God is love' is simply a declaration of intent to live a life dedicated to love. The theory that religious language is symbolic language shares the belief that religious discourse cannot be taken literally. In common with the theory of analogical predication it holds that language is not being used univocally when applied to that which is ultimate.

The question that needs to be asked in connection with symbols, however, is whether it follows necessarily that if they do not point to a reality beyond themselves or have some kind of objective referent, they must of necessity be an expression of the subjective outlook of religious believers. Can it not be maintained that they have a life of their own and that their unity is to be found in the language of religious discourse? Is it not possible to maintain that they are related to one another within the context of religious life rather than because they participate in the reality of that to which they point. If this is so, then the validity and truth of a religious symbol depends not so much on its self-negating quality, or its transparency to the referent for which it stands, as on the life it has in the context of religious belief within a particular tradition and culture. So what Tillich calls the metaphysical ground of being gets its meaning from the symbols used in a particular form of life rather than the symbols deriving their meaning from the ground or structure of being. If that is the case then it is a mistake to assume that we know the reality to which symbols point prior to an analysis of the symbols themselves. To talk of the adequacy and acceptability of symbols and the extent to which they mediate, represent or participate in the ultimate, is to prejudge the issue. We know what it means to speak of the ultimate or the reality of God only from an exploration of the grammar of symbolic language, the language of faith, and from an elucidation of the role symbols play in the context of religious belief.

Notes and References

1 Towards a Theology of Religions

1. Cf. John Hick, *Philosophy of Religion*, New Jersey: Prentice Hall, 1973, p. 129.
2. Heinz Robert Schlette, *Towards a Theology of Religions* (Freiburg: Herder, 1966) p. 16.
3. Ibid.
4. Ibid., p. 17.
5. Paul Tillich, *The Future of Religions* (New York: Harper and Row, 1966) p. 213.
6. Paul Tillich, *Christianity and the Encounter of the World Religions* (New York: Columbia University Press, 1963) p. 43; *Dynamics of Faith* (New York: Harper, 1957) pp. 12–16; *The Future of Religions*, pp. 80–1, 86–7; *Perspectives on Nineteenth and Twentieth Century Protestant Theology*, ed. Carl E. Braaten (London: SCM Press, 1967) pp. xxv, and 213.
7. Cf. Karl Rahner, *Theological Investigations*, Vol. 5 (New York: Darton, Longman and Todd, 1966); John Hick, *God and the Universe of Faiths* (London: Macmillan, 1973).
8. 'Comparative Religion: Whither and Why', *The History of Religions: Essays in Methodology*, ed. Mircea Eliade and Joseph M. Kitagawa (Chicago: University of Chicago Press, 1959) p. 55.
9. Rudolf Otto, *The Idea of the Holy* (New York: OUP, 1962) pp. 4, 8.
10. Cf. Ninian Smart, *The Science of Religion and the Sociology of Knowledge* (Princeton University Press, 1973) Chapter I; J.M. Kitagawa, 'The History of Religions in America, *The History of Religions: Essays in Methodology*, pp. 5–7.
11. Cf. W. Cantwell Smith, *The Meaning and End of Religion* (New York: Mentor, 1964) p. 46, 232, and notes 153, 154.
12. Friedrich Schleiermacher, *On Religion: Speeches to its Cultured Despisers* (New York: Harper and Row, 1958) pp. 40, 54.
13. Ibid., pp. 236, 238.
14. W. Cantwell Smith, *op. cit.*, p. 21.
15. Ibid., pp. 48, 55.
16. Ibid., pp. 114, 134.
17. Ibid., p. 135.
18. Ibid., pp. 141, 162, 175.
19. *The Future of Religions*, p. 81.
20. Karl Barth, *Church Dogmatics*, ed. G.W. Bromiley and T.F. Torrance (Edinburgh: T. and T. Clark, 1956) Vol. I, Part 2, pp. 297–303; 307–10; 325–8; 332–3; 337–8; 353–4.
21. *On Religion*, pp. 211–18; 297–8; 241–3; 250–2.
22. Hans Küng, *Freedom Today* (New York: Sheed and Ward, 1966) pp. 110–24; cf. H.J.D. Denzinger, *Enchiridion*, ed. Karl Rahner (Freiburg: Herder, 1955) pp. 468 ff.

23. Quoted in Owen C. Thomas, *Attitudes Towards Other Religions* (New York: Harper and Row, 1969) p. 206.
24. *Freedom Today*, pp. 132–45; 147–60.
25. *Towards a Theology of Religions*, pp. 94–105.
26. Ibid., pp. 30, 34, 36.
27. *The Future of Religions*, pp. 80, 93.
28. *Systematic Theology* (London: Nisbet, 1968) p. 395.
29. Ibid., p. 389.
30. Ibid., p. 393; cf. *On the Boundary* (London, 1967) p. 48.
31. D.M. Baillie, *God was in Christ* (London: Faber and Faber, 1948) p. 76.
32. For a fuller treatment of Tillich's views on the historical Jesus see my article on the topic in *Studies in Religion*, Vol. 4, No. 2, 1974/5, pp. 120–8.
33. *The Future of Religions*, pp. 86–91.
34. Ibid., p. 86.
35. *Christianity and the Encounter of World Religions*, pp. 54–5.
36. *The Future of Religions*, p. 88.
37. This point has been developed by D.Z. Phillips whose approach to the philosophy of religion I have examined in *The Journal of Religion*, Vol. 58, No. 3, July 1978, pp. 288–302.
38. Cf. D.Z. Phillips' review of Ninian Smart's *The Phenomenon of Religion* (London: Macmillan, 1973) in *Mind*, Vol. LXXXIV, No. 333, January, 1975, pp. 155–6.
39. 'Understanding a Primitive Society' *Religion and Understanding*, ed. D.Z. Phillips (Oxford: Blackwell, 1967) p. 30.
40. D.Z. Phillips, *Religion without Explanation* (Oxford: Blackwell, 1976) pp. 1–3; *Faith and Philosophical Enquiry* (London: Routledge) p. 125; *Concept of Prayer* (London: Routledge, 1965) p. 12.
41. Ludwig Wittgenstein, *Lectures and Conversations on Aesthetics, Psychology and Religious Belief*, ed. C. Barrett (Oxford: Blackwell, 1966) p. 72.
42. *Religion without Explanation*, p. 172
43. Cf. D.Z. Phillips, *Athronyddu am Grefydd* (Llandysul: Gwasg Gomer, 1974) p. 91.

2. A Wittgensteinian Approach to the Philosophy of Religion

1. Kai Nielsen, 'Wittgensteinian Fideism', *Philosophy* 42, No. 161 (July, 1967) pp. 191–209.
2. D.Z. Phillips, *Faith and Philosophical Enquiry* (London, 1970) p. 124.
3. Ibid., p. 125.
4. D.Z. Phillips, *Religion without Explanation* (Oxford, 1976) pp. 1–3.
5. D.Z. Phillips, *The Concept of Prayer* (London, 1965) p. 14; *Athronyddu am Grefydd* (Llandysul, 1974) pp. 9, 44.
6. *Faith and Philosophical Enquiry*, pp. 85–92.
7. *Religion without Explanation*, p. 181.
8. John Hick, *Philosophy of Religion* (Englewood Cliffs, NJ, 1973) pp. 95–6.
9. *Religion without Explanation*, pp. 145–50.

10. See my paper, 'Paul Tillich and the Historical Jesus', *Studies in Religion*, 4, No. 2, (1974–5) pp. 120–27.
11. *Religion without Explanation*, p. 144.
12. *The Concept of Prayer*, p. 10; *Faith and Philosophical Enquiry*, p. 17.
13. *The Concept of Prayer*, p. 12.
14. *Faith and Philosophical Enquiry*, p. 84.
15. S.R. Sutherland, 'Religion and Ethics', *Human World*, No. 5 (November, 1971) p. 44.
16. *Faith and Philosophical Enquiry*, p. 97.
17. Ibid., p. 101.
18. Ibid., pp. 85–92.
19. *Religion without Explanation*, p. 144.
20. See Antony Duff, 'Psychopathy and Moral Understanding', *American Philosophical Quarterly*, 14, No. 3, (July, 1977) pp. 194–95.
21. D.Z. Phillips, *Religion and Understanding* (Oxford, 1967) p. 6.
22. *Faith and Philosophical Enquiry*, pp. 233 ff.
23. *The Concept of Prayer*, p. 9.
24. *Religion and Understanding*, p. 70.
25. *The Concept of Prayer*, p. 22.
26. L. Wittgenstein, *Lectures and Conversations on Aesthetics, Psychology and Religious Belief* (Oxford, 1966) p. 72.
27. *Athronyddu am Grefydd*, pp. 39–43.
28. *Faith and Philosophical Enquiry*, pp. 56–7.
29. *Athronyddu am Grefydd*, p. 91.
30. Michael Durrant, 'Is Justification of Religious Belief a Possible Enterprise?' *Religious Studies* 9, No. 4 (December, 1973) pp. 449–55.
31. D.Z. Phillips, *Death and Immortality* (London, 1970) pp. 38, 42, 45.
32. Ibid., p. 10.
33. Ibid., pp. 18, 61, 69.
34. John Skorupski, 'Review of *Religion without Explanation*' (Glasgow, 1977).
35. *Athronyddu am Grefydd*, p. 133.
36. L. Wittgenstein, *Philosophical Investigations* (Oxford, 1976) sec. 124.

3 Paul Tillich and the Historical Jesus

1. Paul Tillich *On the Boundary* (London, 1967) pp. 49, 50. Cf. Paul Tillich, *The Interpretation of History* (New York, 1936) p. 33.
2. *On the Boundary*, p. 50.
3. Ibid., p. 50; Paul Tillich *Systematic Theology* (London, 1968) II, p. 116 ff.
4. *On the Boundary*, p. 50.
5. Ibid.
6. Tillich describes him as 'the most profound and modern representative of the nineteenth-century theology of mediation' and as a man of overwhelming intellectual ability and religious power. Ibid., p. 47 ff.
7. M. Kähler, *The So-called Historical Jesus and the Historic Biblical Christ*, trans. and ed. Carl E. Braaten (Philadelphia, 1964), p. xii. Cf. Paul Tillich, *Perspectives on 19th and 20th Century Protestant Theology* (London, 1967) pp. 209, 210.

196   *Notes and References*

8.   *Perspectives*, p. 215.
9.   Ibid., p. 227.
10.   Ibid.
11.   *Systematic Theology*, II, p. 112. D. Moody Smith, Jr., in an article on 'The Historical Jesus in Paul Tillich's Christology', *The Journal of Religion*, 46 (January, 1966) pp. 131–47, classifies Tillich with Bultmann on the question of the historical Jesus but points out that Tillich's scepticism reflects his refusal to allow Christology to be affected by the uncertainties of historical investigation rather than any docetic tendencies.
12.   *Systematic Theology*, II, p. 113. Cf. *Ultimate Concern*, ed. D. Mackenzie Brown (New York, 1965) p. 134.
13.   *Systematic Theology*, II, pp. 113, 114.
14.   *The Journal of Religion*, 46 (January, 1966) p. 192. This is Tillich's reply to D. Moody Smith's article in the same issue.
15.   There have been a number of docetic interpretations of Tillich's Christology. Frederick C. Grant, 'Editorial: Paul Tillich', *Anglican Theological Review*, 43:3 (July, 1961) p. 244; Maria F. Sulzbach, 'The Place of Christology in Contemporary Protestantism' *Religion in Life*, 23, (1953–4) p. 212; Kenneth Hamilton, *The System and the Gospel* (London, 1963) p. 163; Bruce J.R. Cameron, 'The Historical Problem in Paul Tillich's Christology', *Scottish Journal of Theology*, 18 (1965) p. 257 ff.; D. M. Baillie, *God was in Christ* (London, 1948) pp. 78–9. Barth's comments on Tillich as collated and recorded by one of his students refers to Tillich's Christology as essentially docetic: Raymond Kemp Anderson, 'Barth on Tillich: Neo Gnosticism?', *The Christian Century* (December, 1970) pp. 1477–81.
16.   The New Being for Tillich is essential being. It overcomes the gap between essence and existence and conquers man's feeling of alienation and existential estrangement. While it is manifested in that personal life to which the name Jesus of Nazareth points, it is not confined to that life. It has been continuously manifested throughout history. *Systematic Theology*, II, pp. 136–44, 155–6.
17.   *Systematic Theology*, II, p. 118.
18.   Paul Tillich, *Dynamics of Faith* (New York, 1958) p. 87. Cf. *Systematic Theology*, II, p. 118.
19.   *Systematic Theology*, pp. 118, 119.
20.   *Dynamics of Faith*, p. 89.
21.   *Systematic Theology*, II, p. 123.
22.   *Dynamics of Faith*, p. 89.
23.   Kähler, *op. cit.*, p. xii.
24.   *Systematic Theology*, II, p. 123.
25.   Ibid.
26.   Ibid.
27.   Ibid. II, p. 132.
28.   Ibid., pp. 131–2. Cf. *Perspectives*, p. 175: 'Can we solve the problem which historical criticism has opened up by a theology of the leap? I do not believe it is possible'.
29.   Paul Tillich, 'A Reinterpretation of the Doctrine of the Incarnation', *Church Quarterly Review*, 147 (1949), pp. 145–6. Cf. *Systematic Theology*, II, p. 132.

30. *Ultimate Concern*, pp. 146–7.
31. *Systematic Theology*, II, p. 132.
32. D. Moody Smith, p. 138. Smith's objection is that transforming power does not guarantee the historicity of the objects of faith. The criterion of transforming power is indecisive.
33. *Systematic Theology*, II, pp. 132–3.
34. Cf. Dorothy Emmet, 'Epistemology and the Idea of Revelation', *The Theology of Paul Tillich*, ed. C.W. Kegley and R.W. Bretall (New York, 1961) p. 213.
35. Cf. Wolfart Pannenberg, who rejects the idea that it is possible for the Christian faith to retreat into 'some sheltered area where it would be immune from historical criticism': *New Frontiers in Theology*, Vol. III; *Theology as History*, ed. James M. Robinson and John B. Cobb (New York, 1967) p. 248.
36. Cf. R.W. Hepburn, *Christianity and Paradox* (London, 1958) p. 5; A.G.N. Flew, 'Theology and Falsification', *New Essays in Philosophical Theology*, ed. A. Flew and A. MacIntyre (London, 1955) p. 98.
37. For further criticisms of Tillich's position from a philosophical point of view compare: Ninian Smart, 'Being and the Bible', *The Review of Metaphysics*, 9:4 (June, 1955) pp. 589–607; 'The Intellectual Crisis of British Christianity', *New Theology*, No. 3, ed. Martin E. Marty and Dean G. Peerman (London, 1966) pp. 20–9; J.H. Thomas, *Paul Tillich: An Appraisal* (Philadelphia, 1963) p. 86.
38. Cf. D. Moody Smith, p. 131.
39. Karl Barth, *Church Dogmatics*, Vol. IV: pp. 2, 247–8. Barth claims that Jesus of Nazareth, the Royal Man, is seen by the community in which the New Testament arose as the Son of God who is also Son of Man and this is how we must try to see him, with the presuppositions of the New Testament. Cf. also Vol. IV: pp. 2, 102, 164 ff. Cf. T.W. Ogletree, *Christian Faith and History* (New York, 1965) p. 204; Van Austin Harvey, *The Historian and the Believer* (New York, 1966) p. 134.
40. When it was suggested to Tillich that he should abandon the attempt to guarantee an historical basis for the Christian faith independent of the uncertainties of historical research and proceed with his theological work on the supposition that Jesus existed, that is, that he should take the risk of historical uncertainty, he rejected the idea. He explained that for him the two risks lay in different dimensions: 'The risk of faith is existential; it concerns the totality of our being, while the risk of historical judgments is theoretical and open to permanent scientific correction' *Systematic Theology*, II, p. 134; cf. *The Journal of Religion*, 46 (January, 1966) pp. 193–4.
41. *Systematic Theology*, III, p. 393.
42. Ibid.; cf. *The Interpretation of History*, pp. 249–50.
43. *On the Boundary*, 50.

4 Truth, Religion and Non-Violence

1. I differ from the view expressed by Joan V. Bondurant who claims that the dialectic implicit in Gandhi's method of *satyagraha* is not dependent

on his metaphysical assumptions nor on his Hindu-based theology, and that his criteria of truth, like those of Marx, lie in the meeting of human need. See *Conquest of Violence: The Gandhian Philosophy of Conflict* (University of California Press, 1971) pp. 192–3.

2. *The Selected Works of Mahatma Gandhi* (Ahmedabad: Navajivan Publishing House, 1968) Vol. VI, pp. 96–7.
3. Ibid., p. 97.
4. Ibid., pp. 100–2; cf. M.K. Gandhi, *Truth is God* (Ahmedabad: Navajivan Publishing House) p. 25.
5. *Selected Works*, Vol. V, p. 382.
6. *Truth is God*, p. 10.
7. Ibid., p. 12.
8. Ibid., p. 11.
9. *Selected Works*, Vol. VI, p. 100.
10. N.K. Bose, *Selections from Gandhi* (Ahmedabad: Navajivan Publishing House, 1948) p. 4.
11. *Truth is God*, p. 3.
12. Ibid., p. 15.
13. *All Men are Brothers*, ed. by Krishna Kripalani (Paris: Unesco, 1958) pp. 70, 76.
14. Ibid., p. 71.
15. *Truth is God*, p. 32.
16. *All Men are Brothers*, pp. 56, 59.
17. *Selections from Gandhi*, p. 254.
18. Ibid., p. 257.
19. W. Cantwell Smith, *The Meaning and End of Religion* (New York: Mentor, 1964) p. 46 and p. 232 notes 153, 154, where Hegel is referred to as the first philosopher to regard religion as an entity preceding all historical manifestations.
20. Friedrich Schleiermacher, *On Religion: Speeches to its Cultured Despisers* (New York: Harper, 1958) pp. 40, 54.
21. Ibid., pp. 236, 238.
22. *Selections from Gandhi*, p. 256. In a discussion I had with Pyarelal in New Delhi he maintained that Gandhi started to search for the one true religion but came to realise that it was wrong to do so.
23. *All Men are Brothers*, p. 59.
24. *Selections from Gandhi*, p. 259.
25. Ibid., p. 258.
26. Paul Tillich, *Systematic Theology* (London: Nisbet, 1968) Vol. I, p. 242; Vol. III, pp. 262–4: *Christianity and the Encounter of the World Religions* (New York: Columbia University Press, 1963) p. 5.
27. Paul Tillich, *The Future of Religions*, edited by Jerald B. Brauer (New York: Harper and Row, 1966) pp. 88–90; cf. *Systematic Theology*, Vol. I, pp. 92–4, Vol. III, pp. 264–285.
28. *All Men are Brothers*, pp. 59–60.
29. Ibid., p. 56.
30. Ibid., p. 81.
31. *Truth is God*, p. 4.
32. D.Z. Phillips, *Some Limits to Moral Endeavour*, Inaugural Lecture (University College, Swansea, 1971) p. 7.

33. *The Encyclopedia of Philosophy* (New York: Collier-Macmillan, 1967) Vols 5–6, p. 120.
34. *All Men are Brothers*, p. 82.
35. Aldous Huxley, *Ends and Means* (London: Chatto and Windus, 1941) p. 52.
36. *Selections from Gandhi*, p. 162.
37. *Truth is God*, p. 38.
38. *Selections from Gandhi*, p. 155.
39. *Truth is God*, p. 38.
40. *All Men are Brothers*, p. 42.
41. Peter Winch, *Morality and Purpose* (London: Routledge and Kegan Paul, 1969) p. 181.
42. Ibid., p. 186.
43. Ibid.
44. *All Men are Brothers*, p. 92.
45. *Selections from Gandhi*, p. 156.
46. *All Men are Brothers*, p. 91.
47. *Selections from Gandhi*, pp. 175–6.
48. Ibid., p. 165.
49. *All Men are Brothers*, pp. 89–90.
50. *Selected Works*, Vol. VI, p. 230.

5 Gandhi's Concept of Truth and the *Advaita* Tradition

1. N.K. Bose, *Selections from Gandhi* (Ahmedabad: Navajivan Publishing House, 1948) p. 92.
2. Ibid.
3. *Vivekachūdāmani of Śrī Śankarācārya*, edit. Swami Madhavananda (Calcutta: Advaita Ashrama, 1970) p. 98.
4. Ibid., pp. 74–6, 145–6.
5. Ibid., pp. 131–2.
6. *The Vedānta Sūtras of Bādarāyana, with the Commentary by Śankara* trans. George Thibaut (New York: Dover, 1962) II, pp. 1, 33.
7. Ibid. III, pp. 2. 18.
8. Rudolf Otto, *Mysticism East and West* (New York: Macmillan, 1972) pp. 19–23.
9. Ibid. p. 34.
10. M.K. Gandhi, *In Search of the Supreme*, I (Ahmedabad: Navajvan Publishing House, 1931) p. 196.
11. *The Selected Works of Mahatma Gandhi* (Ahmedabad: Navajivan Publishing House, 1968) Vol. VI, p. 108.
12. M.K. Gandhi, *Truth is God* (Ahmedabad: Navajivan Publishing House, 1955) p. 44.
13. Ibid., p. 12.
14. Ibid., p. 10.
15. *Selected Works*, VI, 97.
16. L. Fischer, *The Essential Gandhi* (New York: Vintage Book, 1962) p. 229.

17. *Selections from Gandhi*, p. 47.
18. *Truth is God*, p. 11.
19. Stewart R. Sutherland, *Goodness and Particularity*, Inaugural Lecture (Kings College, London, 1979) pp. 12, 13.
20. *Truth is God*, p. 15.
21. *Mysticism East and West*, pp. 50–3.
22. *Truth is God*, p. 16.
23. Ibid.
24. *All Men are Brothers* (Paris: Unesco, 1969) p. 71.
25. Ibid., p. 75.
26. Ibid., p. 57.
27. Ibid., pp. 58–61, 77, 88.
28. *Truth is God*, pp. 5–7.
29. Margaret Chatterjee, *Gandhi's Religious Thought* (London: Macmillan, 1983) p. 105.
30. Gandhi would find it difficult to accept Otto's analysis of the manifold world as the antithesis of the One which is the real above the many (*op. cit.*, pp. 63–71). *Avidyā* or ignorance may obscure the real nature of the empirical world, but that does not make the manifold the antithesis of the One. Perhaps Otto's terminology is too Hegelian for Gandhi.
31. M. Hiryanna, *Outlines of Indian Philosophy* (Bombay: George Allen and Unwin, 1973) p. 310; *The Vedānta Sütras*, IV, i. 15.
32. *All Men are Brothers*, p. 81.
33. *Truth is God*, p. 4.
34. *All Men are Brothers*, p. 58.
35. *Truth is God*, p. 28.
36. *The Essential Gandhi*, p. 229.
37. *Truth is God*, p. 10.
38. S.K. Saxena, 'The fabric of self-suffering in Gandhi', *Religious Studies*, XII, 2 (1976) pp. 239–47.
39. *All Men are Brothers*, p. 59.
40. *The Complete Works of Vivekānanda*, I (Calcutta: Advaita Ashrama, 1970) p. 356.
41. Ibid., II, p. 133.
42. Ibid., II, pp. 254, 334, 381.
43. Ibid., I, p. 17.
44. Ibid., II, p. 253.
45. Ibid., I, p. 373.
46. Ibid., I, pp. 374–5.
47. Ibid., I, pp. 325, 365.
48. Ibid., II, pp. 153, 235–6.
49. Ibid., I, pp. 389–90.
50. Ibid., III, pp. 246–7.
51. Ibid., I, p. 20.
52. Ibid., IV, p. 481.
53. Ibid., I, pp. 317–18, 324.
54. Ibid., II, p. 388.
55. *All Men are Brothers*, pp. 54, 56, 59; *Selections from Gandhi*, pp. 245–7.

6 Gandhi's Philosophy of Education

1. *The Selected Works of Mahatma Gandhi* (Ahmedabad: Navajivan Publishing House, 1968) Vol. VI, pp. 96–7.
2. M.K. Gandhi, *Truth is God* (Ahmedabad: Navajivan Publishing House, 1955) pp. 11, 20.
3. Ibid., p. 10.
4. Ibid., p. 32.
5. *Selected Works*, Vol. V, pp. 350–3; Vol. VI, pp. 109, 114.
6. *Truth is God*, p. 139.
7. Louis Fischer, *The Essential Gandhi* (New York: Vintage Books, 1962) p. 229.
8. *Selected Works*, Vol. VI, p. 294.
9. 'What is Education', *Navajivan*, 28 Feb. 1926. Quoted in Raghavan Iyer, *The Moral and Political Writings of Mahatma Gandhi* (Oxford: Clarendon Press, 1987) Vol. 3, pp. 377–9.
10. M.K. Gandhi, *All Men Are Brothers* ed. by Krishna Kripalani (Paris: Unesco, 1958, 1969) p. 151.
11. Ibid., 157.
12. Margaret Donaldson, *Children's Minds* (Glasgow: Collins, 1978, 1981) pp. 127–8.
13. *With Gandhiji in Ceylon*, p. 109. Quoted in *The Moral and Political Writings of Mahatma Gandhi*, Vol. 3, p. 382.
14. *Selected Works*, Vol. VI, p. 521.
15. *All Men Are Brothers*, p. 153.
16. *Selected Works*, Vol. VI, p. 526.
17. Nimal Kumar Bose, *Selections from Gandhi* (Ahmedabad: Navajivan Publishing House, 1948, 1972) pp. 284–5.
18. *The Essential Gandhi*, pp. 236–7.
19. *All Men Are Brothers*, pp. 153–4.
20. *Selections from Gandhi*, pp. 283–4.
21. *Selected Works*, Vol. VI, p. 519.
22. *Selections from Gandhi*, p. 298.
23. *English Works of Raja Rammohun Roy* (Calcutta: Sadharan Brahma Samaj 1945–51) pp. 59–61.
24. *Autobiography of Dayananda Sarasvati* (New Delhi: Manohar Publications, 1978) p. 65.
25. *An Autobiography* (London: Jonathan Cape, 1972) pp. 15, 16.
26. Rabindranath Tagore, *Towards Universal Man*, (Bombay: Asia Publishing House, 1961) pp. 222–3.

7 Religion and Religions: Gandhi and Tillich

1. *All Men are Brothers*, ed. Krishna Kripalani (Paris: Unesco, 1958) pp. 56, 59.
2. N.K. Bose, *Selections from Gandhi* (Ahmedabad: Navajivan, 1946) p. 254.
3. Ibid., p. 257.

202 *Notes and References*

4. W. Cantwell Smith, *The Meaning and End of Religion* (New York: Mentor, 1946) p. 46, and p. 232 notes 153, 154, where Hegel is referred to as the first philosopher to regard religion as an entity preceding all historical manifestations.
5. Friedrich Schleiermacher, *On Religion: Speeches to its Cultured Despisers* (New York: Harper, 1958) pp. 40, 54.
6. Ibid., pp. 236, 238.
7. W. Cantwell Smith, *op. cit.*, p. 135.
8. Ibid., p. 55.
9. *Selections from Gandhi*, p. 256. In a discussion I had with Pyarelal in New Delhi he maintained that Gandhi did start to search for the one true religion but came to realise that it was wrong to do so.
10. *All Men are Brothers*, p. 59.
11. Ibid., p. 75.
12. Louis Fischer, *The Essential Gandhi* (New York: Vintage Books, 1962) p. 229.
13. Paul Tillich, *Ultimate Concern: Tillich in Dialogue* (New York: Harper, 1965) p. 34: *Christianity and the Encounter of the World Religions* (New York: Columbia University Press, 1965) p. 34.
14. Paul Tillich, *Systematic Theology* (London: Nisbet, 1968) Vol. I, p. 242, Vol. III, pp. 262–4.
15. M.K. Gandhi, *In Search of the Supreme* (Ahmedabad: Navajivan, 1961) Vol. 3, pp. 108–9.
16. Paul Tillich, *The Future of Religions*, ed. Jerald C. Brauer (New York: Harper, 1966) pp. 89–90. Cf. Paul Tillich, *Systematic Theology*, Vol. I, pp. 92–4, Vol. III, pp. 264–85.
17. *All Men are Brothers*, p. 75.
18. *Selections from Gandhi*, pp. 303–4. Cf. M.K. Gandhi, *Truth is God* (Ahmedabad: Navajivan, 1955) p. 104 ff.: *The Selected Works of Mahatma Gandhi* (Ahmedabad: Navajivan, 1968) Vol. VI, p. 287.
19. Paul Tillich, *Dynamics of Faith* (New York: Harper, 1957) p. 125.
20. *Selections from Gandhi*, p. 259.
21. Ibid., p. 258.
22. *Systematic Theology*, Vol. I, p. 242; Vol. III, pp. 262–4; *Christianity and the Encounter of the World Religions*, p. 5.
23. *The Future of Religions*, pp. 88–90; cf. *Systematic Theology*, Vol. I, pp. 92–4, Vol. III, pp. 264–85.
24. *All Men are Brothers*, pp. 59–60.
25. Ibid., p. 56.
26. *Selections from Gandhi*, p. 259.
27. Cf. D. Z. Phillips, *Faith and Philosophical Enquiry* (London: Routledge, 1970) p. 233 ff.
28. *Selections from Gandhi*, p. 256.
29. *In Search of the Supreme*, Vol. 3, pp. 61–2, 69.
30. *All Men are Brothers*, pp. 61, 63.
31. *In Search of the Supreme*, Vol. 3, p. 83.
32. Ibid.
33. *The Essential Gandhi*, pp. 234–5.
34. *In Search of the Supreme*, Vol. 3, p. 17.

35. *All Men are Brothers*, p. 65. Note the view of John Hick in *The Myth of God Incarnate* (London: SCM, 1977) p. 175 ff., where he describes the phrase Son of God as a phrase to be taken metaphorically and not literally and refers to the claim that God can only be known through Jesus, the Son of God, as a literal interpretation of mythological language.
36. *In Search of the Supreme*, Vol. 3, p. 18.
37. Paul Tillich, *Christianity and the Encounter of the World Religions*, pp. 33–7
38. Simone Weil, *Letter to a Priest* (London: Routledge and Kegan Paul, 1953) pp. 29–33.
39. *The Essential Gandhi*, p. 234.
40. *In Search of the Supreme*, Vol. 3, p. 29.
41. Ibid., p. 54.
42. Ibid., p. 39.
43. *Truth is God*, p. 75.
44. *In Search of the Supreme*, Vol. 3, p. 155.
45. Ibid., p. 169.
46. *Christianity and the Encounter of the World Religions*, p. 79.
47. *The Future of Religions*, pp. 33–4.
48. Paul Tillich, *Perspectives on Nineteenth and Twentieth Century Protestant Theology*, ed. Carl E. Braaten (London: SCM Press, 1967) p. 213.
49. *Systematic Theology*, Vol. I, p. 18.
50. *The Future of Religions*, p. 93.
51. The same view is developed by W. Cantwell Smith in *The Faith of Other Men* (1963), especially in the section on 'The Christian in Religiously Plural World'.
52. Cf. Simone Weil, *op. cit.*

8 Liberation Theology: Bonhoeffer and Gandhi

1. Gustavo Gutierrez, *A Theology of Liberation* (London: SCM Press, 1974) p. 269.
2. Ibid., p. xi.
3. Ibid., p. 6.
4. Ibid., p. 13.
5. Ibid., p. 15.
6. Ibid., p. 36.
7. Ibid., p. 145.
8. Ibid., p. 67.
9. Ibid., p. 175.
10. Ibid., p. 176.
11. Ibid., p. 177; cf. p. 155.
12. Ibid., p. 159.
13. Ibid., p. 194.
14. Ibid., p. 200.
15. Ibid., p. 222.

16. Juan Luis Segundo, *The Liberation of Theology* (London: SCM Press, 1977) p. 75.
17. Ibid., p. 81.
18. Ibid., p. 82.
19. Ibid., p. 85.
20. Ibid., p. 84.
21. M.K. Gandhi, *In Search of the Supreme* (Ahmedabad: Navajivan, 1948) Vol. I, p. 131.
22. *Op. cit.*, p. 145.
23. Dietrich Bonhoeffer, *Letters and Papers from Prison* (London: Fontana, 1959) pp. 106–8.
24. Ibid., p. 124.
25. Ibid., p. 104.
26. Ibid., p. 93.
27. Julio de Santa Ana, 'The Influence of Bonhoeffer on the Theology of Liberation', *The Ecumenical Review*, 28, No. 2 (April, 1976) pp. 188–97. Quoted in G. Clarke Chapman Jr., 'Bonhoeffer: Resource for Liberation Theology', *Union Seminary Quarterly Review*, Vol. XXXVI, No. 4, Summer, 1981.
28. *Letters and Papers from Prison*, pp. 19, 123–4, 142–3, 163–4.
29. *The Cost of the Discipleship* (London: SCM Press, 1951) p. 56.
30. Jose Miguez Bonino, *Christians and Marxists* (Michigan: Grand Rapids Publications, 1976) p. 40; cf. G. Clarke Chapman Jr., *op. cit.*, p. 231.
31. Dietrich Bonhoeffer, *Gesammete Schriften*, II, p. 182.
32. Dietrich Bonhoeffer, *Ethics* (London: Fontana, 1964) p. 67.
33. *Letters and Papers from Prison*, p. 128.
34. John D. Godsey, *The Theology of Dietrich Bonhoeffer* (Philadelphia: Westminster Press, 1960) p. 264.
35. Dietrich Bonhoeffer, *Act and Being* (London: SCM Press, 1962) p. 90.
36. Gustavo Gutierrez, *op. cit.*, p. 168.
37. *Ethics*, p. 69.
38. *Ethics*, p. 70.
39. *Letters and Papers from Prison*, pp. 109–110.
40. Gustavo Gutierrez, *op. cit.*, pp. 155–9, 175–7.
41. Dietrich Bonhoeffer, *Christology* (London: Collins, 1966) pp. 23 f., 43 f.
42. Gustavo Gutierrez, *op. cit.*, p. 194.
43. *In Search of the Supreme*, Vol. 3, p. 17.
44. M.K. Gandhi, *All Men are Brothers*, ed. Krishna Kripalani (Paris: Unesco, 1958) p. 65. Cf. John Hick, *The Myth of God Incarnate* (London: SCM Press, 1977) p. 175 f.
45. Louis Fischer, *The Essential Gandhi* (New York: Vintage Books, 1962) p. 229.
46. Ibid.
47. N.K. Bose, *Selections from Gandhi* (Ahmedabad: Navajivan, 1948) p. 47.
48. M.K. Gandhi, *Truth is God* (Ahmedabad: Navajivan, 1955) p. 28.
49. *In Search of the Supreme*, Vol. 3, p. 108.
50. Cf. Glyn Richards, *The Philosophy of Gandhi* (London: Curzon Press, 1982) p. 80 f., for a fuller treatment of this topic.

51. *All Men are Brothers*, p. 69.
52. *Letters and Papers from Prison*, p. 124 f.
53. *Ethics*, pp. 360–1.
54. *The Selected Works of Mahatma Gandhi*, ed. Shriman Narayan (Ahmedabad: Navajivan, 1968) Vol. VI, p. 247.
55. Ibid., p. 246.
56. *All Men are Brothers*, p. 120.

9   Modern Hinduism

1. This essay was originally published in *The World's Religions*, edited by Stewart Sutherland, Leslie Houlden, Peter Clarke, Friedhelm Hardy (Routledge, 1988).

10   Vivekānanda and Essentialism

1. *The Complete Works of Swami Vivekananda* (Calcutta: Advaita Ashrama, 1970) Vol. II, pp. 382–3.
2. Ibid., Vol. VI, p. 17.
3. Ibid., Vol. I, p. 388.
4. Ibid., p. 356.
5. Ibid., Vol. II, p. 133.
6. Ibid., pp. 254, 334, 381.
7. Ibid., Vol. II, p. 333; Vol. VIII, p. 188.
8. Ibid., Vol. I, p. 17.
9. Ibid., Vol. III, p. 460.
10. S. Radhakrishnan, *Indian Religions* (New Delhi: Vision Books, 1979) p. 102.
11. *The Complete Works of Swami Vivekananda*, Vol. III, pp. 278–80.
12. Ibid., Vol. II, pp. 252–3.
13. Ibid., Vol. III, pp. 278–80.
14. Ibid., p. 424.
15. Nalini Devdas, *Svami Vivekananda* (Bangalore, 1968); P. Bishop, *The Raja Yoga of Vivekananda and the Integral Yoga of Aurobindo* (London, 1974). A post-graduate student of mine, John Prentice, refers to the views of Devdas and Bishop in his article on Vivekānanda in the *Scottish Journal of Religious Studies*, Vol. XII Number 1, pp. 46–55.
16. *The Complete Works of Swami Vivekananda*, Vol. II, p. 374.
17. Paul Tillich, *The Future of Religions*, ed. by Jerald C. Brauer (New York: Harper and Row, 1966) pp. 86–91.
18. *The Complete Works of Swami Vivekananda*, Vol. VI, p. 17.
19. Ibid., pp. 82–3. We might well ask whether Gandhi was not profoundly influenced by the neo-Vedāntism of Vivekānanda for the cornerstone of his philosophy is his concept of Truth (*Satya*) which he equates with God.
20. F. Schleiermacher, *On Religion: Speeches to its Cultured Despisers* (New York: Harper, 1958) pp. 15, 16.

21. Ibid., p. 39.
22. Ibid., pp. 211–13, 217.
23. Cf. Stewart R. Sutherland, *Goodness and Particularity*, Inaugural Lecture, Kings College (London, 1979) pp. 12, 13.
24. *Indian Religions*, p. 13.
25. *The Complete Works of Swami Vivekananda*, Vol II, pp. 382–3.
26. Ernst Troeltsch, 'Historiography', *Contemporary Religious Thinkers*, edited by John Macquarrie (New York: Harper and Row, 1968) p. 90.
27. Ibid., p. 90.
28. Ernst Troeltsch, *The Absoluteness of Christianity and the History of Religions* (London: SCM Press, 1972) p. 41.

11 The One and the Many: Radhakrishnan's Concept of Religion

1. 'Understanding a Primitive Society', *Religion and Understanding*, ed. D.Z. Phillips (Oxford: Blackwell, 1967) p. 30.
2. *In Search of the Supreme*, ed. V.B. Khar (Ahmedabad, 1931, Vol. I) pp. 27–8.
3. Ibid., p. 230.
4. S. Radhakrishnan, *Indian Religions* (New Delhi: Vision Books, 1979) p. 102.
5. E. Troeltsch, *The Absoluteness of Christianity and the History of Religions* (London: SCM Press, 1972) p. 91.
6. Ernst Troeltsch, 'Historiography', *Contemporary Religious Thinkers* edited by John Macquarrie (New York: Harper and Row, 1968) p. 90.
7. Ibid., p. 90.
8. A. Toynbee, *Christianity Among the Religions of the World* (Oxford University Press, 1957) pp. 103–5.
9. Ibid., pp. 111–12.
10. Schleiermacher, *On Religion: Speeches to its Cultured Despisers* (New York: Harper and Row, 1958) p. 40.
11. Ibid., pp. 236, 238.
12. Ibid., pp. 15, 16.
13. Ibid., pp. 48, 49.
14. Ibid., p. 38.
15. Ibid., pp. 211–13.
16. Ibid., pp. 215–17.
17. Ibid., pp. 217–18.
18. Ibid., pp. 214, 224–5.
19. Ibid., pp. 227, 245, 247, 249.
20. Ibid., pp. 251–2.
21. *The Complete Works of Swami Vivekananda*, Vol. II (Calcutta: Advaita Ashrama, 1970) p. 297.
22. Ibid., Vol. II, pp. 382–3.
23. Ibid., Vol. IV, pp. 82–3.
24. Ibid., Vol. II, pp. 252–3.
25. Ibid., Vol. IV, p. 17.

26. G. Richards, *A Source Book of Modern Hinduism* (London: Curzon Press, 1985) pp. 185–6.
27. Ibid., pp. 186–7.
28. Ibid., p. 186.
29. Ibid.
30. S. Radhakrishnan, *Eastern Religions and Western Thought* (Oxford University Press, 1940) p. 347.
31. S. Radhakrishnan, *An Idealist View of Life* (London: Allen and Unwin, 1961) pp. 97–8.
32. S. Radhakrishnan, *The Hindu Way of Life* (London: Allen and Unwin, 1964) pp. 125, 129.
33. S. Radhakrishnan, *Eastern Religions and Western Thought*, p. 83.
34. *An Idealist View of Life*, pp. 108–9.
35. Ibid.
36. *Indian Religions*, p. 13.

12 *Śūnyatā*: Objective Referent or Via Negativa?

1. E.B. Cowell (ed.) *Buddhist Mahāyāna Texts* (New York: Dover Publications, 1969); F.J. Streng, *Emptiness: a Study in Religious Meaning* (New York: Abingdon Press, 1967) Appendix A; Edward Conze, *Buddhist Wisdom Books* (London: George Allen and Unwin, 1970).
2. *Buddhist Wisdom Books*, p. 81.
3. Ibid., p. 82.
4. Masao Abe, *Zen and Western Thought*, edited by Wiliam R. La Fleur (Honolulu: University of Hawaii Press, 1985; London: Macmillan, 1985) p. 93.
5. *Mūlamadhyamakakārikās*, xv, 10.
6. *Op. cit.*, p. 83.
7. M. Hiryanna, *Outlines of Indian Philosophy* (London: George Allen and Unwin, 1973) pp. 220, 222.
8. *Mūlamadhyamakakārikās*, xxv, 20.
9. D.T. Susuki, *Outlines of Mahayana Buddhism* (New York: Schoken, 1970).
10. *Op. cit.*, p. 98.
11. T.V.R. Murti, *The Central Philosophy of Buddhism* (London: Allen and Unwin, 1968).
12. Cf. Ninian Smart, *Doctrine and Argument in Indian Philosophy* (London: Allen and Unwin, 1969) pp. 54, 223.
13. *Emptiness*, p. 149.
14. Ibid., p. 143, 224; cf. Nāgārjuna, *Vigrahavyāvartanī: Averting the Arguments*, p. 22.
15. *Mūlamadhyamakakārikās*, xxvii.
16. L. Wittgenstein, *Philosophical Investigations* (Oxford: Blackwell, 1963) pp. 133, 255.
17. Ibid., 109, 128; cf. Murti, pp. 163–4.
18. *Mūlamadhyamakakārikās*, xiii. 8; *Vigrahavyāvartanī*, 21–9; 57–9; 64–9.
19. *Emptiness*, p. 148.

20. Cf. Ninian Smart, *op. cit.*, p. 55; Masao Abe, *op. cit.*, p. 512; Edward Conze, *op. cit.*, p. 78; Murti, *op. cit.*, p. 226.
21. F.J. Streng, *op. cit.*, p. 151.
22. Hsueh-Li Cheng, 'Nagarjuna's approach to the problem of the existence of God', *Religious Studies*, xii, 2 June, 1976, p. 215.
23. *Mūlamadhyamakakārikās*, I.
24. Ibid., xxiv, 19.
25. Ibid., xxii, 11; xv, 10.
26. Ibid., xxiv, 1–5, 10, 14, 18, 20, 40.
27. Ibid., xxiv, 36.
28. Ibid., xxv, 6, 13, 18.
29. Ibid., xxv, 20; xi. 1.
30. Ibid., xxii, 7, 13–15.
31. K.V. Ramanan, *Nāgārjuna's Philosophy* (Delhi: Bharatiya Vidya Prakashan, 1971) p. 16.
32. See note on *śūnyatā*, ibid., pp. 338–9.
33. *Mūlamadhyamakakārikās*, xxv, 24, 25; xiii, 8.
34. Ramanan, *op. cit.*, pp. 39, 41.
35. Ramanan, *op. cit.*, p. 44.

13 Conceptions of the Self in Wittgenstein, Hume and Buddhism: An Analysis and Comparison

1. This point has been developed admirably by J.R. Jones in 'How do I know who I am?', *Aristotelian Society*, Vol. XLI, 1967, pp. 1–18. I am indebted also for some valuable suggestions by D.Z. Phillips.
2. Ludwig Wittgenstein, *The Blue and Brown Books* (Oxford: Blackwell, 1958) p. 69.
3. The phrase is used by John V. Canfield in an interesting article on 'Wittgenstein and Zen', in *Philosophy*, Oct. 1975, Vol. 50, No. 194.
4. Ludwig Wittgenstein, *Philosophical Investigations* (Oxford: Blackwell, 1963) 304.
5. 'Wittgenstein's Notes for Lectures on "Private Experience" and Sense Data', *Philosophical Review*, July 1968, pp. 278–9.
6. *Philosophical Investigations*, 11, 23; *The Blue and Brown Books*, pp. 67–8.
7. *Philosophical Investigations*, 432.
8. Ibid., 413.
9. It is claimed that the analogical argument delivers us from solipsism by constructing a bridge to the other self. If so it destroys its own foundation.
10. P.F. Strawson, *Individuals* (London: Methuen, 1964) p. 102.
11. *Philosophical Investigations*, 412.
12. *Philosophical Review*, July 1968, p. 282.
13. Ibid., pp. 298–9.
14. *The Blue and Brown Books*, p. 68.
15. *Aristotelian Society*, p. 2.
16. *Philosophical Review*, p. 308.
17. Ludwig Wittgenstein, *Zettel* (Oxford: Blackwell, 1967) pp. 220–5.

18. David Hume, *A Treatise of Human Nature* ed. L.A. Selby-Bigge (Oxford, 1965) Book I, Part IV, pp. 259, 257. Cf. N. Kemp Smith, *The Philosophy of David Hume* (London, 1941) p. 96.
19. David Hume, *Dialogues Concerning Natural Religion*, Part IV, from *Hume on Religion* (London, 1963) p. 134.
20. *Treatise*, p. 254.
21. Ibid., p. 261.
22. *The Philosophy of David Hume*, p. 98.
23. Ibid.
24. *Treatise*, Appendix, pp. 635–6.
25. Ibid., p. 259.
26. Ibid., p. 261.
27. Ibid., p. 262.
28. *Buddhist Scriptures*, trans. Edward Conze (London: Penguin, 1959) p. 188.
29. Ibid., p. 149.
30. Ibid., p. 193.
31. Ibid., p. 196.
32. Ibid., p. 194.
33. Ibid., p. 196.
34. Christmas Humphreys *Buddhism* (London: Penguin, 1959) p. 88; *The Wisdom of Buddhism* (London, 1960) p. 77.
35. T.V.R. Murti, *The Central Philosophy of Buddhism* (London: Allen and Unwin, 1968) p. 25. Cf. Edward Conze, *Thirty Years of Buddhist Studies* (London: Faber, 1967) p. 12.
36. Walpola Rahula, *What the Buddha Taught* (London: Gordon Frazer, 1959) pp. 62–64.
37. *Buddhist Scriptures*, p. 196.
38. *What the Buddha Taught*, p. 65.

14 Symbols and Religious Language

1. A.R. Radcliffe-Brown, *Structure and Function in Primitive Society* (London: Cohen and West, 1952) p. 143. Cf. J. Skorupski, *Symbol and Theory* (Cambridge University Press, 1976) p. 117.
2. T. Parsons, *Structure of Social Action* (London: Free Press, 1968) p. 416. Cf. Skorupski, *op. cit.*, p. 118.
3. Mary Douglas, *Natural Symbols* (London: Barrie and Jenkins, 1970) p. 11.
4. Paul Tillich, 'The Religious Symbol', *Religious Experience and Truth* Barry and Jenkins, ed. Sidney Hook (New York University Press, 1968) pp. 301–2.
5. Paul Tillich, 'The Meaning and Justification of Religious Symbols', *Religious Experience and Truth*, pp. 3–11.
6. Ibid., p. 4.
7. Bernard J.F. Lonergan, 'Reality, Myth, Symbol', *Myth, Symbol and Reality* ed. Alan M. Olsen (Notre Dame University Press, 1980) p. 31.
8. Ibid., p. 34.

9. Jaques Waardeburg, 'Symbolic Aspects of Myth', *Myth, Symbol and Reality*, p. 43.
10. Paul Ricoeur, *Interpretation Theory: Discourse and the Surplus Meaning* (Fort Worth: Texas Christian University Press, 1976) pp. 41–68.
11. Paul Tillich, 'The Meaning and Justification of Religious Symbols', p. 5.
12. John Hick, *Philosophy of Religion* (New Jersey: Prentice-Hall, 1973) pp. 69–71.
13. Ibid., p. 71.
14. Ibid., p. 69.
15. R.B. Braithwaite, *An Empiricist's View of the Nature of Religious Belief* (Cambridge University Press, 1955) p. 18.
16. Ibid., p. 24.
17. Ibid., p. 27.
18. Cf. D.Z. Phillips, *Religion Without Explanation* (Oxford: Blackwell, 1976) pp. 141–2.
19. Braithwaite, *op. cit.*, p. 23.
20. Phillips, *op. cit.*, p. 143.
21. Ibid., p. 144.
22. Hick, *op. cit.*, p. 83.
23. Paul Tillich, *Dynamics of Faith* (New York: Harper, 1958) p. 45.
24. Ibid., p. 42.
25. Paul Tillich, *Theology of Culture* (Oxford University Press, 1959) p. 45.
26. Hick, for example, insists on the factual and not merely symbolic nature of belief in the love and power of God, *Philosophy of Religion*, p. 83.
27. *Dynamics of Faith*, p. 46.
28. 'The Religious Symbol', *Religious Experience and Truth*, p. 304.
29. Ibid., p. 306.
30. Hick, *op. cit.*, p. 83.
31. *Dynamics of Faith*, p. 47.
32. Ludwig Wittgenstein, *Lectures and Conversations on Aesthetics, Psychology and Religious Belief* (Oxford: Blackwell, 1966) p. 56.
33. Ibid., p. 72.
34. See D.Z. Phillips, *Faith and Philosophical Enquiry* (London: Routledge, 1970) p. 17.

Index

211